# Sexy at Seventy

## *A Spiritual Quest*

**Eva Maria Chapman**

Page intentionally left blank

Published by PublishingPush.com

Page intentionally left blank

# Contents

Preface .......... vii

Chapter 1. Sexless Cronedom Beckons .......... 1

Chapter 2. Nuns and Perverts .......... 33

Chapter 3. Jake Enters My Life .......... 65

Chapter 4. The Party Has a Surprise in Its Tail! .......... 83

Chapter 5. Golden Delicious .......... 97

Chapter 6. Facing Madness in Deep, Dark Peru .......... 107

Chapter 7. Kimberley: The Party World Revs Up .......... 131

Chapter 8. Meeting the Pilot—60/30 Party .......... 151

Chapter 9. The Saint, the Sinner and Parties! .......... 175

Chapter 10. Russian Roots .......... 193

Chapter 11. Isha .......... 217

Chapter 12. Becoming My Own Queen Bee and Owning My Russian Bar Girl .......... 235

Chapter 13. Fall from Grace .......... 263

Chapter 14. Road to Recovery .......... 309

Chapter 15. Getting Old .......... 335

Chapter 16. The Party Is Over .......... 357

Chapter 17. A Tribute to Poonie .......... 367

Chapter 18. Kundalini Tiger ........ 379
Chapter 19. The White Tigress ........ 397
Chapter 20. The Future ........ 415
Dr Eva Maria Chapman's Bio ........ 426

# Preface

2004 was a bad year. My first grandchild died at two days old, my youngest sister descended into madness and my husband of 25 years, fell in love with a beautiful woman the age of my daughter. These events were profoundly traumatic, but the last is what this book is mainly about. I had to get my man back. But how? Especially when I was being stalked by the Dowager of Decrepitude and weighed down by societal messages that I was used up, done, past it. Well, I turned and faced that dowager head on. I kicked myself up my sorry backside, dyed my hair black, donned black leather gear to match, and out I went. As you do when you are 58 and on the brink of cronedom. I had no idea at the time that this event would lead to a dramatic self-re-evaluation that would lead me to becoming a sexy and spiritual woman at seventy. Fulfilled, satisfied, desirable and happy. I intend to continue on that journey.

Page intentionally left blank

# 1

## Sexless Cronedom Beckons

Just to show what a mammoth effort this was, I have to go back a few steps. To a time when I thought that the era of me being an attractive woman was well and truly over; when Cronedom, the repulsive figure that she is, began cackling gleefully, especially when I turned 50. I hated turning 50, even though the blow was softened when Jake, my husband, took me to Luxor.

Two days before the trip, I had an 'I am 50' panic, and bought three Wonder-bras. I had never owned one and brandishing a pink, a black and a white, I felt I was facing my 50s with some weapons. I had good boobs and I was going to show them off before they drooped into sad, wrinkly sacks.

We were on a Nile cruise so everyone dressed for dinner. I wore each of my Wonder-bras with aplomb. On the final night, at a dress-up, Egyptian style affair, my cleavage, in its pink Wonder-bra looked fetching through the gold coins of a skimpy harem piece. All eyes were on me. I felt I was giving the 30-somethings a run for their money.

There was only one problem. It was January and the evenings were cold. I ignored my mother's words, etched into my soul, 'You must always cover your chest or you will get sick.' By the time I returned to England, I had a severe chest infection and was ill for weeks. But I still felt it was worth it! A final bash at being the Belle of the Ball. Or so I thought.

And that sadly was what I felt; my Belle of the Ball days were over. The year 2000 was only three years away. As a child, I'd always dreaded the year 2000. I would be 53. Just horrible. Unimaginable. How would I ever cope?

Not well I'm afraid.

As the 21st century progressed, I was passing clots as big as plates. Yes, it was the bloody menopause. Regular as clockwork, my ovaries decided to give up the ghost. Big time. I ran out of my allotted quota of eggs. In my head, I stopped being a woman. I became a crone. An old bag with no juice.

As Cher famously said, 'Being 50 sucks. Men stop looking at you!'

I believed her, so dutifully I dried up. Then came the wrinkles. Then the extra rings of apple around my middle. Started wearing big, loose floppy tops. Mind you I had it lucky. Very few grey hairs. I hexed the first grey pubic hair that dared make an appearance when I was still in my 40s. I pulled it out, shrieking 'Fuck off you little white bastard'. It and its poxy little friends never dared to grow back.

I did everything to get the sexy thing going again. My lack of success was deeply depressing, as I had always been a very sexy woman. Lots of Jacuzzis. Just get that jet in the right place! But it was a bit like a frenzied drubbing on a cock's comb that had lost its colour and its owner its crow. So as compensation, I began to watch the daily word contest game, Countdown. I would record it and replay and replay until I got all the words right. I was once an English teacher, so at least I was good at words.

After early retirement, Jake and I moved to the West Country of England. I felt doomed to bedeck myself in floral dresses and join the Women's Institute; doomed to be one of those women who do church flowers, sit on committees and play indoor bowls. Life was grim; a downhill slide. Countdown was my daily succour; the Cloudy Bay Sauvignon evening quotient climbed imperceptibly and insidiously beyond the second glass.

Yes, the ageing thing was battering me senseless. A vain woman and old age are rarely comfortable partners and I am a very vain woman, a gibbering wreck at its cruel door. My diary at the time demonstrates my total obsession with how I looked. In my meditation practise I tried, with little success, to rise above this obsession and float serenely into older age. I failed.

## January 2001

**Monday**: Oh God, I'm 54 now- can I still get away with being in my early 50s? At least I've retired early and can look forward to painting holidays.

Went into the nearest village and peered at the notices. Oh dear!

Yoga for the over 50s.

Volunteers to visit the elderly.

Bell-ringers wanted.

Help!

Came home in despair; performed woefully on Countdown; seethed at one of its presenters, Carol Vorderman. How dare she look so sexy and still be in her 40s.

**Tuesday**: The end of the world has come! In a Department Store changing room! While I was inured to the sight of bulges in the garish mirrors, I spotted something far worse. Despicable creatures emerged from the loose bits around my jawline. J***s. Now that's a four-letter word that should be banned. I threw on my clothes and stumbled out in panic. At home where all the mirrors are strategically placed in dark corners and lit by soft lighting, the j***s didn't look so evil, but I am shaken to the core.

**Wednesday**: JOWLS. Sounds like 'howls'. That's what I want to do. HOWL. I hate the word. I have barely managed to put up with my eyelids collapsing, a sprouting moustache and the inexorable march of crows' feet. How I can cope with JOWLS? They are just too cruel.

**Thursday**: Obsessed all day. I even looked ****s up in the Oxford dictionary. The descriptions 'dewlap of cow' and 'crop of bird', were enough to send me racing to the mirror and frantically experimenting with little tucks under my ears. I could see how a nip here, tuck there could restore my jawline. Till now I've been anti facelifts with the best of them. I stalwartly paraded the banners, 'I'm beyond what I look like', or 'it's the inner person that counts', or 'cosmetic surgery is patriarchal butchery', or 'I must rise up above the shallowness of youth-obsessed society.' But now the banners lie in tatters of empty rhetoric. I am feverishly leafing through the pages of a woman's magazine, past the galleries of flawless young women, past the plethora of anti-wrinkle creams, past the promises of youthful 'sun-kissed' skin, and pounce avidly on the substantial section of cosmetic surgery adverts at the back.

**Tuesday:** Saw Mary Archer speak at a charity event. I scrutinised her face for signs of ageing. She is older than me but doesn't seem to have jowls. Has she had a facelift? It was with great comfort that I watched Ab Fab and noticed Joanna Lumley has beginnings of loose bits on her cheeks.

**Wednesday:** Definitely a 'wanting-to-have-a-facelift' day. Joanna Lumley says she wouldn't be against a facelift. She is my age. I wonder how long she can last out. Disappointingly, Julie Christie succumbed to the surgeon's knife at the age of 57. I can sympathise. In California, she was sick of bumping into women, older than her and looking like she was their mother.

**Friday:** Decide to go to Over-50s yoga.

Read somewhere that doing the shoulder stand brings blood to your face and stops sagging jawline. Wonder how long I need to stay inverted for my face to fall the other way? I stopped Yoga yonks ago when I ruined my back trying to keep up with the lithe 20-year-olds. But this class is different. I am the youngest. A spring chicken. There are a couple of Lady Somethings in their seventies and all the rest are older than me. I scrutinise their faces to see how they are standing up to the ravages of time. Doesn't look pretty. But they don't seem to care.

Jake was busy doing what he loved best, gardening. He cleared brambles, built walls, fixed barns, planted vegetables, an orchard and even got some beehives. Once a month, donning smart suit and tie, Jake travelled to London to teach senior civil servants how to think differently for the National School of Government. The kids stayed for weekends here and there. Steve came back from India, Paul came down from Scotland, Gary cycled from Wales and Lucie was engaged to Matt. I continued my yoga classes. Jake often found me in an inverted posture in the living room.

'You'll hurt your neck again doing that.'

'It's inverting my jowls.'

'Oh, come out and dig up some potatoes. That will sort you out.'

I grimaced. Jake always said this to irk me. It was my stepfather's favourite refrain when I wanted to go out as a teenager. Sasha refused to speak to me for over thirty-three years when I had the temerity to run away from home at twenty. But we managed a wonderful reconciliation before he died of cancer. While I nursed him, he had told me how growing potatoes had saved his family from starvation in 1930's Ukraine. The only one of my family I now saw was my younger sister Alexandra, who was confined to a nursing home in Australia. Severe postnatal depression and the death of Sasha had thrown her into a severe debilitating schizophrenia that had claimed the life of our mother, Olga.

I rubbed my neck as I came out of my pose. Jake was right. My neck felt decidedly wonky. I decided I hated the shoulder stand. (a) I couldn't do it (b) it fucked my neck (c) and being face to face with my stomach rolls was horrifying.

At least I didn't fart every time I changed position, like poor old Lady Satchwhistle.

Perhaps I should emulate Cher and Dolly Parton who had totally remodelled themselves with the surgeon's knife and looked fantastic.

'Don't you think so, Jake?'

'Good God, no,' said Jake. 'They look like giant fake Barbie dolls.'

And then he'd say, 'Darling I love the way you are', and remind me of the banner, 'It's the inner self that counts.'

And I'd say, 'Well, if that's the case, what's wrong with remodelling the outer bit so the inner self has a nicer-looking outer self to shine out of!'

He'd say, 'What's wrong with it is, that if you have plastic surgery, I'll divorce you.'

'Oh, Jake that's so mean,' I'd say. 'Especially when you get better looking with age!' I was rolling in the double chins and looking decidedly frumpy.

However, I was secretly pleased, even if I did pronounce him a bully who was stifling my freedom just like my father had. Jane, a dear friend in her mid-sixties with iron-grey hair, masses of wrinkles and huge flapping jowls, just laughed at me and said it was wonderful to grow wrinkly and old. With friends and husbands like these, perhaps I would be spared the degradation of being hoisted on the petard of vanity and sacrificed to youth culture. That's what I thought on a good 'I-don't-want-a-facelift' day.

I was helped by what Robert Redford said about facelifts; that having one was like cutting out a bit of your soul and he 'didn't give a damn' if his face fell apart. I admired Helen Mirren, another older actress who had not succumbed to the knife. That such a sexy one dared to play the frumpy housekeeper with wrinkles galore in Gosford Park. A heroine.

I wasn't sure that heralding facelifts as liberators, that enabled women to exercise choice over their bodies, was a good argument- especially when assailed by the battery of procedures available; surgical nips and tucks; botox to freeze wrinkles; lasering to shed outer layers; collagen implants; chemical peels; it just went on and on. I laughed at author Kathy Lette's observation, that women who have liposuction on their backsides in order to plump up their lips, will forever talk through their asses! And good old Brigitte Bardot! She claims she loves every one of her wrinkles. Encouraged, I gazed intently at my jowls in the mirror, tried to love them, but failed miserably. I saw a programme about cosmetic surgery where a woman kept a video diary. Ghastly. Besides the terrible pain, she now had permanent lack of colour pigmentation from laser surgery gone wrong. Her cosmetic surgeon was eventually struck off for disfiguring a multitude of women. Pre- facelift, she was a giggly, happy, wrinkly woman. And a year later she had lost her laugh and wished she had her wrinkles back. That programme brought me back from the brink of deciding to go for a facelift. I threw myself into meditation again, trying to shore up 'it is the inner self that counts.' To little avail. I ping-ponged between the pro and con arguments as I peered in the mirror, wondering whether the jowls looked any better. Didn't seem to.

I decided I should get healthy and do a detox. Too many delicious glasses of Cloudy Bay could be ageing me.

## February 2001

**Monday**: I feel a bit like an ageing Bridget Jones. e.g.

9st 4lb, alcohol units - 4; chin whiskers - 8; moustache whiskers - 82 (one side worse than the other!)

No. of times looking at wrinkles in mirror - 19

Supplements (including Yam pills) - 11

Minutes looking for lost reading glasses - 65

Likely percentage odds on getting a facelift - 70%

Minutes spent on thinking about a facelift - 45

No. of stomach rolls - 4

Diet books flicked through - 5. Settled on Carole Vorderman Detox Diet.

Articles on cosmetic surgery - 4

**Tuesday**: 9st 3lb (started Carol Vorderman's detox diet)

Alcohol units - (ditto)

Moustache whiskers - raggedy 28 (faulty waxing strip from catalogue)

Likely percentage odds on getting a facelift - 49% (influenced by ghastly programme about facelift gone badly wrong)

Minutes spent on thinking about a facelift - 3 (ditto)

Minutes looking for lost reading glasses - 0 (bought 6 cheap pairs - one for kitchen, car, handbag, by TV, lounge, bed)

No. of pull-ups - 30 (will have got rid of disgusting rolls and have flat stomach in no time)

**Wednesday:** Weight -? (Carol Vorderman Rule No 1 'Do not weigh yourself')

Alcohol units - 0

Time spent looking for organic wheat-free breads, flours, etc - 6 hours (included having to buy another pair of cheap reading glasses - couldn't read the small print on the packets)

Money spent on organic wheat-free, dairy-free food - £205 (!)

Minutes spent thinking about a facelift - 0 (totally obsessed with new diet)

No. of reading glasses lost - 2

Supplements - 15 (have to add milk thistle, spirulina, kelp and chlorella to clean out the liver)

No. of pull-ups - 0 (did my back in doing 30 the day before)

**Monday:** This morning I was sort of doing the plough when I noticed something new and ghastly. The flesh on my thighs is beginning to hang off my bones. I've always had skinny, taut legs. The elasticity seems to be going. Bloody menopause! That's what it is. Oestrogen levels dropping fast. Wish I hadn't read Germaine Greer or Leslie Kenton and had taken HRT instead. And my sex drive is non-existent. 'What's the point?' a little voice says in my head. 'No eggs left in the ovary sacs - no possibility of any babies - the womb is as barren as a pig's bladder - what's the point of sex? At least HRT still pumps oestrogen around- the body is tricked into thinking it is young.'

**A week later**

At the moment, I am winning. Just. I don't think I will have a facelift. I'm going to put NFL (no facelift) after my name. I sound a bit like my old hippy days when I marched behind the NLF flag in Australia! (National Liberation Front for Vietnam). I am so pleased that I don't live in California. I think that would be too difficult and I wouldn't last out. Ram Dass (formerly Richard Alpert who with Timothy Leary popularised LSD, and now a spiritual teacher) says that people like me, obsessed with how they look, live in Channel 1 dimension. There are so many deeper dimensions to life, like the emotional, intellectual and spiritual. I know this and have meditated for years. But I am VAIN with a capital V. Meditation or not, I HATE getting old. I don't want to be caught up in political correctness about how I SHOULD feel about getting old or pretend I am on a deeper Channel when I'm not. Many of my friends think I'm daft and should have got over this age thing long ago. They look down on the Chers and Dolly Partons of the world. They think I'm insecure and should be relying on a deeper sense of self.

I have followed many spiritual practices to develop my other channels and get out of my obsession with my looks. I was an Enlightenment master for over 20 years, exploring deeper layers of myself. I contemplated my third eye so I could turn my attention inwards. This worked for a while but I didn't want to pretend that I was above caring about my wrinkles when I wasn't. I am a product of this youth-obsessed society and continually bombarded by advertising, magazines, men leaving their wrinkly wives for younger models and the never-ending stream of new, fresh-faced, flat-stomached nineteen-year-olds who pour on to the streets.

So, my own battle continues. My husband still insists he will divorce me if I have a facelift. He said this was the face he married and he doesn't care how wrinkly it gets. Will I, in the words of another diehard NFL Observer writer, be the 'only prune left among all the peaches'?

## March 2001

Oh no - the worst has happened. NECK WRINKLES! Now, these are really bad. I DO NOT WANT A TURKEY NECK! I DO NOT! I am now obsessed with looking at women's necks. I want to know how old they are and when it gets REALLY bad. What I mean by REALLY BAD, is when a large wrinkly bag hangs from the chin like a turkey's crop. I'm on the way. At the moment in certain lights, vertical striated wrinkles are making their unwelcome entrance into my Channel One life. If I pinch my skin at the back of my neck they disappear. I wonder if I can grow my hair to hide a permanent peg at the back of my neck. Jake is amused.

'Why are you so worried? I can't see anything wrong with your neck.'

'Men won't look at me anymore.'

'Darling, if you think men look at your neck, you are sadly mistaken. They'll look at your tits, your arse, and your pretty face. But they won't look at your neck.'

I'm not in the slightest bit convinced.

I continue with concentrating on my third eye and gobbling yam pills. They are supposed to be natural oestrogen!

**A week later**

9st 2lb, (all that worry about neck wrinkles)

Alcohol units - 16 (ditto)

Pubic grey hairs – 0 (they don't dare grow back, but I am developing a worrying bald patch on my mound of Venus - (if only that part of my anatomy lived up to this moniker)

Chin whiskers - 12

Moustache whiskers - (stopped counting in horror)

No. of times looking at neck wrinkles in mirror - 28

Yam pills -11

Minutes looking for lost reading glasses - 20 (I now have fifteen pairs all over the house, but often lose the whole lot; thinking of having a pair in the shower - can't distinguish the shampoo from the conditioner!)

Likely percentage odds on getting a facelift - 99%. Has shot up because of neck wrinkles.

Minutes spent on thinking about a facelift - 90

No. of stomach rolls - 3. Stomach lifts and worrying about neck have helped

I am now an avid fan of the television programme 'Nip and Tuck'. It is the best therapy to put me off facelifts. The operations look terrible. And the depiction of America as a sad, Channel One-obsessed nation, leads me to a comfortable smugness. This smugness is helped by the fact that I have rapidly increased my collection of scarves. Scarves! What wonderful inventions. I can so effortlessly drape one around my neck and in certain lights, can look in my thirties.

## April 2001

Lady Lovepringle refuses to do the sun worshipper. Partly because she can't. Her long, dog-walking limbs don't seem to bend any more. Well, she is eighty. She also refuses to meditate - regards it as highly suspect claptrap. To her, yoga is just exercise for health - none of this mumbo jumbo, spiritual wholeness claptrap. She thinks my ability to stretch is amazing. I'm the only one in the class who can do the cow's head both ways. She demands loudly, what's the point of twisting your arm awkwardly up your back? I chip in with 'it stops dowager's hump!' I bite my lip. Is that the beginnings of one between her shoulder blades? She shuts up. Can't help feeling smug and young! I may have jowls but at least I don't have dowager's hump. However, I love Lady Lovepringle as she thinks I am about 43.

**Later**

I may look 43 to Lady Lovepringle, but I was horrified to notice that the wrinkles above my eyes now have their own wrinkles. This is particularly depressing, as I had launched myself into a state of delusion that I could go on looking younger for a few years because of neck scarves and feather boas. These aren't the big, flashy, feather boas, but just the more discreet-looking ones which have soft, tiny feathers and do a great job of hiding neck wrinkles. But when your eye wrinkles develop wrinkles of their own, what can you do, short of a facelift? I have seriously approached Jake about a facelift again. But he is adamant - facelift and certain divorce.

'It's not fair,' I rail. 'You just get more handsome and debonair and younger women find you attractive - and young men just do NOT find women with wrinkly wrinkles dancing on top of deep eye wrinkles, sexy.' Even if they are sporting sweet little feather boas around their neck.

Many of my women friends have got caught in the crossfire.

'I can't believe that you let your husband dictate what you can do with your face!' they say, indignantly. 'What a bully.' And there I am looking soft and sad with my feathery neck frill. Downtrodden and put upon.

'But Jake, are you sure you will find me sexy when I've got a turkey gobble neck?' I ask over morning tea.

He sighs in exasperation. 'The fruit cage needs to be weeded, you know!'

**Next Day**

Weight -9st 0lb (continuing worry about neck wrinkles - although I have noticed that older plump women's necks look pretty good.)

Alcohol units - 12 (heard that alcohol dehydrates the skin and makes it look wrinklier, so have to balance that against the minimum amount of wine I need to send me into sweet oblivion)

Pubic grey hairs - 0 (they still don't dare grow back)

Diameter of bald patch on mound of Venus - 2 inches (in fact have begun shaving top bit - I think it's called a Monte Carlo or some other principality!)

Stomach lifts - 10

Over coffee, I talk to Isla who is still in her thirties and a gorgeous former Page Three model. 'Come with me to Goa,' she says, 'to the Marble Clinic - they do cosmetic surgery there for a quarter of the price - and you can stay and recuperate - and no one need know.'

'But why do you want to go?' I say, looking at her stunning face.

'Oh, I'd like a tit lift and to get rid of these smile lines.' Her tits are gorgeous and so are her smile lines.

But for my parchment neck, I am sorely tempted!

Should I take HRT? Ignore Leslie Kenton and Germaine Greer? Surely artificial oestrogen rollicking through my neck capillaries would halt the avalanche of wrinkles?

In a cake shop in Totnes, I met Jocasta. She was still a snip in her early forties and she, with her husband Vincent, would become very important in our lives. She talked me out of taking HRT.

'That won't make you younger. You are just as old as you feel,' she said.

'It's all right for you to talk – you've still got eggs. What's the point of feeling sexy if you have no eggs!'

'Oh, Eva, it is poppycock that you lose your sexuality when your eggs run out. You need Horny Goat. That will do the trick.'

'Horny what?'

'Horny Goat.'

'Where do I get that?'

'Green Life online.'

I bought six packets and, threw out the yam pills. Useless.

Didn't help that Jake laughed his annoying, greying head off when the Horny Goat arrived and chuckled, 'Horny goat for an old goat!'

These pills rapidly became like flies to a frog. Didn't seem to do much good. But gave me some hope.

I walked through the nearest market town. Not one man looked at me. When I walked with my daughter, Lucie, the guys always looked at Lucie. I felt invisible. I spied some builders on a building site. Not one whistle. Cher was right; in your 50s, you become invisible to guys. Germaine said she was glad and relieved, as they would now appreciate her for her brain. I would gladly trade my PhD for just one whistle. I sighed and headed on home to the highlight of the day; Countdown. At least I could use my brain trying to beat the contestants. Now I became really depressed. 'When would this Horny Goat start working?' I swallowed 2 whole packets. Not a flicker of interest in my genital area. I did participate in sex, but I felt Jake was getting short-changed. He had married a woman who used to be sexy. That seemed so long ago. I was now the wrong kind of hot. Hot flushes! Several times a night. I had read an interesting theory that hot flushes demolished impurities and burnt off toxins in order to pave the way for deeper wisdom. But when they kept me awake at night, the fact that this was preparing me for being a fully-fledged wise witch when I turned 56, did not offer much solace.

I had to do something drastic. I dyed all my clothes purple. Even my underwear.

Lady Lovepringle was aghast when I turned up every week to yoga in different shades of purple. That's all I wanted to wear.

Then some real excitement. My daughter was getting married and she wanted me to make her wedding dress. We chose the silk together and Lucie designed the dress; a sexy, silk affair with a bustle which curved beautifully around her shapely figure. I had fun making a purple outfit for myself and a purple pillbox hat. I also made the wedding cake, all 5 tiers, which needed the beating of several buckets of white icing. I scoured the hedgerows for violets and primroses that I sugared and left to dry on the window sills. The trouble started when I started eating them. They were delicious and I became addicted. Jake got pretty worried when I wore my purple dressing gown all day, gobbling sugared violets by the score. They were giving me a slightly stoned feeling. It was nice. I'd then sit with a tray of sugared violets and chomped through them as I watched Countdown.

Jake put his foot down. No more sugared violets. He said I was acting loopy and should pull myself together.

The wedding was wonderful and I presented Lucie with a quilt for which several female family members had created a square.

After the excitement of the wedding, life became tedious again. I carried on wearing purple and secretly quaffed sugared violets when Jake wasn't looking.

The years rolled by. I continued going to yoga and trying to develop my third eye. I just became more glum and depressed. My sporadic attempts at meditation did not lift me out of the doldrums. I felt I was falling deeper into a dark, sexless, unspiritual cavern.

Jocasta encouraged me to continue with Horny Goat.

'You must give it time.'

'I've given it 3 years and not a flicker.'

Jake and I were invited to an ecstasy party in Totnes, Devon. I had missed the rave scene of the 90s. Jake and I were busy being academics, running a business, leading meditation groups and bringing up four teenagers. I had also been scared off ecstasy by the unfortunate and much-publicised death of Leah Betts in 2001. So, I went to the party with some trepidation. But hey, I was a purple loony, with no eggs and serious addictions to Countdown and hedgerow flowers. What did I have to lose?

Going to a party in Totnes, a very trendy town in Devon, is something else; certainly better than joining the WI. People were on serious health kicks. Bottles of super-greens replaced beer, spirits and wines. These were slurped down with sugarless cakes made with Spelt flour and goji berries. The music was amazing and the ecstasy pure. Hey, this was a healthy rave! I took a half a pill, Jake a whole one. After a bout of nausea (was it the super greens?), I started to feel really good. Jake and I danced to the jaunty rhythms. Hey, this was great. What a shame we had missed the rave scene. I really got the meaning of being 'loved up'. Everyone looked beautiful, especially my husband. Jake and I couldn't keep our eyes and hands off each other. While the effect of the drug wasn't particularly sexual, it was very sensual. The best thing about it was that our hearts opened up to each other. We talked and talked and talked. Jake explained how he missed the meditation groups we used to run together. These Zen type, Enlightenment Intensives were our passion and our joint spiritual path for many years. But Jake told me what he missed most, was me. We had been together for over 25 years. We had brought up four children together. We had run a successful business together. We had roamed the world together. Which foggy planet had I disappeared to? What happened to the vibrant, sexy woman he had married?

Our Totnes friends were great hosts. They had attached a marquee to the back of their living room and had filled the space with velvet cushions, low lighting and music. It was the perfect atmosphere in which to begin the long road of reconnection. Life was looking better. My daughter was pregnant with her first child and bloomed with health and happiness. Jake and I looked forward to grandparenthood.

However, things were about to change dramatically. Yes, this was 2004. I was 57.

My sweet grandson died tragically and unexpectedly at two days old. I was at the hospital and witnessed how devastating it was for my daughter and her husband. For the next few months, I forgot about my obsession with my appearance and looked after my daughter who was plunged into inconsolable grief. Meanwhile, in Australia, my sister Alexandra was going from bad to worse and was deteriorating rapidly in a mental institution. She had a small child, Henry, who lived with his father, a recovering alcoholic, and who gambled away any money I sent. I had to fly out and help sort out the situation. Fortunately, Lucie and her husband went to Australia for a holiday, so I could continue supporting her.

While I was away, Jake and I were invited to another ecstasy party, but with friends in London. This group of friends had participated in the Enlightenment Intensives we used to run. I was in email and phone contact with Jake and encouraged him to go without me.

He went. And that is when it happened. He fell in love with HER. He didn't put it like that when he emailed me. He didn't realize it then. In fact, Jake said I must come to the next ecstasy party, which was scheduled a few weeks after I returned from Australia, shortly after my 58th birthday. He told me the party he went to without me was great, and he had very close contact with everyone. One of those people was Stella and she really opened up to him. I didn't think anything of it. Jake and I had been her meditation teachers and she had him up on a pedestal. I trusted Jake totally. I was otherwise engaged with my sister's rapidly deteriorating health and the messy situation with my nephew in Melbourne.

It took a while after I returned, for the penny to drop. I noticed that Stella was phoning Jake every day. I still didn't think anything of it as Stella was having problems with her husband, Brett, who was a recovering heroin addict. Near my 58th birthday, a picture of Stella came up on the screensaver of the computer we kept in the living room. I should say at this point that Stella was bald, by choice. It suited her. She had sweet, elfin features and looked like a beautiful, serene sphinx. When Jake looked at the photo, I could see he was smitten. 'I really miss her,' he said.

'You what?' I said, aghast. 'You miss her?' It was then I knew this was trouble. I felt my heart being wrenched from my chest. Had I lost Jake? I took a deep breath, looked at him squarely and said, 'I want you to tell me everything that happened at that party.' So, he did. The two of them had been ensconced on a sofa together and she had told him painful things about herself. I knew what that was like. I had experienced how ecstasy opens up the heart. I also knew that ecstasy blurs boundaries and brings up sensuality. I wanted to know exactly what boundaries had been blurred.

'Did you kiss her?'

'Well ... er … No.'

'What does 'well ... er …' mean?'

'I nibbled her ear.'

'You what?'

‘I nibbled her ear.’

‘You nibbled her ear?’ I was horrified. Jake might as well have told me he had shagged her. But this felt even worse. Nibbling someone’s ear felt extraordinarily intimate. Especially when she was young and beautiful with no hair to hide the offending ear.

‘Why?’

‘Well we were really close and her ear looked very inviting, so I licked it.’

I was beside myself with jealousy. I was reminded of Ally MacBeal, an American TV drama, in which an adulterous kiss between the main protagonists caused a major scandal. This felt like a similar betrayal. Jake and I talked long into that night.

But something totally unexpected happened! My sexuality came back like a tsunami. I suddenly transformed into a wild, sexual panther. I even became a morning woman. Jake had always wanted a woman who likes sex in the morning. I had been pretty sexy before menopause, but never in the mornings. Always felt like a dead dodo at sunrise, what with morning breath and sleep-filled eyes! But not anymore. I was rampant. Jake didn’t know what hit him. He loved it. I was not going to even let him think about that bald bitch and her sphinx-like ears. The sex was electrifying. I noticed that I began to look better - my breasts were perkier and my eyes glowed. This was much better than Horny Goat and any facelift.

The ecstasy party in London was looming up. I ditched my purple clothes and bought tight leather trousers and a leather jacket. I also ditched my blonde curls, dyed my hair black and had it cut in a spiky style. I was going to this party and claiming my husband back, big time.

Little did I know that this blast of sexual awakening, after several years of being a dried-out husk of a woman, would launch me into a fearsome self-re-evaluation. I would become, to my total surprise, a sexy rampant flirt in my 60s. And with this came a re-emergence of my spiritual self. Really? Sexy at 70 and spiritual?

In order to understand what happened at the party and how this unbelievable transformation happened, I must go back further. The seeds had been set in every fibre of my being since birth. I was born to a sexy mother in a dark, spiritual time. So, the sexy, spiritual thing was woven deeply in a tangle of distortion that I am unravelling to this day.

# 2

# Nuns and Perverts

My umbilical cord was still a decaying stump when I was initiated into my first religious cult.

Time: January 9th 1947 Anno Domini.

Setting: Prague, mediaeval capital of the Holy Roman Empire.

Emissary of Pope Pius X11 - Father Josef Pasek

At the time of my birth, Prague was enjoying a brief political respite between Nazism and Communism, but was gripped by the coldest winter for a hundred years. In the freezing chapel of the St. Apollinaire Maternity Hospital, Father Josef Pasek branded me with the sign of the cross. As icicles multiplied on the eaves of the church, he dropped an extra blob of holy water on my unsuspecting brow to counteract the fact that I was spurus illegitimus incertris patris (the cult's fancy way of saying 'bastard of a hit-and-run father'). As well as the stain of the cross, I was saddled with the Christian names, Eva Maria. Eva meant mother of all life, and Maria, 'the mother of God'. Heavy duty. A lot to live up to.

My grandmother hated my mother, Olga, a refugee from Ukraine and the family's kitchen maid. She wanted Olga to disappear out of her son's life so she could keep me. For this reason, she inculcated me into the cult of Catholicism, even though my mother was Russian Orthodox. The grandmother encased me into her holy chrysalis and shot evil dagger eyes at the barbaric peasant girl who bore me. But Olga, the unholy one, filched me away in the dead of night, escaped Communist Czechoslovakia and walked across war-torn Europe with me in tow. She was aching to return to her family in Ukraine, but knew that being accompanied by a child born out of wedlock, she would be a disgrace. According to Sasha, my stepfather, Olga fucked her way across Europe; according to my mother, she had to prostitute herself to feed me. Whatever the truth, she was well and truly tainted. By association, so was I, as Sasha would never fail to remind me when I was a teenager. 'You' he often said, 'are a whore just like your mahder.'

On a boat full of refugees bound for Australia, my future stepfather watched disapprovingly as my mother, in a fetching swimsuit, was chased by a bunch of sailors. They were trying to catch her to throw her into a swimming pool of blue dye, the custom as the ship crossed the equator. She returned a while later giggling, hair all blue, to find me being taken care of by Sasha. I was three years old and felt safe with this serious young man, who despite being outraged by Olga's flirtatious antics, fell in love with her.

From an early age, I was preyed upon by all manner of people, both sexual and religious, pulled in extreme directions of apparent piety and degrading lust. Australia seemed full of sickly-looking nuns in long, white habits, or retarded perverts with shifty eyes and bulging trousers. The first of the latter unsavoury bunch was Dave, a farmhand on a sheep station where my mother was sent to as a kitchen maid soon after we arrived in

Australia. Sasha had reluctantly left us to work on the hydro-electric power scheme in Tasmania. Dave offered to drive me to the nearby country town, Wagga Wagga, to buy me some slippers. The excruciating clarity that these came with a price, shattered my three-year-old innocence with such force that it has taken me a lifetime to find an even keel. We stopped on the way to Wagga Wagga, where Dave would buy me a pretty dress or a new doll. I remember the sickening, sour feeling that assailed me the first time. I didn't yet speak English but quickly learnt the age-old language of prostitution. He had told my mother, before the journey, that he would buy me slippers with bells on them. To my refugee mother, Australia had been sold as a land of milk and honey. This must be the beginning, she thought, so was enthusiastic and totally trusting. Dave did not have cold, cruel eyes or wear jackboots or any other insignias of the totalitarian hell from which she had escaped. To a three-year-old girl who had known deep hunger, cold and few possessions, slippers with bells seemed the most desirable objects in the world. I jumped into the truck with princess stars in my eyes.

The denouement was ugly; a jumble of dark, pulsing hairiness being rubbed on a very private place. 'This is very good for you,' he purred. 'And shhhh, this must be our little secret,' he said, putting his fingers to his lips. I wore the slippers on my feet on the way home, the bells jingling. My mother didn't seem to notice the lack of joy in my face.

I struggled privately with the words 'this is good for you' over the next few weeks, translating them into my native Russian. I was not sure at all if what Dave did in his truck was good for me. After a few more desirable acquisitions, I decided that regardless of Dave's constant shushing with his fat fingers, I must check with my mother. Was him rubbing the thing in his trousers on my 'buhta' good for me?

I never got an answer. My mother went white and rushed from the room. This was followed by lots of shrieking from somewhere in the large house. I never saw Dave again. Then I did what a lot of children do; I temporarily forgot the encounters in the truck. I always remembered Dave as having a long, red nose.

The nun appeared on the lawn of the house my mother and stepfather acquired in Adelaide. Sasha had landed a job at Holden's factory and flown Olga and me over to join him. A voice emanated from the pasty-faced form swathed in white robes and clinking crucifix.

'Hello, Eva.'

I was shocked. She was like an apparition who had materialised out of thin air.

'How do you know my name?'

'Ah!' Her thin lips attempted a smile. The cross around her waist rattled. Her eyes disappeared into her skull. 'God knows everything.'

Another white being floated out from the veranda, accompanied by my anxious-looking mother. The Catholic Church had come to claim me. And unfortunately, as I would discover, cultish tentacles are supremely difficult to escape.

I felt spooked. The nuns were creepy and scared the wits out of me. They wanted to enrol me in the local Catholic school. My parents were not keen. My mother's Russian Orthodoxy had lapsed and my stepfather was a secret Jew. Their experiences in the last ten years had ground any concepts of goodness, religion, or God into the earth where their loved ones had perished.

At this time, there were three religions vying for superiority in South Australia; Anglicanism, Methodism and Catholicism. The nuns represented Catholicism and its drive for new recruits, especially those who had 'Roman Catholic' stamped on their refugee papers. My parents didn't understand what the nuns were talking about but received the message that somehow they must feel guilty - my mother could only get rid of the nuns by promising to take me to the local Catholic church the following Sunday.

'It is behind the football oval,' said pasty face. 'And bring eggs,' she added, noticing our chooks.

My mother, who spoke little English and found the rules of this new country strange and confusing, donned a peasant scarf and dutifully led me around the football oval to the church. Church? Now St. Vitus Cathedral in Prague - that is a church; shining and magnificent, an epiphany in stained glass, lording itself over that fairy-tale city. What accosted our eyes that dismal Sunday in impoverished post-war Adelaide, was a large piece of curved, corrugated iron with a cross stuck on top. After grabbing our eggs, the nuns herded us on to makeshift benches. A tortured-looking bloke in a loincloth was perched awkwardly on a plinth, his eyes like that of the nuns, disappearing upwards. We were harangued in an alien tongue for what felt like hours. I had picked up a fair bit of English but understood very little of what transpired, except that somehow or other the mangled bloke on the cross had a lot to do with it, and furthermore whatever he was suffering seemed to be my fault. My mother was then exhorted to turn out her purse and asked to bring more eggs and money next Sunday. We left, bewildered, but with little incentive to return. At least my mother did not succumb to the order that I should be sent to the local Catholic school.

We had moved into our house in Pudney Street and had a boarder, as well as chickens, to make ends meet. This man with shifty eyes seemed to like my long plaits and stroked the ribbons with which they were woven. My mother, newly vigilant, shrieked at him. I found out a lot later that the reason the police came to arrest him soon after, was that he was a convicted paedophile. It was great to have my mother look out for me, but it seemed that the resident paedophile and the Wagga Wagga incident had ignited all the paranoia and suspicion she thought she had left behind. She became increasingly fearful and would not let me out of her sight, which became another kind of burden. In addition, she was completely neurotic about how much I ate and beat me if I couldn't eat. She had watched her brother pine away and die during Stalin's enforced starvation of the Ukrainian peasants in the 1930s, a time she referred to as 'the hungry years'.

Before too long, I was begging Mama to take me to church again. Not because I was drawn to the sanctity of the corrugated iron; nor that I was impelled to unravel the mystery of the mangled man - he was already creeping unbidden into my dreams - but because of Religious Instruction. Although I escaped Catholic school, I did not escape Catholic Religious Instruction, which was foisted upon me every Wednesday morning at my local school. I was the only migrant in the school and as well as learning English, had to learn all the spoken and unspoken rules of an alien culture. I actually loved school, progressing quickly with all my lessons, but dreaded Wednesday morning Religious Instruction. RI, as it was called, dominated my week for the next seven years. Every Wednesday morning, I had to kneel on my bony knees on an uneven wooden floor, rosary in hand and repeat ‘Our Father’ and ‘Hail Mary’ over and over again for what seemed an eternity. I had no idea what I was praying about and certainly didn't understand what ‘the fruit of thy womb, Jesus’, meant. I also had to intone the Apostles’ Creed, which made me feel uncomfortable as I was claiming to believe all this stuff that didn't mean anything to me. ‘I believe in the Holy Catholic Church’ just conjured up images of the corrugated iron monstrosity up the road. I was given a Catechism. Barely able to read English yet, that slim little book was sinister and terrified me. I was ordered to memorise long lists of mortal and venial sins which, when committed by me, apparently pierced the body of Jesus Christ and caused him great suffering. This was worrying and extremely puzzling as I tried to come to grips with this and the new culture I had landed in. I looked at the picture of the suffering Christ, his heart looking all red and bloody and wondered how I was causing his pain.

The catechism commanded that I go to church every Sunday and take Holy Communion and confession. I didn't even know what these things were. All I knew was that if I didn't do them, I was committing a sin. Our RI instructor was a Father somebody or other to whom I took an instant dislike. He leaned over my desk and pierced me with pebble eyes and foetid breath, 'DID YOU GO TO CHURCH LAST SUNDAY?' Petrified, I stammered that I had been once.

'ONCE! YOU MUST GO TO CHURCH EVERY SUNDAY!'

I ran home and begged Mama to take me. "Maybe" she would say and each Sunday rolled by and we didn't go. Wednesday would inevitably descend upon me and after all the knee-crunching Our Fathers, Hail Marys and communions of saints, I would await the foetid onslaught. By then I had sussed the difference between venial and mortal sins. Venial sins, like lying, meant that I went to Purgatory. Mortal sins meant I went to Hell. I wasn't exactly sure when these dire things would happen to me but Purgatory sounded a bit better than Hell- even though it was a much longer word and harder to spell. 'Yes I did go to Church last Sunday,' I lied, trying to banish the spooky image of Jesus in the catechism. It was the stuff of nightmares; a disembodied head of Christ. Thorns pierced his head trickling rivulets of blood, and his eyes were permanently riveted towards heaven. Sanpaku, it is called. Close to death. The image was so horrible I could see it glowing at me in the dead of night. The worst thing was that the catechism insisted that it was definitely my fault. Apparently, every time I committed a sin, I was piercing his flesh; every bad thought I had, drove him further into sanpaku. He even died because of me. I was barely six years old. My guts were tangled in his thorns. I was dead in the water. The cult had me by the entrails.

I suddenly developed mysterious stomach pains every Wednesday. My mother was puzzled; the teachers were puzzled; Father Foetid-breath was puzzled. I couldn't explain to anyone that it was Jesus who was freaking me out. Sometimes the pains were severe enough to convince the teachers I needed to lie down. But most of the time they did not save me from the RI ordeal. The countless Wednesdays rolled into countless years.

I soon discovered something even more sinful. Whether or not I had been prematurely stimulated by the Wagga Wagga episodes, or I was just born highly sexed, I noticed I experienced a great deal of pleasure when I rubbed Nonda on my 'buhta'. Nonda was a brown velvet clown given to me my grandmother and who escaped with us over the border from Communist Czechoslovakia. He was my most beloved soft doll. I took to rubbing with him a lot, and at a very early age, I was surprised to tip over into an explosive release. I instinctively felt I couldn't ask my mother about it and felt that the whole experience belonged firmly in the Sin box. It was strangely comforting. Fear transmogrified into overwhelming bursts of pleasure. As I learnt when I was older, there's nothing wrong with a good 'wank', and the release probably kept me sane. But at that time, I believed it was terribly wrong. Every time I rubbed Nonda, I promised the guy with the bloody red heart that this would be the last time. Of course it wasn't. Jesus, as well as Nonda, continued to get a sinful drubbing.

At age seven, as a break from weekly Hail Marys and her mysterious 'woom', I went away to a Methodist camp in the Adelaide Hills. I loved it and was glad to escape from my increasingly erratic, unhappy mother, who hated her new life in Australia and was always screaming, breaking dishes and slapping me around the head. As well as being the cause of misery and suffering to Jesus, apparently I was also the cause of all her suffering too. If it hadn't been for my sojourn in her 'woom', she could have gone back to her family in Ukraine whom she missed terribly. She had married my stepfather when I was five. And just like I had forgotten Dave and his sexual intrusions, I forgot that my stepfather was not my real father. Sasha had become Tata very quickly and smoothly. I told everyone at camp that I had attended my parents' wedding. I had loved that day, as my mother was in an unusually good mood and had let me wear my hair loose and curly, instead of in the plaits she normally insisted on. The Methodist organiser took great interest and asked me all about the wedding day.

'Are you sure that it was your mummy and daddy who got married?'

'Yes,' I said proudly.

'And how old were you again?'

'I was 5.'

She called another supervisor over. 'This little girl says she was at her parents' wedding!'

'Really?' I saw the woman's eyes shoot up in surprise.

I thought to myself, "what's the matter with these people. Doesn't everybody go to their parents' wedding?"

When I returned from camp, a baby sister had miraculously appeared. I was pleased to have an ally. But she seemed to make my mother worse. We were looked after by a Mrs Taplow on weekends. She was a staunch Methodist who took me to her church every Sunday, accompanied by her aged father and bachelor brother who had a walleye. Didn't like them much. But they were nowhere near as grim or scary as the Catholic bunch, so I asked my teacher if I could change to Methodist Religious Instruction. Miss Wesley, rimless glasses perched on potato nose, looked at me as if I was asking to have sex with the devil. She fixed me with a stare that chilled my blood. Even her name, as Methodist as they come, did not save me.

'I - beg - your - pardon?' Very cold, very curt and very measured. My resolve began to drain down to my prayer-ravaged knees.

'Please can I change to Methodist RI?' Small wheedling voice. 'Don't be so ridiculous,' she snapped. 'Don't you know who you are? You are a ROMAN Catholic.' She emphasised the word "Roman", piercing me with steely eyes. 'Don't you know what that means?' Other than being scared witless for years, no I didn't. 'It means, Eva, that once you are a Roman Catholic, you are always a Roman Catholic. Being a Roman Catholic is a privilege. The Pope in Rome....' She paused as she crossed herself, 'is our Earthly Father and we Roman Catholics are all special in the eyes of God. So, I don't want to hear any more of this nonsense. Off you go!'

So there I was; thrown back into the cauldron of mortal sin, Hail Marys and fear. Nonda the clown continued to get a drubbing. Would I ever escape? As an adult, participating on Enlightenment Intensives was a perfect means of putting all this nonsense into perspective.

I continued to go to Methodist Sunday school, but I now had to succumb to the attentions of Mrs Taplow's 80-year-old father. During Sunday afternoon tea, he would put me on his lap and tickle me. It started off harmlessly enough until the tickling took on a decidedly unpleasant turn. One day he poked his fingers under the elastic of my pants. I would try to squirm away from the gnarled, probing fingers, my giggling reaching a hysterical squeal which would earn me a stern admonishment from the pious Mrs Taplow. If I escaped to the kitchen, the bachelor brother would be standing there fiddling with the bottom of his white singlet and fixing me with his one good eye.

Once a year I was invited to June Read's birthday party. It was here that the depth of sexual trauma I was suffering became clear. The Reads owned a local factory and lived in a large house. One of the wonderful things they bestowed upon us party guests was a home cinema. This was an extraordinary treat in the 1950s and we watched all manner of cartoons and slapstick comedy. In the latter, some little guy was always being thrashed by some big thug. I was surprised that images of these scenes would steal their way into my nocturnal affairs with Nonda. I would climax at the thought of being savagely beaten. I didn't tie together this torrid development of my sexual fantasies with the fact that my mother, in a screaming fit of uncontrollable rage, would often literally beat me black and blue, with a leather strap that hung behind the bathroom door. I would be embarrassed to change my clothes for Physical Education in case anybody noticed the welts and bruises on my body.

My stepfather cycled to the Holden's car factory every day, where he worked double shifts as an oxy-welder. I often waited for him in the little wooden station house by the railway line near our house. I was disturbed by the strange drawings on the walls which seemed rather rude to me. A couple of older boys laughed at me as they explained what they meant. I felt uneasy with stories they told me of a girl called 'Fuckerada.' So rude and terrible. One afternoon one of the boys asked me to lie down on the bench and pull up my dress. I refused. He started to push me down. I screamed, 'my father is coming.' The boys ran off. I waited anxiously and was so glad when my father did appear on his pushbike. I loved my dad and wished he would be around more to protect me from my mother who did not seem to be able to look after my baby sister properly (I often had to reluctantly stay home from school when she couldn't cope) and had more raging fits, taking her turbulence out on me. We went to stay with Mrs Taplow and her strange Methodist relatives more often. Her father died; I wasn't too sad about that, so I only had to avoid the bachelor uncle who unnerved me with his roving walleye.

We were also shunted off to a German couple, who had moved in up the road. They had a son, Charlie, who was a little older than me. He and I liked to climb over the barbed wire of a disused munitions factory and play among the large cement pipes. It was in one of these pipes that Charlie took my pants off and did 'experiments' on my 'buhta'. I didn't know what was better, staying with the Methodists, staying with my mother's increasing volatility or staying with the Germans.

At home, things were increasingly intolerable. My mother's moods were getting worse. Even though my father had bought her a brand-new house, she was not happy. She refused to sleep with my father in their brand-new double bed. Her violence towards me also increased and my sexual fantasies became more masochistic.

This development wasn't helped by a book I found under the new double bed. The 'House of Dolls' was a shockingly vivid portrayal of what happened to young Jewish women who were abused both sexually and physically in Nazi concentration camps. To this day I shudder at what I remember of the graphic descriptions of torture, shame and humiliation. I would secretly devour the lurid pages of this book. This horrific world became alive in technicolour in my masturbatory fantasies, where I would work myself into a violent orgasmic crescendo as I imagined myself being treated as the scum of the earth and beaten mercilessly by vicious Nazis. A big split was developing- between my secret, shocking inner world and my sweet innocent exterior.

My mother became increasingly suspicious of me and accused me of all sorts of things. When I was eleven years old, it was 'I know why you are waiting for the postman.' She thought I was in love with him. Or 'I know what you were doing with Alexei in the darkroom!' Alexei was the son of a neighbour. 'I know what you were doing with David in the library.' David was a boy at school.

My mother decided that she hated my father and tried to leave him a few times. She suppressed her own sexuality deep within herself and projected it out. It felt that my sexuality was being twisted into a lurid, cruel, unhealthy form. Would I ever come out of that?

And spiritually, my life also felt twisted and very dark.

Then a ray of light pierced the darkness, surprisingly in the form of the evangelist Billy Graham. He visited Adelaide in May 1959 as part of an Australia-wide tour to spread his message. Mrs Taplow and her family took me to see him at the Wayville Showground. She was suspicious of this charismatic American, but felt obliged to go because the Methodist Church was supporting Graham's crusade to help initiate a Christian revival in Australia. We were among a 65,000-strong throng, a huge audience for Adelaide which, in the 1950s, was little more than a large town. The pious inhabitants of this quiet city of churches were curious about this preacher who was sweeping the world with his fiery mission. But, also wary. I stood on a hill, watching Billy Graham speak from a lectern. The Taplows were tight-faced at the unfolding spectacle. 'What a charlatan,' muttered Mrs Taplow. I was initially sceptical too as all my brushes with organized religion had been dire, but soon I became transfixed by what he was saying in his sonorous voice. I remember something like;

'You are perfect as you are and my message to you is one of love.'

This struck me in the chest. I felt he was speaking to me personally. Me, who believed I was so full of ugly sin and whose skinny body had endured all sorts of assaults, both external and self-inflicted- who felt tormented by the sheer ugliness of the dark world around me- who felt terribly guilty about being alive- whose mother screamed every day 'I wish you had never been born. It is all your fault- you are the cause of all my misery.' Who made me kneel for hours on a coir mat in the toilet as punishment. Me, who believed I had caused terrible suffering on the afflicted Jesus, whose every dirty sin was like a new nail being driven into his soft body. I was way beyond redemption.

Here, in the mouth of a man with a strange accent and an open face, was a new message.

'I tell you that Jesus loves you, just as you are.' This sounded like a different Jesus from the spooky, suffering one I had learned about in the catechism. Evening was settling over the Wayville Showground. Candles were lit around Graham's lectern. Billy Graham paused and a choir of women in white robes began to sing, 'Just as I Am.'

I was transported to a heavenly place where I knew without doubt, "I am perfect just as I am." This was a totally revolutionary experience in my world.

'If you want to come forward and receive the love of Jesus and allow him to dwell within you, walk down now.'

I looked up at the face of Mrs Taplow. The set of her mouth was grimmer than ever. Disapproval emanated like a black haze from all the Taplows.

'It's time to leave,' she barked, grabbing at my arm. 'Let us get away from this nonsense.'

But I did not allow her to drag me into the devouring blackness of her world. I made the decision to move forward.

The Taplows stared, horrified, as I walked down to the candle-lit heaven below me. I took a huge risk and moved towards light and love. Towards a spiritual connection that warmed my heart.

This Bill Graham sojourn lasted for two years. I received some slim volumes of the Gospel according to Matthew, Mark, Luke and John, which I enjoyed reading. I was also part of a well-organized Crusade support system. It took me through a dark time when my mother fell into severe mental illness that took her on a grim journey, further and further into the bowels of various grim Adelaide mental institutions. A rabbi's prayer that I have heard since, 'Let me not die while I am still alive" reminds me of the day when I knew I had lost my beautiful mother for good. I couldn't find her in the reception house she lived in, so went looking for her. In the bowels of the hospital, I spotted her in a long line of shuffling women in shabby clothes. I knew it was over for me and her as she was claimed forever by an unfathomable darkness.

She told me that she was the real Queen of Australia and I was a spy masquerading as Debbie Reynolds. 'You can't fool me,' she pronounced. 'And you are always up to no good whenever my back is turned'. When I was sixteen, she accused me of having sex with my stepfather. It went on and on.

After Olga was locked away permanently in a mental institution and Sasha took over, I drove my already confused sexuality into deep hiding. I was not allowed out at all; I was forbidden to cut my hair or to wear makeup. Once, when he found me in bed with curlers, he ripped them from my head. 'You whore, just like your mahder!' When, at the age of seventeen, he caught me holding hands with a boy, he bashed me across the head several times and said, 'No boys till you are 21.'

I would go to University on the bus, looking like the serious student he approved of- hair tied back, long skirt, no makeup. I emerged from the bus exactly twenty-one minutes later, skirt hitched up, coloured tights, mascara, lipstick, hair loose, looking like a babe. And I was a babe. University time was boy-hunting time!

My only slim rudder through this tumultuous time was the tiny conviction that I was perfect and Jesus loved me just as I am.

I ran away from home (literally) at twenty, in the dead of night, my father in his underpants chasing me with a broom shouting what a whore and Jezebel I was. I had committed the grave sin of coming home at one a.m. from a party. He was waiting, in a rage.

I was actually a virgin but had secretly engaged in heavy petting with a number of boys. So, my mother and father were right on one level. Boys would only have to touch me and I was off. It is a wonder I never did go all the way and fall pregnant, which was the all-consuming fear of my parents and many parents of the girls I knew. Two months after leaving home, I fell in love with Ken who ran the college student newspaper. I was his virgin and that was sacred to me. I only wanted him and during the next few years we were inseparable and the sex was good. We were also Anarchists. This became my new religion. Our commune became a hotbed of intrigue and plotting against the state.

I shocked my future mother-in-law when I said all churches should be destroyed as they were built on the bones of the poor and downtrodden, in service to the greedy and powerful. I dismissed Billy Graham and his Jesus claptrap firmly and buried them in a deep and shameful recess of my mind. I would sometimes break into a cold sweat in my dreams as my anarchist friends jeered at me when they discovered I was secretly a Billy Graham lover. I stamped out such revisionist nonsense by learning long tracts of Marx, Bakunin and Camus off by heart. I would drop these casually into conversation, earning respect from my comrades and another great shag from Ken.

The big fly in the ointment came when sexual liberation hit Adelaide. I was not into it at all, but all our friends were and unfortunately so was my new husband. Jealousy carved a deep scar across my heart.

Our child Lucie was born a few years later but the damage had been done.

I decided to bury any more vestiges of love or romance in the dark abyss into which Billy Graham had sunk.

Ken received a scholarship to the Sorbonne to do a PhD, so we moved to France with our child, who was only a few weeks old. We both became intrigued by Sigmund Freud and Wilhelm Reich and started to climb out of the confines of our Anarchist enclosure. A friend in London invited us to what he called a 'Reichian weekend'. This was dubbed a Marathon as it started on Friday at midnight and continued until Sunday midnight, with only four hours' sleep. The weekend blew both our minds and catapulted us into the therapy and Human Potential movement. It also led to the break-up of our marriage. I had closed off to Ken. With the deliberate quashing of my love for him, I quashed all the sexual feelings towards him as well.

We managed the split amicably and lived in a large commune in North London. Here, a new religion swamped us. This was the religion of a therapeutic community based on the Synanon Encounter movement that had originated in New York in the late 60s. This involved a lot of letting rip and yelling at each other. Breakfast was always followed by a 'slips' encounter, which involved picking up slips of negative comments that people had written over the last 24 hours and then screaming them out, e.g. 'Shelley, you left your dirty mug on the mantelpiece and I hate you.' Similar bouts happened in the evenings. We all screamed a lot, believing that our suppressed emotions were better out than in.

There was a lot of fun too. Luke Reinhart's book, 'The Dice Man', was all the rage. This combined our former Anarchistic leanings with our new psychotherapeutic adventures and we quickly became 'Dice Game' crazy. This involved setting ourselves six daring options and then rolling the die. The option that was called had to be acted out, for example running around the neighbourhood naked. So many evenings were spent enacting outrageous dares. One of these involved Brinsky doing a striptease on the kitchen table. He had been Ken's and my best friend in Adelaide. I noticed his shapely legs and fell in love. We began a relationship. From then on, a lot of the encounter groups and screaming involved Ken and Brinsky raging at each other, about me.

Meanwhile, I did as many Marathon groups as I could and trained to run them. The leader of these was Denny Yuson, who had brought Synanon to the UK. He looked like a shorter version of Jimi Hendrix and he soon realized that being a group leader got all the girls to want to drop their knickers. This led to the break-up between him and his wife Leida, who escaped to Poona and became a disciple of Bagwhan Shree Rajneesh. Meanwhile Denny's Marathons became more and more extreme. On one, for example, all the women, eyes bandaged, had to lie naked in a big circle, their heads at the centre of the wheel. Then the men, also naked, had to caress our pubic region. Why I subjected myself to this torture is beyond belief - I screamed and screamed and screamed. It was totally horrible. However, I did have a lot of historical rage and revulsion to scream out, so it may have been a blessing.

I wasn't sure what the point was of these exercises, but I did lose my inhibitions about being naked. We did all sorts of structures, which in retrospect seemed like one big, long, sexual orgy. There was, for example, the Snake-pit, where we writhed around naked on a pile of mattresses. We engaged in all sorts of sexual exploration, including with the same sex. Some of the exercises I found very useful, especially one where we explored each other's bodies. I discovered that no two vaginas were the same and every woman had a different-size clitoris, labia and vulva. I also lost my inhibitions of being weird or different. I was unique. All men's penises were so different too. I never forget one guy who could make his penis spin like a helicopter.

In one encounter group, we were doing a hidden agendas session. This involved saying out loud something very risky about oneself or another in the group. I had a particular aversion to a male participant with a long red nose. The point of the exercise was that one's projections often harboured unconscious memories. It worked. I remembered Dave, the farmhand, and his long red nose and his sudden disappearance when I dared tell my mother what was happening on the front seat of his truck. The repressed memory came flooding back. I relived the scene and was grateful to the man with the long red nose. Facing this helped settle a little of my disturbed sexual history but there was still a long way to go.

Most of these groups took place in a North London venue, Quaesitor, where I experienced a gamut of New Age psychotherapies including Gestalt, Psychodrama,

Psychosynthesis and Bioenergetics. I found it all very helpful in healing my fractured past, so decided to train to help others in the capacity of a psychotherapist.

As part of my training to become a Human Potential psychotherapist, I underwent a three-day experience called an Enlightenment Intensive. I really didn't want to do it. I did not believe in 'spiritual claptrap' as I called it. I had put Billy Graham in that box and thrown it away. The leader was Charles Berner, recently returned from India where he had been initiated by his Yogic guru, Kripalu. During this three-day process, we had to contemplate one of four questions, Who Am I? What Am I? What is Life? What is Another? We then punctuated the contemplation by communicating with a partner. There were 100 participants, so every exercise was with a new partner. Each exercise lasted 40 minutes, 5 minutes each way. I was soon plunged into great darkness and pain. For several hours, I suffered the most intense migraine. At age fourteen, when my mother disappeared further and further into insanity, I had started developing these migraines. I re-experienced the intense agony of losing her to madness, a forlorn kid watching her mother consumed by a haze of drugs, electro-shock therapy and finally a lobotomy. I experienced all that misery, accompanied by sporadic blindness, alternating with shooting, zigzagging arrows of flashing lights that assailed my brain. I vomited in a bucket many times. My partners swam before my eyes. I felt I was dying. The aim of the group was to have a change of state of consciousness- called Enlightenment. Sounded like gobbledygook to me. Berner said that wanting to die was part of the process and that I must persevere. Even though my world was falling apart, I decided to go along with the bearded weirdo on his dais. Eventually, through all the pain, fracturing and splintering, I bumped into a central part of me which seemed to hold the whole shebang together. I went up to Berner and said 'I am me'. Could it be this simple? He smiled- 'That is just the first level! Keep going!' The next day I was outside during a walking period where I pondered the question on Life. I sat in the garden of the Buddhist monastery, gazing at the flowers, the peacocks and the trees. I realized I just couldn't see them. Life was hidden behind a vale of tears. I cried and cried. Desperation pierced my body in waves. I felt that this was what life was- one never-ending travail of despair and misery. I was sobbing so much I didn't hear the bell and a monitor came to fetch me back into the room. As luck would have it, the only seat left was in front of an attractive guy. I tried to run away. I didn't want anyone to see me in my blotchy, snotty state, let alone him. The monitor led me firmly to my place and said 'Communicate to your partner.' So, I just continued sobbing and wailing and spluttered that life was just totally tragic. In the middle of my despair, he placed his hand on my knee in sympathy. Suddenly the world changed- his touch sent a powerful current of sexual energy right through me. I was shocked. One minute I was in the depths of agony and the next minute I was ablaze with sexual fire. I turned towards Berner, who was sitting on his raised dais at the far end of the room. He was shining and looking straight at me. He felt the shift in my consciousness through the throng of 100 people. Then I knew. There is no way that words can adequately convey this change of state. I experienced that life just IS, always, and I can choose how I experience it from moment to moment. I had had a similar experience with the birth of my daughter. My relationship with her father was difficult and I was terrified and alone as I went into labour. How could such a miserable unworthy being as me be capable of giving birth? My daughter as she slithered out was so perfect and lovely, I realized that I must be okay to have produced something so beautiful.

The experience of life on the Intensive galvanized a truth, deeply buried, that I had a choice in every moment. It also blew the top of my head, off, literally- I was catapulted right out of a narrow constraining viewpoint into a cosmos of brilliance. I felt blessed by a transmission of Truth through Berner, from his guru Kripalu.

I was again on the path towards light and love, or to what I call 'real' spirituality.

In my second marriage to Brinsky, it was me who had the roving eye. Even though he was a loving husband and a great father to my two children, Lucie and Steve, I was closed off to intimacy with a man, on a deep level. On a trip to Paris, I fell for a Frenchman. It led to the breakdown of my marriage.

I dumped the Frenchman and went on a sexual binge with men in their twenties; well, boys I should say, most of whom were quite disappointing. I didn't flirt. I just picked men up. I was thirty-two and determined to have the adolescence that I felt my father denied me. Probably the most shameful thing I did was go to discos at the Open University (where I was doing a PhD), leave the kids asleep in the back of the car, pick up a guy, take him home then get him to look after the kids next day as I slept off a hangover.

It felt I was still rebelling against the constraints my father had put on me in my teenage years.

# 3

## Jake Enters My Life

It seemed very easy to pick men up and use them as babysitters, but I obviously needed much more in my life.

The sparks from Billy Graham, my daughter's birth and the Enlightenment Intensive, simmered somewhere deep within my depraved soul. They gave me a new impetus toward my self-exploration. I wanted to wake up more. I started reading Ken Keyes' 'Handbook to Higher Consciousness' and practised the awareness exercises diligently. I also wanted a man, not another boy- someone who could stand me down, and at the same time not drive me away. I had a habit of turning men into my father which, I discovered in my work as a psychotherapist, a large proportion of women on the planet often do. I prayed for a man who could bust through all that. I also wanted a stable relationship, within which to bring up my children. These days it is called the Law of Attraction. In the late seventies, I was doing my own version, called a 'Creative Law'. And it worked.

I was reading 'Handbook to Higher Consciousness' in the Open University refectory, when a girl walking past, was arrested by the front cover of the book.

'That looks interesting,' she said. 'What's it about?'

So, I told her and described my work as a psychotherapist.

'I'm Lara and I live in an experimental commune and I think my housemates would be very interested in you, especially my partner, Peter. Come on over.'

A week later, I was invited to participate in the Christos experiment, a past life process that three people in the commune were trying out. Peter and I were to be each other's guides even though we hardly knew each other. I gave him the first instruction.

'You have to imagine your feet are six inches longer than they are.'

'No. I can't imagine them any longer than they actually are.'

This man was a hard-nosed scientist, a Professor of Physics at the age of thirty-four and running a successful Energy Research group. I had a job on my hands. As a psychotherapist, I had developed a lot of patience, so after half an hour of gentle suggestion, he was finally able to imagine his feet a tiny bit longer. That little tweak at his imagination was the breakthrough that was needed. After that, the process was easy and we launched into the most extraordinary experience of a past life. He became Jake, a Shropshire lad in the 19$^{th}$ century, who was hanged for poaching at an early age. For a variety of reasons, Peter adopted this name a couple of months later.

So, in essence, I was the first person to meet Jake. In return, he met a 14$^{th}$-century mad woman, the life I experienced when it was my turn. It could have been real or it could have been an allegory for my own background at the hands of a schizophrenic mother. It didn't really matter. What mattered was that Jake was not phased or put off in the slightest, even though I spent most of the time screaming and freaking out. This man just held the space for me beautifully. His patient acceptance of a deeply mad part of me was very healing.

This was the first of many bizarre and wondrous interactions between Jake and me which hinted at the hand of destiny. The next time we met, for example, was when we bumped into each other on a train which broke down at Watford Junction for three hours. We talked non-stop the whole time. We discussed our attitudes to relationships and both discovered we had been through the gamut of sexual liberation and experimentation, and deep down we each craved an intimate monogamous relationship; however not with each other at this stage, as we were not sexually attracted to each other; yet. But we loved the way each other thought.

Soon after this long conversation, I went to a midsummer night's party held at Jake and Lara's house. I took my kids and when I arrived, I realized I had forgotten my two-year-old son's plastic pants to cover his nappy. (these were the days before Pampers)

'No problem.' said Jake, whipping a plastic bin bag out of a drawer. He cut off the corners, fitted it, tied it at the waist and hey presto, plastic pants. I was impressed. The kids were put to bed upstairs in bunk-beds belonging to Jake's kids, who always came to stay in the holidays.

I'd gone with my latest young pick up and was dismayed to find two other boyfriends at the party. All three wanted to hang out with me. To avoid problems, I asked Jake and Lara if I could sleep with them. Jake and Lara were famous for three-way relationships. I had been through that whole trip several years earlier when I had lived in hippie communes in Adelaide. I had also experimented with every sexual persuasion one could think of in the many Marathon Encounter groups in which I had participated.

'Of course,' they both readily agreed.

That first night I fell asleep and kept my clothes on. As I left next morning, Jake murmured, 'A pity you kept your clothes on.'

'Mmmmm,' I thought, quite liking the glint in his eye.

It wasn't long before I was in a three-way sexual relationship with Lara and Jake. Lara encouraged it as she was having a second three-way with another couple. She was into polyamory and believed that this was a necessary evolutionary step and that monogamy was retrograde. I didn't mind too much as it suited me not to be committed to anyone, yet. Brinsky had also started living with a pretty woman, ten years younger than me.

The proverbial thunderbolt of love struck me a month later when I joined the members of the commune with my two children, Jake's two and their three cousins, on a camping holiday in Cornwall. We had stopped for lunch on the way and as Jake rested on a wall, bathed in sunlight, I saw the glimmer of goodness in his green eyes and I was struck by his kindness and generosity. I knew, then and there, he was the man for me. Slight problem. Two of his girlfriends were also on the camping trip. On the first evening, Jake came to visit me in my tent and stayed. Everything changed. Both internally and externally. The sex was electric. The earth moved, literally! A Force 10 gale which had been brewing over the Irish Sea, hit our campsite soon after. Tragically fifteen people died in the Fastnet race nearby. Our seven tents were totally flattened; the campsite wrecked, but I had found my man.

The three-way relationship continued – Jake was still committed to working it out with Lara. I snapped. I wanted Jake to myself and told him so. Lara became my interrogator. What kind of reactionary step was I trying to take here? Did I live in the Dark Ages? Belinda, the other girlfriend, was there too.

After several hours of fruitless argument, I left. As I walked home, I felt exhilaration. I had said my truth whatever the consequence, whatever the political correctness, whatever my retrograde sexual politics. The clear truth was that I wanted Jake to myself! It took another few weeks to untangle the physical relationship and another few months for Jake to free himself of Lara's charms. Lara went off and joined her other three-way relationship and Jake moved in with me. He told me that it had made a big difference to him when I had said I wanted him to myself. 'No-one had ever said that to me before,' he said.

Jake was attracted to the Human Potential therapy world I had been immersed in and wanted to know all about it. I described all the processes that I knew and had participated in, and we tried out some of the techniques together. Ever since his imagination had been ignited during the Christos experiment, Jake was ready to soar and try everything. He built a soundproof den in my bedroom and off he went on an intense journey of self-exploration. We thumped out our aggression on cushions; we attended all manner of workshops including regression, bioenergetics and psychosynthesis. Unfortunately, Jake was still hooked sexually on Lara. While I was in London working as a psychotherapist, she would visit, flashing her eyes. Once she wanted to show a butterfly she had tattooed in an intimate region of her body. I was relieved when Jake resisted her charms.

Jake and I attended a primal integration workshop where we screamed a lot and relived our births. At this workshop, Jake discovered the neurotic basis of his sexual attraction to Lara. He had always been attracted to rejecting women and wanted to break that pattern. With me, he felt he could- I was against type. We didn't need to have, he said, a 'romantic' relationship. Although I understood all this intellectually, I was not happy. I watched people snogging on railway station platforms and felt pain. I wanted that to be Jake and me. I felt like the adolescent girl who had not had enough of that kind of romantic love. I craved it.

Finally, Lara, Belinda and the other commune members moved out of Jake's house. I moved in. A small room upstairs was converted into a den where we continued exploring our psyches. We also used the hallucinogen psilocybin, consciously, to explore our inner worlds and psychological makeup. Jake could not remember his childhood and psilocybin opened up much of his early past. On one trip, I was thrown into the deep split within my sexual self- the sweet innocent little girl who coexisted uncomfortably with the voluptuous serpent queen. The raging lust of the latter threatened to splinter the fragile veneer of the former. A huge battle ensued as I tried to contain the rampant serpent that writhed and twisted deep within me. I thought I was going mad. How could I live with two such opposing sides of my femininity? I dared show Jake my terror, my brokenness, my madness. Most importantly I dared show him my intense jealousy. After having squashed it in my first marriage, I was allowing it up again and the pain that entailed.

We saw Lara at a party. Jealousy clawed my insides. I told Jake how I felt- I dared show him my vulnerability. He immediately pulled me on his lap and held me tightly for the rest of the party. As a result, I then dared show him my shy sexual self. Behind her emerged a sexy, serpent queen whom I began to accept as part of me. We became closer and Lara began to fade. Belinda visited some time later and confessed to me that she had also been in love with Jake and that she had been in awe of me the night I said I wanted him to myself. She wished she had had the courage to do the same.

Jake and I continued to work on ourselves using a variety of self-discovery techniques. The personal growth process I was most enthusiastic about and wanted Jake to experience was the Enlightenment Intensive. However, the main practitioners lived in the US. Jake found a book written by Jeff Love, about the Creative Law, another precursor of the law of attraction. Jeff Love had been the monitor on my first EI who had brought me, a snivelling wreck, back into the room. He was now a fully trained EI master. Jake did the 7-step creative law process to have him come to the UK. Miraculously it worked. Jeff Love was coming to London. Jake and I signed up.

On the 2nd day of the Intensive which was held in central London, Jake had a direct experience and walked around beaming rays of love. I avoided him. I couldn't stand it as I was immersed in a heavy process of my own and was angry that he had arrived there before me. I hadn't slept for two nights and was sobbing and screaming and feeling totally hopeless. On the third morning, during walking contemplation, I was in a cemetery near Old Street. I had a headache and severe nausea. The facial twitch I had developed as a teenager was back in full force – a sure sign of my madness and imperfection. I felt I had swallowed so much bullshit in my life and it was killing me. All the introjections of being a 'no good' person, of being a second-class citizen, of being mad like my mother, flooded my being. All the therapy I had done on myself to 'clear my shit', had clearly not worked. All the communication and crying and screaming I had expressed on this very Intensive, could never 'fix' the seriously flawed and totally imperfect being I was. I was a hopeless case whose mouth twitched in an ugly way. I believed I could only be blessed with an enlightenment experience if my twitch would be healed. A large undigested head of Christ with san paku eyes was stuck permanently in my craw- a symbol of my imperfection and sin. I suddenly had a violent urge to vomit, so found a cardboard box and spewed this Christ and all the poisonous introjections lodged in my system, into the box. When I had finished, I felt weak but strangely calm. I sat on a bench and asked myself the question 'What am I?' At that moment, a pigeon hopped past on one leg. Despite having only one leg, the actuality of this pigeon's existence burst through all my limiting perceptions. I had a facial twitch; the pigeon had one leg. We were both perfect as we were, even with all our imperfections. I was blasted into a change of state. I knew without a doubt what I was. I ran back to the venue and up to Jeff Love and said. 'I just am. I am.' It was a deeper level of what I had touched with Billy Graham all those years before.

'Beautiful,' he said.

Our first Enlightenment Intensive together was brilliant for our relationship. I managed to reconnect to my own worthiness and not try to suck it up obsessively from Jake. That was driving him away.

Shortly after that, Charles Berner came to the UK to do a Masters' Training course. I signed up and Jake participated in a 2-week Intensive in the UK and a 6-week in California. We were hooked on the process.

While Jake was away, I was paranoid that he would fall in love with someone more enlightened than me, more sexy than me, more together than me.

The opposite happened. He came back radiating even more love. And what's more, he directed it at me. He had decided that I was the one for him and that he would give himself to me totally. This is what I had always dreamed of, this is what I had always desperately wanted, this is what I had ached for. And here it was in all its glory.

And what did I do? Did I surrender and accept this beautiful love? No. I actually couldn't stand it. It felt too much. Too overwhelming. I ran away. I closed off. I withdrew.

Jake wanted to marry me. I stalled for two years. I was still technically married to my second husband. I delayed the divorce. I found it too difficult to let such deep love and commitment in.

The split between the icy cold girl and the serpent queen was still too huge.

Enlightenment Intensives were the battleground on which I continued facing down my demons. Both Jake and I became passionate about participating in them and mastering them for other people. We had got so much out of each of the illuminations that we had both received, as well as the continual in-depth explorations of what made us tick. I especially liked the space and time the process gave me, to explore my tumultuous past. The process worked and we wanted others to benefit as well.

Gradually the ice began to melt. I finally got divorced. I worked hard on my resistance to allowing Jake in. I began a process called Mind Clearing, another set of techniques devised by Charles Berner. By a quirk of fate, Berner had moved to Adelaide, the very place to where my parents had migrated when I was three. I participated in a two-week, 4 hour a day, one-to-one Mind Clearing Intensive. It seemed appropriate that I should be dealing with all my childhood stuff in the place where all the traumas occurred. But it was also where I had fallen in love with my first husband and experienced the consequences of sexual liberation and the methodical closing down of my heart.

Mind Clearing worked. I felt some of the steel bars around my heart beginning to melt. I made dramatic progress.

Finally, Jake and I set a date for our wedding.

As well as the Registry Office wedding, we had our own ceremony at home where we personalised our vows. The vow I had struggled with most was that of forsaking all others. I didn't want to give up all the other men on the planet. And here was the most delicious man, right in front of me. I made the vow. We also made the vow that our relationship would be based on Truth and that Jake and I would be each other's guides on our path to God. These vows served us in great stead and would be tested to the limit in the years to come.

I relaxed. Our marriage was happy. Commitment to one person wasn't so bad after all. My children liked the fact that their mother was settled at last. An unexpected bonus was that my two kids and his two kids loved the union. From then to this day, they see each other as siblings and adore each other.

We continued with our joint passion, which was running Enlightenment Intensives. This was in addition to Jake heading a department at the Open University, and me running psychotherapy training groups. Jake began to run several two-week EIs in which I participated. I then went to Austria and participated in a 6-week Intensive run by Satya, Berner's chief disciple. It was gruelling for me. I faced so much stuff about my mother and her madness. My face decided to continue exhibiting its twitch, which I had to show to every participant. It was humiliating and I felt I was displaying my insanity day after day after day. On day 32, I had my reward. I knew without doubt that we humans loved each other profoundly, always had and always would. Paradoxically, this made sense of all the suffering I had endured. I felt great peace.

A few months later, the ashram in Adelaide exploded. Satya left her husband and spilt the beans on the hidden sexual exploits of her guru, Berner. He was hounded out from the ironically-named Eternal Truth Foundation. He and his girlfriend/chief follower wrote and asked if they could have refuge in our house. Satya immediately warned us that Berner would destroy our relationship like he had destroyed all other relationships, including hers. She also threatened to expose us to the News of the World if we allowed this evil devil into our house.

I was a bit worried by this threat, but my gratitude to Berner and his techniques overcame my fear. Fortunately, Jake and I had never gone along with the ashram, eternal truth stuff. We also thought the power Satya and other people gave Berner was crazy.

We had the guru in our attic for ten weeks. Our relationship did not fall apart. But Berner did try to convert us into new disciples. We knew the traps to avoid falling into a disciple trip. Flattery was one of the chief lures. It came in many forms.

'You are highly-evolved beings.' We ignored it.

'You are both ready to receive this esoteric knowledge.' We ignored it.

'You are the chosen ones to continue this path.' We ignored it.

However, he did tell us a great deal of the teaching he had received from Kripalu, his Yogic guru, which was valuable. Berner also supervised the Sahaja Yoga meditation which I had been doing since the first Enlightenment Intensive when the top was blown off my world. This was a surrender meditation and had been bringing up deeper levels of my sexual trauma, especially the masochistic fantasies that often still plagued me. I just couldn't get them out of my head. Berner encouraged me to accept and allow these fantasies to come up and relive them. I did so and it was very confronting. After a few weeks, the practise culminated in a vivid dream in which I was being beaten with different coloured whips by a beautiful set of clowns, in a sadomasochistic orgy. The sadists were men in brightly-coloured costumes and masks. I had read 'Story of O' in my 20s, which had further fuelled my masochistic fantasies. As I experienced an orgasm in the dream, I felt something dark and slimy being expelled from my body. Permanently. 'Boga' it was called in the yogic tradition. Since that day I have not had another beating fantasy. The healing of my sexuality has taken many more twists and turns and continues to evolve. But this was a big step on that journey and a pivotal one.

Sahaja Yoga was a powerful meditation which required surrender to the Divine, but required a teacher further along the Yogic path. Berner had strayed off this path and was now a disgraced guru. Like many gurus, he had abused his students sexually. Moreover, he did not act in the way I expected an enlightened person to act; his breath smelt; and he would eat all our biscuits in one sitting. He justified his sexual exploits with his students, by claiming they were part of an ancient yogic tradition. Sounded like bullshit to us. We were glad when he finally left, but as I did not then have a reliable teacher for my Sahaja Yoga, I stopped the process.

Jake and I continued running Enlightenment Intensives. For all his failings as a guru and spiritual teacher, Berner had taught us some amazing techniques. His importance in our life was immense and we wanted to honour that. We bought and renovated a large manor house so we could run the groups at home. I had now also trained to be a Mind Clearer and was training others. Unbeknownst to me, these techniques would become very handy when I turned 58 and I had to get my man back; when I had to confront Stella, the beautiful bald sphinx, and let her know that Jake belonged to me. Little did I know that instead of her, it would be me in the firing line.

# 4

## The Party Has a Surprise in Its Tail!

The party is happening at Brett and Stella's London house. Many of our friends from meditation days are there. They are all a little shocked by my appearance. I was their Enlightenment Master, was blonde and curly and favoured wearing soft, flowing skirts. Now I have black spiky hair, am wearing black leather jeans and jacket, with a determined gleam in my eye. I look sassy.

Stella is wearing tight jeans; when she bends over, I can see a pink thong outlining her curvaceous backside. She looks up at Jake, all doe-eyed. I have my work cut out.

We all take some ecstasy. I again only take a half a tab; I suffer a bout of nausea and there has not been a hint of spirulina in sight. I put it down to a particular inherited aversion to drugs that runs in my family. My mother suffered severe side effects from lithium when it was poured down her throat in the 1960s and I had been battling for years with psychiatrists to take my sister Alexandra off the drug Olanzapine, which seemed to be locking up her joints. So, I find drugs, both illegal and medicinal, difficult – I can't even have a sleeping pill. I live with the nausea but it passes after fifteen minutes or so. The party is warming up. Brett and Stella, the same age as our kids, had embraced the rave scene in their twenties. They both dabbled with other drugs and Brett had got hooked on heroin. Enlightenment Intensives had helped him get through his addiction. Two other couples, Angie and Will and Gerry and Irma, are present. All have participated in Enlightenment Intensives with us.

The ecstasy starts to do its heart-opening magic and the ambience in the room is lovely. I see how young and glowing

Stella is, but it doesn't bother me. I feel so feisty in my leather gear and Jake seems to appreciate this new hot woman he is with. Stella's friend Angie, who is training to run Enlightenment Intensives, asks me to tell the group about Mind-Clearing, the therapeutic process I had practised and trained others to do. Angie wants to learn about it, so very confidently, I say, 'Hey I will demonstrate one of the techniques, right here, right now, one that deals with guilt.' I turn to Gerry who had practised the process, and say, 'you up for it?'

'Yes,' he says. The group gathers around.

'Gerry, I will give you the guilt-clearing instruction, "Tell me something that you have done that in your own estimation you should not have done."

Before Gerry can answer, Jake interrupts. 'Gerry, are you sure you want to do this? I suggest you ask Eva the question.'

'Okay,' I agree. Jake has a point. Gerry need not be put on the spot. Foolishly, I make a mental decision to say the first thing that comes into my head. I have participated in many Enlightenment Intensives with these people, and they have heard everything about me, the good, the bad and the very ugly. So, I am confident that no stone has been left, unturned. Gerry turns to me and says.

'Tell me something that you have done, that in your own estimation you should not have done.'

Oh, hell and damnation, the first thing that pops into my head is unbelievably bad. My inner censor snaps to attention.

"No way, baby, are you going to confess THAT!!"

Damn the ecstasy. It is unearthing an embarrassing secret buried deep in my subconscious. Jake doesn't even know about this yet. Everybody's eyes are upon me. The doe-eyed sphinx glows in her thong. And to think I started this. Damn. What has risen unbidden, is an incident that occurred twenty years earlier. Jake and I were running an Enlightenment Intensive in Devon and during a break, I sneaked off to a public telephone booth, to phone a man I had fallen in love with. To tell him I missed him.

"You must not confess this!" commands my inner censor. I desperately try to think of something less incriminating. But nothing pops up.

I remember the instruction. Is this something I've done that in my own estimation I should not have done? Definitely. I am so ashamed that I sneaked off without Jake's knowledge. Jake knew everything else about this chap but not this. It had been a difficult time in our relationship and I thought we had got through it. But I had never told him about the telephone call.

And hey, I can't say this here in front of these people. Enlightenment Intensives are about Truth with a capital T. I was always telling these very people, 'the truth shall set you free.' They look up to me as a 'truth seeker.' And here is this example of me being two-faced and doing the opposite. I can't say this, especially in front of Stella. I'm here, in my black biker gear, to see her off for being intimate with my man. I'm the injured party here, right? I'm not going to confess that I broke the rules and snuck off to talk to another man I was in love with. There is a deathly hush in the room. Where can I run? No less-incendiary confessions bubble up in my mind. Only me telling this guy I miss him. But there's something about ecstasy that gives you courage. I blurt out the lugubrious confession to Gerry. I see his eyebrows arch in surprise. I hear Stella gasp. The leather of my trousers chafes uncomfortably against a sheen of sweat.

'Thank you,' says Gerry and gives me the next instruction in the guilt-clearing process. 'Tell me something you have failed to do, that in your own estimation you think you should have done.'

It is blindingly obvious. I should have told my husband.

I turn to Jake. He is looking at me intensely. I move towards him and blurt out. 'Oh Jake, I am so sorry I did that and kept it secret.' His eyes burn.

'I am so sorry it has taken me 20 years to tell you that.' My remorse is genuine and deep. Tears fill my eyes. I realize how much I love this man, and how profoundly sorry I am for keeping this secret from him. His eyes are dark, unfathomable. It is like a deep opaque barrier between us is being faced.

'I promise I will never lie to you again.'

"Dammit," my inner censor is freaking out. She feels helpless in the face of ecstasy, which is well known as a truth drug. She desperately dredges up her arsenal of weapons which lie in a scattered heap.

"You can't promise that!" she shrieks. "That's too hard. Your whole persona is built on secrecy." This is true. My parents were spawned in Stalin's Russia. The only way to survive was to lie. And I had become an excellent liar. I had hidden my sexuality for example.

I ignore the inner turmoil. Jake's eyes clear and I feel I can see straight into his heart. I see the vestiges of hurt that me falling for another guy has deposited there.

I say, 'I don't ever want to hurt you again.'

We fall into each other's arms. It is a sweet moment. The rest of the group stand as witnesses. Jake and I gently extricate ourselves from each other. I feel a weight has been lifted. I am feeling as light and clear as a fluffy grass seed in the wind. I turn to the group.

'There,' I say, 'that is an example of guilt-clearing in action. You examine yourself and decide, in your own estimation, if there is something you did or failed to do in your life. You bring it into the light, have it received by someone; feel the remorse; put it right and you can go on. But I tell you what a breeze it is, under the influence of ecstasy. Anyway, now lets all dance. This is a party after all.'

The rest of the evening was great. Jake and I only had eyes for each other. We noticed that Stella was cosying up to Brett. I had got my man back but in the most unexpected way.

The next day Jake and I debriefed over breakfast. We believe that anything discovered while under the influence of intoxicants has to be gone over again, straight and sober. That way we can bring it permanently into our life. It did feel permanent. I felt a deeper understanding between us. I marvelled at how efficient the universe was in resolving this particular crisis in our relationship. What had stung my heart just a few days earlier was Jake saying how much he missed Stella. It seemed like a dart had found its way into a hidden crevice in my heart and uncovered my secret of missing another man. The combination of guilt-clearing and ecstasy did the rest.

'And your courage,' said Jake softly.

We felt closer than we had for a long time. By hiding the secret of Tom within myself, I was holding out on Jake.

I had fallen in love with Tom when I was 38. I believe that is a dangerous age for married women. Many of my girlfriends at the time had fallen for other men and created havoc in their marriages. For me, the unsettling spectre of future cronedom was already casting a shadow over the future.

"Uh oh, I'm nearly 40 – it's not going to be much longer that I will be young and sexy and will be able to pull a man. Can I still pull a man?"

The opportunity arose when I went to run a three-day training group in Bath for an organization that Tom was involved with. I was to stay with him and his wife and children. He picked me up at the railway station and informed me that his wife and kids had gone to visit her mother.

'Oh!' I said, somewhat taken aback. Tom was the proverbial tall, dark, handsome type. I briskly dismissed his allure. I was happily married and so was he. Besides, he was only 30- he couldn't possibly be interested in an old bag like me. And anyway, I had work to do- and a group to run. All was fine and very professional for the first two days. The evenings were spent with the clients and I would fall exhausted into the spare bedroom in Tom's house. On the last evening, we walked to his home together and the energy between us began to shift. He looked like a dreamboat in the moonlight.

'I liked the way you worked with the clients,' he said looking down at me from his 6'3" height. 'You are so cool and professional.'

Now that was a turn on for me. All my life I have believed I am totally uncool and not in the least bit professional. I am scatty and my hair is an unruly mass of curls- the proverbial dizzy blonde. So, the 'cool professional' type I longed to be, glowed inside, and the way he looked at me made something else glow as well. Uh oh, we were walking towards temptation; towards an empty house.

'I'm going to miss you when you go tomorrow', he said simply. Shit.

'I'm going to miss you too.' The words came out of my mouth before I could rein them in. I was sliding on a slippery slope. I was 38. Could this be the last time I could pull such a gorgeous bloke?  The song, "This could be the Last Time," droned in my brain.

When Tom took my hand, the charge was electric. We reached his house and sat in the living room, gazing at each other.  It felt so romantic. I felt I had not had enough romance in my life. I still craved it. it. I was so hurt when Jake didn't want a romantic relationship when we first met – this just added to my craving for heart-melting moments like these.

'Sleep with me,' he said. I gulped. An image of Jake sprang up in front of me.

'No, I can't,' I spluttered. 'I'm in a monogamous relationship.'

'Oh, are you?' he said. 'Sherry and I are in an open relationship.' This was news to me.

'What, she wouldn't mind if you……'

'Well, no. In fact, she had a sexual relationship with her therapist.'

'How was that for you?'

'Difficult, but as a result, we decided to open up the marriage. But we are committed to staying together.'

'Hmmm', I said. 'For me that wouldn't work. And besides, I would have to tell Jake. We have that commitment to each other and to telling the truth.'

Oh, I was being so sensible. I just wanted to jump him then and there.

'Well, just lie next to me in the bed,' he said. 'We could just go on talking there. It is really cold down here.'

Ah temptation, how tantalising you are.

"You've only one life." screamed the denied girl inside of me. "Go for it."

"Remember your vow to forsake all others." A stern admonishment from the sensible one.

A compromise.

'Okay, but we mustn't touch.'

So that's what we did. It was torture, but we managed to keep a respectful distance.

Next morning, we had a bath together. That was pretty bad.

With huge difficulty, I told Jake when I got back.

'Did he touch you sexually?'

'No.' Phew, thank God for that. It took me a few more weeks to tell Jake about the naked bath.

Twenty more years to tell him about the secret phone call.

And now we were now processing the ecstasy party. It seemed we were square. One ear-licking felt well and truly balanced out against sleeping all night with someone, having a naked bath together and a secret phone call.

But the real damage both ways was the intimate 'falling in love' thing. That was yet to be fully worked through.

But in the meantime, the sex between me and Jake continued to be good. It turned out it had nothing to do with lack of eggs or hormones. As the intimacy between us deepened, so did the passion. And the romance!

The packets of Horny Goat lay forgotten in the back of the cupboard.

Page intentionally left blank

# 5

## Golden Delicious

Soon after this party, Jocasta and Vincent invited us to a weekend party in Wales. It was put on by a group of people who had first partied together in the height of the rave scene in the early 90s. Julie Devine, who would become a great friend of ours, and her friend Sephie had arranged the event. As the partygoers were all 15 – 25 years younger than us, I went with some trepidation.

I was in my late fifties. How would a near pensioner fare? But hey, I had rediscovered my sexuality. I had also finally seen that I had great legs and I wanted to show them off. Since being told I had chicken legs when I was in my teens, I had hidden my legs for the next forty years. Despite Jake telling me they were great, I didn't believe him. When I looked down upon them, they looked like emaciated chicken bones. Then I made the startling discovery that if I looked at them from down low in a full-length mirror, they didn't look half bad. In fact, I started prancing about in shorts and skirts and thought 'Wow, they are okay.' So, I went to the party determined to show them off. After all, I only had a few years before the meat fell off my bones.

The party was in a swank hotel in the Welsh countryside and lived up to its name, Golden Delicious. Sumptuous gold hangings were swathed over the entrance, hallways and dance rooms. A young man and two delectable young women, decked in little else but gold spray, enticed us in, offering us Golden Delicious apples, piled high on platters. It looked like something out of a Fellini set. All party-goers had to make their entrance down a grand stairway, glittering in gold.

I wore the same scant, triangular, gold coin affair I had bought in Luxor where Jake had taken me on my $50^{th}$ birthday. It showed off the pink Wonderbra and my new-found legs to perfection.

With many misgivings, I stood at the top of the stairs on Jake's arm. Jake wore a Rod Stewart wig and leopard skin pants. We were a couple of ageing 1960's hippies attempting to hobnob with serious 1990's ravers. I was afraid we might look ridiculous? As we started our descent, a luminous young couple swooped upon us, saying, 'You two look amazing. We want some photos.' While she wielded her camera, her man, looking debonair in a gold cap, started a sexy dance with me right there on the landing. His girlfriend flirted outrageously with Jake. It took my breath away; such a brilliant start to the weekend.

Neither Jake nor I could believe how many people 'hit' on us over the next couple of days. Age did not seem to matter one jot. Most of the party-goers were successful professionals who now had children. They were here in a reunion with their raver day mates, to relive old times. The party was a blast. I received so many compliments on my legs, which emboldened me to show them off more. And Jake had a devoted army of giggling girls who made believe he really was Rod. Even without his Rod wig, Jake looked sexy.

I was struck again by the unfairness of it all. In this society, men got more attractive as they got older. But where were the sexy older women? Yes, there were the cougars- but they were usually in their 40s. Then there was the facelift generation. How many women with falling necklines graced the front of magazines? None. Perhaps occasionally on the front of a Saga magazine. It wasn't fair.

A girl with gypsy-like curls made a beeline for Jake. Flattered, he flirted with her. I felt uncomfortable as my heart constricted. I still felt raw and vulnerable from the Stella episode. It also reminded me of times in my early twenties when I lived in a commune, and the man I was crazy about would be flirting with another woman and would sometimes end up in bed with her. It was so painful. I would be so jealous and be admonished by other communards: 'jealousy is a false emotion', 'nobody owns anybody', 'sexual liberation forever.'

One particular New Year's Eve, my partner was chatting up a voluptuous 15-year-old. I was the ripe old age of 22, already feeling old. I knew my man wouldn't be kissing me at midnight. It would be that under-age minx. I felt powerless and insane. I ran out of the party, drove my car to a river and screamed. I screamed and screamed till midnight came and went, then I sobbed till dawn. Jealousy was twisting my insides into a torment of pain. I couldn't bear it. I couldn't go on. I shut something down that night. I refused to ever feel that hurt or rejection again.

I am now in my late 50s. I watch Jake flirting with Jinny with the impossible gypsy curls. She is about 28 – less than half my age. And I – I'm an ageing grandmother. The tears well up from the pain deep within me. I grab Jake's hand and take him to the chill out area.

'What's up, babe?' Jake looks concerned.

'I am insanely jealous of that young gypsy. I need you to stop giving her the eye.'

'Okay, babe.' Jake takes my face tenderly in his hands.

'I hate the fact she is young and beautiful and nubile. I hate being so old.' The tears come down. Jake kisses my tear-stained cheeks.

'Eva, I want you to know it's you I love.' He hugs me hard.

'But, what about my wrinkly neck?'

'Hey, you are so silly. I guarantee that no man here is looking at your neck. You are just gorgeous. It's you shining out that is important.'

Something deep within me lets go. Jake leads me up to bed and we have electric lovemaking. Sexual healing, I would call it. Later when Jake is falling asleep, I am wide awake. I hear the music reverberating throughout the hotel.

'Jake, I have to go down and dance some more,' I say.

He gives me a drowsy kiss. 'You go, darling.' I'll look forward to you snuggling up with me later.'

I returned to the dance floor and started to dance. I suddenly noticed that everywhere I looked, guys were giving me the eye. I was shocked. And they were good-looking men. When I was young there were many guys from whom I was continually escaping. I couldn't believe it. But it was true.

After a few more dances, I found I was getting more and more confident. It felt great. Jake was right. None of these guys seemed to notice my neck.

Over the next couple of days, we met people whom we would get to know over the next few years. Chloe and Julie, who were great DJs, became close friends, as well as DJ Sparkie. Poonie, a stunning blonde and Greg, her tall, handsome husband, a brilliant DJ and doctor, welcomed us warmly to their party world. Poonie flirted effortlessly and I was in awe of her. We chatted to her at breakfast where she was canoodling with Greg. I did not know at this point that Poonie would become a very important role model for me. I liked them both immediately, especially the way Greg had carried her off over his shoulder the night before.

Jake and I were feted as the Golden Oldies and this description would fit us well over the next decade. Some people thought we were famous tantra teachers. We began to get great feedback on how good we were together- this would eventually launch us into fully embracing our relationship as a spiritual path.

Life was looking up; especially when Lucie became pregnant again and gave birth to a healthy, divine little boy.

Jake and I discovered 4-wheel driving and went on some spectacular adventures in different parts of the world. Cronedom, which had been stalking me so viciously in the last few years and had sucked the life out of me, seemed to have withdrawn. She skulked in a dark corner, shielding her eyes from the sexy woman I was becoming and tut-tutting. 'You can't avoid me forever!''

Although I well and truly had my man back, the temporary intimacies we had formed with other people in our dalliances with Stella and Tom, still needed to be unearthed and healed. Then, as if on cue, Jocasta and Vincent threw us another outlandish invitation which would lead unexpectedly to a deeper layer of healing in our relationship.

Page intentionally left blank

# 6

## Facing Madness in Deep, Dark Peru

'Come to the Amazon with us to take ayahuasca', said Jocasta.

'What a silly idea' I said. I had had quite enough excitement recently, what with going to parties and dressing up. I was also knitting for my grandchildren (another was on the way). The crone whispered from the corner 'Ignore them. You have been outrageous enough lately. You need to wind down and get ready to draw your pension.' So, what was this crazy new caper?

Jocasta and Vincent wanted us to accompany them to the middle of the Peruvian jungle to try the jungle medicine, ayahuasca, with a Shaman. These were the early days of Western people trying ayahuasca, which has now become widely popular.

Having sampled various psychedelics in the past, I wasn't particularly attracted to what I saw as just being a new version.

'What about piranha fish, malaria and anacondas? And besides, Ayahuasca makes you vomit spectacularly,' I told them. We had tried ayahuasca already in a Sante Daime ceremony in the UK. (In 1930 Brazil, Raymond Irineu, an illiterate rubber tapper, had an ecstatic vision of the Virgin Mary. He built the Santo Daime Church, now legal in Brazil, based on this vision that uses ayahuasca as a sacrament.)

As well as being peeved by having to sing Portuguese hymns, I spent a lot of time in the loo, throwing up. Going to Peru was of greater interest to me, as it felt like a more genuine way of trying the 'medicine' with traditional Shamans from the Amazon jungle, without the Virgin Mary overlay. My relationship with drugs has had a fraught history since watching my mother being destroyed by the first wave of psychotropics that flooded mental hospitals.

There were other associations as well. When pot hit Adelaide in the late 60s, all my friends got into it. It rendered me totally paranoid so I hated it. Pregnancy saved me from the first experimentation with LSD. When I did try it a couple of times in Paris when I was 25, I was plunged into a terrifying, temporary psychosis. I was thrown back to when I escaped Communist Czechoslovakia as a three-year-old. Innocuous looking Parisian postmen on pushbikes transmogrified into evil Russian border guards on motorbikes, all intent on killing me. My ego was very weak and the contents of my unconscious spilled out and nearly drowned me. This was well before I discovered the work of Stanislas Grof, which used LSD very effectively to help people face such nightmarish parts of their psyches and heal them.

Later, when I lived in the therapeutic commune in London, drugs were frowned upon. The commune had been based on Synanon-style encounter groups, where many people had been recovering addicts from alcohol and other drugs. This suited me, as at that time I didn't like the effects of drugs upon me. When Jake and I pursued Enlightenment Intensives, both as participants and as leaders, this was also a 'straight' path. The aim was to discover the nature of reality and spirit, without the use of drugs. So, I always had had a saint hat on in relation to taking drugs as recreation. However, I also noticed that people who had taken hallucinogens seemed a lot more open than those who hadn't. Their doors of perception had been widened, as famously described by Aldous Huxley. They had seen a glimpse of a world outside their normal perception. These people usually did well on Enlightenment Intensives and in Mind-Clearing therapy.

There were times that Jake and I specifically used drugs to expand our knowledge of ourselves. This was successful and liberating. Jake helped me get through my paranoia which was acute, especially with cannabis. I would become terrified and felt I was being watched and judged. This meant I had to communicate what I was frightened of and this was scary as it was often Jake and what was going on in our relationship! Getting through this was liberating and led to several breakthroughs in us really understanding each other's reality. We dubbed our cannabis sessions as 'joint reality'. When I had tried psilocybin and encountered the Serpent Queen, I had to show her to Jake. Inside the cocoon of terror lived a sensual Bohemian woman who was aching to expand, let go and be herself. She would not be totally free until she was in her 60s as we shall discover.

However, I also firmly believed that I should really acquire greater consciousness without drugs. This is why I was attracted to 'pure' gurus like Ching Hai, a Vietnamese nun, whom I followed for a few years. All main spiritual paths recommended eschewing drugs. I was torn between the two versions of how I should spend my life. Jake and I had found a way around this dilemma by splitting our lives into what we called Pilgrim phase and Hedonist phase; three to six months each. We found that this way we could have the best of both worlds- the saint and the hedonist.

However, with our introduction to ecstasy, we saw the huge benefits of this drug to relationships. On further investigation, we found that it had been used like this in America before being banned. And the benefits felt permanent, as long as the experiences were grounded by talking about it afterwards, as we did after the ecstasy party when I confessed to Jake. In fact, I found ecstasy effective for me personally, as it helped me unburden my secrets more easily, and in this way free me from their sticky webs.

With the advent of the hallucinogen ayahuasca into the west from the jungles of South America, a new strand entered this hedonism versus pilgrim dilemma. It gave the name 'medicine' to our hedonistic path. Ayahuasca was a plant medicine purported by its practitioners to have a huge power to heal.

Ingesting ayahuasca was akin to imbibing a healing force, an entity of love that could teach you and heal you. This had been heralded by Carlos Castaneda along with peyote in the 1970s.

'Oh, come on,' pressed Jocasta. 'It will be an amazing adventure.'

So, I casually said,

'We are going to Canada this summer to do more 4-wheel driving. If it is right for us, we will only come if the timing fits.'

I shouldn't have said that. The timing fitted in perfectly. Soon I was buying jungle clothing impregnated with mosquito repellent, and reading everything I could about Peru and Shamanism

What we were being propelled into? Little did we know that the South American adventure would eventually lead to deeper understanding of what had brought Stella so dramatically into our lives.

We flew to Lima and then Iquitos, a city hemmed in the northeast corner of the Peruvian rainforest. An overnight ferry chugged down the Amazon for twelve hours, deeper into the jungle, as I swathed myself in mosquito repellent. Then we switched to canoes as we branched out on a smaller river to a dank, malaria-infested corner of Peru. No rain had fallen for a month and this tributary of the Amazon was running low. Our canoe was heavy, laden with water and supplies for our intrepid group of seekers, who were winding their way further and further into the labyrinth of the jungle, to visit a remote Shamanic group. When the canoe got stuck, I had to put aside my terror of various poisonous creatures that lurked in the mud and sank in over the side, to push. I was engulfed in the sweat and odour of this shaded paradise which exploded with life. And incredible beauty. As monkeys cart-wheeled through their leafy highways above, an orange butterfly licked the salt from the nostrils of a yellow-spotted turtle basking on a rock. Tramping through the jungle next day, I had to put aside more terrors such as tree snakes unfurling onto my head, tree frogs shooting lethal arcs of poison and black tarantulas waiting to strike. The jungle turned out to be much more benign than any of my fantasies.

We were searching for barks, leaves and vine roots for the ayahuasca brew we would be making and drinking, its active psychedelic ingredient being DMT. This medicinal concoction was purported to bring healing visions and great insights. I watched fascinatedly as the Shamans performed their gathering rituals. Smoke was blown on each tree from which bark had been taken, and thanks were sung to the tree spirits in a haunting mixture of Spanish and Quechua, the ancient language of the Amazon tree people. As with the orange butterfly and the turtle, life here was as much about symbiosis as survival. Clouds of Blue Morpho butterflies drifted by as we spent hours pounding vine roots before adding them to the leafy, barky concoction that boiled away in a giant cauldron over a roaring fire. As I pounded, I lurched between excitement and scepticism. My work as a meditation teacher led me to be wary of 'hallucinogenic fixes'. However, there was something magical about creating the brew from scratch and watching it being impregnated with the mystery of the jungle.

We imbibed the foul-tasting liquid that evening, in a ceremony that was carried out in a large area on stilts, swathed in mosquito netting. I liked the fact that we all were asked to make an intention. As I had been struggling a lot with trying to heal my dysfunctional family in Australia, I asked for healing for myself. The Shamans sang haunting icaros or spirit songs. These, accompanied by the rustling of their leaf rattles or shacapas, invoked the healing spirits of the plants that we had drunk. Fireflies pinpointed the blackness of the night and the jungle closed in around us, enveloping us with the sounds of a million forest creatures.

The first effects of the juice were beautiful if not unnerving. The incantations and rhythmic rustling of the shacapas, ushered in troupes of rainbows that danced into the halls of my mind. This rainbow world was not unlike the psilocybin trips I had taken in the English countryside around a campfire. I thoroughly enjoyed the kaleidoscope of colours which seemed to pop and sway with the background chorus of tree frogs.

A most beautiful tree spirit materialised in front of me. He smiled at me benignly and welcomed me on this healing path and commended all my efforts of journeying to discover more truth. I could see all the roads I had ventured along, merging to this point. The Shaman then sang an extraordinary incantation over me and I was surrounded by thousands of tree spirits - some of them were hoary and old-looking, world-weary and serious; others were fierce and angry; others sad. But they all had one thing in common; they loved me seeing them and recognizing them. They comprised an anthem of tree spirits, all loving me. In turn, I felt beautifully recognized- they saw me as a powerful, funny, light being and I seemed to bring a smile to their faces, even the morose ones. I had never really had an experience like this before and it opened me to another world of plants and animals that I would return to later in my journeying.

This particular visit was five days long and we undertook three ayahuasca ceremonies. The first was totally glorious; I felt I was queen of the jungle and welcomed by all beings residing there. But the second trip was horrifying. I vomited and vomited and felt myself drowning in a dark barrel of snakes. I thought this was the end and I would die. The Shaman again sang over me and his assistant started to bathe me with water. I felt myself disentangling from the snakes and rising above them to a glorious place. I was spread-eagled on the altar of love and surrounded by ancient Ayahuasca queens who poured their love into me and sprinkled me with multi-coloured flowers. They radiated light and their bodies were made of a myriad of multi-coloured jewels, all glittering in hexagonal shapes. They were welcoming me into their world and I felt like a trembling novice.

'But I am not like you. I am too unworthy of this splendour.' I said.

'Oh, you are so worthy. We honour the struggle you have been through in your life and the journey you have taken. You are so welcome to sit at our table. We have so much to teach you.'

The third journey started again with dancing rainbows, when suddenly my vision was flooded with 1950s' Adelaide people.

1950s' Adelaide people! This was the last thing I was expecting. I was in remote Peru. I'd drunk a medicine that was supposed to bring amazing visions. Anyone who has ever met 1950s' Adelaide people will concur that 'amazing' is not an adjective likely to be used. My rainbow world was flooded with them and they were effortlessly making even rainbows look ugly. They bundled in so closely, I could smell afternoon tea and lamingtons on their breath. I tried everything to push them away and think of other things but to no avail. In desperation, I called upon the one Shaman who spoke English, and complained that I was being bombarded by weird, ugly people from my childhood, and try as I might, I couldn't get rid of them.

'Yes,' he said 'I can see what you mean.' He seemed to be entering my vision and peering at them. I was intrigued. How could that happen? Was he seeing what I was seeing? But by now, all rationality seemed redundant. The Shaman said these people would only go away if I learnt why they were there. To help me uncover this mystery, and accelerate the process, he started shaking his shacapa over me and singing a resounding icaro. That was quite an experience. I watched as my hideous, unwelcome companions grew bigger, more garish and overpowering. I was thrown back through time, to how I felt about them as a small child. Synapses between then and now snapped. The awkward shapes loomed above me, threateningly, demonically. I was terrified of them, as I had been then. They were the people at whose ungainly feet I had been thrown as a three-year-old Eastern European refugee in 1950. They were my new masters and I was at their mercy. The Shaman was right with me. The shacapa and the Quechua chants were reassuring as I shivered and shook. Then something even more frightening started to happen. The faces and bodies of my masters started to disintegrate alarmingly, and dark forms emerged from behind them, who looked at me reproachfully. I knew who I was seeing- these were people who had also been at the mercy of the British Empire, but more than a century earlier. The 1950s' country bumpkins who were once my lords and masters, inhabited Adelaide for only a tiny slice of time, and represented a thin veneer behind which danced the shadows of a far older race; a race who had lived and breathed for 40 000 years where Adelaide once stood. My fear vanished. I finally saw something that had been flitting at the edge of my consciousness all my life, and now, at last, I knew what it was. When I went to Adelaide in the 1950s, I didn't even know about the existence of its original inhabitants. South Australian History began in 1836. The Indigenous Kaurna race had been blanched from the record. I did not spot an Aboriginal person until I was twelve.

I came out of the ayahuasca journey with a book thrumming in my head and for the next year I researched it. I had written my first book about the place where I and my parents had come from, and now I wanted to write a book about where we had landed. Both books were about overcoming being the child of madness. That was a big legacy to conquer. Even though I had done a lot of work on facing my mother's schizophrenia, I still felt a fear that madness might subsume me as it had my sister. I knew I still had to face that fear and planned to return to Peru.

When came back to the UK, I went on another Sainte Daime journey with apprehension. A bad decision. I felt brainwashed by a vision which was not my own. I did not want to sing Portuguese hymns about Mary planting flowers in my garden; very beautiful but not my original experience. My past history of distorted religious dogma and my adventure with Enlightenment Intensives had instilled in me an overriding desire to find out my own truth, not be buffeted by someone else's. And I had swallowed enough bullshit that purported to be spiritual. I escaped the ceremony to the toilet, freaking out, vomiting, and feeling I was going mad. I was saved by the Peruvian queens who flooded my consciousness and encouraged me to stay strong within my own truth.

This, along with my desire to heal my madness trauma, saw me going back to Peru within a year. I felt that ayahuasca and my ancient queens could help me. Jake wasn't particularly keen but agreed because I wanted him by my side, to hold my hand while I faced my madness demons once and for all. We decided to make a bigger trip out of it and went via Iguazu Falls and Machu Picchu. The Iguazu Falls are one of the amazing wonders of the world, but it was there that I got very drunk on Limoncello and tripped and had a bad fall. I hurt my coccyx which bugged me for the rest of the trip, caused me lasting back problems and eventually nearly bust up my marriage. We then journeyed to Cusco, and once we had got over altitude sickness, made our way to a hotel on top of Machu Picchu. We met a friend who suggested we take mescaline and offered to send us a Shaman.

'Yes Jake, let's do it!' I said, throwing all caution to the wind.

Jake was wary. 'You have injured your coccyx and in two days we will be flying to Iquitos and imbibing more hallucinogens. This doesn't sound sensible.'

I could see Jake's point but felt compelled to do it, which was very uncharacteristic. Inside, a battle raged. The hedonist thought, 'What a laugh; you, an ageing granny, taking mescaline on top of the world!' But the pilgrim freaked out. 'Are you mad? This could really tip you over into insanity before you even have had a chance to heal it with ayahuasca.'

But I was adamant. I wanted to go for broke, even against Jake's better judgement, even though I was terrified. Something strange was driving me. I stayed up half the night learning phrases in Spanish like 'Take me to the hospital' in case the mescaline would make me very ill.

Next morning, I desperately hoped the Shaman wouldn't turn up, but he did and took us along a path that would lead down into the Machu Picchu ruins. We stopped at a little clearing and he got out his jar of pale green liquid from the San Pedro cactus plant, named thus as ingestion of the juice is supposed to get people 'to reach heaven while still on earth'. The Shaman did an incantation over the juice and gave us some to drink. I drank a minuscule amount, afraid of its effects, especially as the Shaman spoke very little English.

Predictably, I felt ill and crawled into some undergrowth to spew from both ends. I heard the Shaman say to Jake in halting English, something like. 'She can't go in there- there are snakes and deadly spiders.' I just didn't care. I was so ill and felt I belonged with the creatures of this dank jungle. I felt unclean and slimy and wanted to slither about like a serpent. Meanwhile Jake was flying high, literally. I eventually ventured out and we descended upon the fabulous vista that is Machu Picchu. Jake was leaping about like a jumping bean, soaking up the amazing energy of the place- especially from the magnificent mountain that all the ruins faced.

'You are my brother', he shouted out to it. I stumbled along and was struck by Jake's radiant face. It was in striking contrast to his wife- a pale, bedraggled, wretched creature crawling miserably down the path, confronted by her husband who was now throbbing as a manifestation of the male centre of the Universe. By now the Shaman had scuttled off- we were too much for him. As I gazed at my husband, it struck me forcefully why I was putting myself through all this suffering. Similarly, as with psilocybin and ayahuasca, I could clearly see all paths had led to this moment. The mescaline had the effect of bringing into consciousness and clarity, why I had insisted on taking mescaline here. I was finally emerging from the nausea and my purpose was crystal clear.

'This is my gift to you,' I said. 'I wanted you to see how magnificent you are. I wanted to bring you here to the male centre of the universe to recognize what an amazing man you are. That mountain reflects your glory. I am so sorry that I have lost sight of how extraordinary you are and that I have withheld secrets from you. This withholding was a way of diminishing you.' I was fully claiming my man as the spiritual and magnificent being he is. We had a beautiful moment in which Jake hugged me and received my gift.

He then climbed up on to a pinnacle to take in the grandeur of the mountain that in spiritual traditions is the male centre of the universe; pulsing, potent, magnificent. He called out to the mountain. 'I am in my 60s and don't have much time left. What shall I do for the rest of my life?'

'Be guided by your wife,' came back the unequivocal answer. He returned to me and said, 'I have been told it is you who must guide me.' Another magical moment between us.

As we flew from Cusco to Iquitos, we debriefed our powerful mescaline trip. Jake was puzzling. 'I feel I have been guided by you in the past,' he said. 'When did it stop?'

It was true we had been guided by each other. It was a central part of our marriage vows. What had gone wrong? When had we stopped guiding each other on our spiritual path? We had reconnected after I had fallen in love with Tom and left that liaison behind. We both thought long and hard. And then it dawned on us. It was seven years before when Jake had run a six-week Enlightenment Intensive in the manor house where we lived. I chose to be a participant and Jake had built me a quaint garden cabin for the duration. As we had both participated in each other's Intensives before and had been each other's Masters many times, we did not anticipate that this would be a problem. But it was. Having Jake as my Enlightenment Master for two weeks was fine, but for six weeks it had, unbeknownst to us, caused a huge crack in our relationship, the depth of which was not illuminated until now. He could not be my EI Master AND my husband for such a long period.

The cause of the crack seemed quite innocuous at the time. My behind was sore from sitting on chairs and I wanted Jake to bring in some orange armchairs from the shed. He did bring them in, but after the next walking contemplation, I walked in, sat down, looked around and could not see them. I realized he had taken them out. I froze. 'How dare he?' I went up and asked why. He answered that he would discuss the reasons at the end of the Intensive and I must continue with the process. I was incensed and spent the next half day screaming that he was the greatest fascist in the universe- I hated him- and deeply questioned how I could possibly be living with such a bastard! I spent some sleepless nights. I just couldn't get past the injustice of it. I even attempted to instigate a rebellion among the other participants in order to have the orange chairs reinstated. That night I had a powerful dream in which I was with my real father in Prague. It was clear that his mother really hated my mother and wanted her to go away and leave me behind. I woke up bereft. I felt powerless. Someone had decreed that I could not have my parents together, the consequence being that my real father had been banished forever from my life. Jake, as Master, had decreed that I, his wife, could not have the orange chairs in the room. Unconsciously I closed off a deep part to him. I ceased to see us on a spiritual journey together. Jake, my husband, could not be my Master. As we unravelled this state of affairs, we saw the truth of it. I had not only stopped trusting Jake as a husband, but had given up on my spiritual connection with him, as well. This could have also explained some of my former sexual shutdown. As we realised the depth of this fissure in our union, it came like a blinding flash why Stella had come into the picture. She had crept through the fissure- she was giving Jake something that I had stopped giving him. She was acknowledging his magnificence and his spirituality. The realization was profound. We revisited and renewed our vow of being on a journey to God together.

We arrived in Iquitos more solidly together than we had been for seven years. Next stop; to face my madness. This time I ate a diet of jungle rat, herbal concoctions and plantains for nine days and participated in five ceremonies. The Shamans taught me how to confront all my fears. With their help, and Jake by my side holding my hand, I entered a dark world where my fears lurked. I examined them one by one and managed to shrink them into cages. I walked past the cells like a warden, checking insane inmates. I felt myself becoming in control of my fears rather than them controlling me. If I felt myself falling into the dungeons where deranged inmates came running at me (as they really had done when I had visited my mother in her Adelaide lunatic asylum), I would take a couple of deep breaths and just gently blow them back.

I also learnt how to choose between realities. Often at the beginning of the trip when the ayahuasca plunged me mercilessly into a vortex of weird realities, I could just step back and observe them all, and choose to travel up the spinning cycle towards a place of calm and beauty. The icaros which the Shamans sang, were so pure and exhilarating- I felt myself spiralling up to a high altar, a little like the one at Macchu Picchu, where I was bathed in love.

During the last ceremony in Peru, I saw my body as a spaceship that I was steering. I wondered if I was capable of being in control of my life. 'Of course, you are,' said my queen guides. 'Who else is going to steer your ship if it's not you?' I noticed I was wearing a red and gold suit but it didn't quite fit, a bit baggy. 'You must grow into this sexy outfit- fill it with your voluptuousness. Accept who you actually are in all its glory. Do not dim or hold yourself back. Who you actually are may surprise you.' I took these words with me when we left Peru.

This was a portent for the future in a way in which I could not possibly foresee. It would still take time for me to have the exact fit of an exotic costume, to drive this spaceship that was my life.

Many of my friends became addicted to ayahuasca, believing it to be a miracle cure-all. But I knew that any of the progress I had made on these plant-induced journeys, was a supplement to all the hard work I had done in countless hours of deep self-inspection, and that real management of one's tumultuous inner babble came from this. For example, during my first LSD trip, before I had done any work on myself, my fragile ego collapsed, the contents of my unresolved terrors flooded my mind and I lost grip of 'here and now' reality. The plant medicine, ayahuasca, does alter brain chemistry to the extent that you clearly see your trips, but that is only the beginning. Aldous Huxley firmly believed that psychedelics, as he coined them, were able to open the doors of perception but that was all it was, an opening, just an illumination and only the beginning of the long trudge of bringing it into reality. I saw how glorious I could be, but to REALLY be glorious and to REALLY accept myself, was hard work. As I was to find out.

As a result of this intense journeying together and unearthing and healing profound trips, Jake and I became more solid on so many levels. I wrote 'Butterflies & Demons' about the intertwining of my life with the history of Adelaide's inhabitants, both old and new. In writing it, I experienced a deeper level of healing. The intention for self-healing I had made at the beginning of the Peruvian journey, had evolved in a surprising way.

Page intentionally left blank

# 7

## Kimberley: The Party World Revs Up

The next summer, Jake and I were invited by Jocasta and Vincent to a three-day festival in the country, continuing to propel us into new exciting adventures. This festival was hyped up to be the best private party in the world. And exclusive. Famous people frequented it, enjoying the anonymity.

In the early nineties, a group of Londoners had teamed up with a group of aristocrats, whose parents owned a big pile in the depth of the country. Together they started to throw these amazing 'Kimberley' parties every summer. Two of the

Londoners were the gorgeous Poonie, whom we had met at the Golden Delicious party, and her brother Ben. Ben, an actor, had found what he really loved to do- organizing sumptuous parties where people could come together for three days, let their hair down and live in love. Everyone was encouraged to bring something to give to others. There was a large healing area which Poonie managed, where party-goers were treated to a variety of treatments including massages, Tibetan sound healing, reflexology and other healing practices. In the beautiful grounds, dripping with strawberries, was an extravagant light garden which looked amazing at night, and down a windy path was a spectacular shrine. I had seen such a shrine at Golden Delicious as well, made by the aptly-named Loveshine Sarah. Jake and I felt lucky to be invited, so we borrowed a friend's campervan and off we went.

It was everything it was cracked up to be. The party started with a gathering in the main tent where Allegra Taylor, Ben and Poonie's mother, led an opening ceremony which included a meditation and orientation towards loving acceptance of oneself and each other. To us seasoned meditators this was wonderful- like a merging between hedonist and spiritual worlds. We were then asked to hug a stranger. This opening ritual served as an invitation to plunge into a few days of revelry. Afterwards, we were treated to a saucy and electrifying cabaret. On the Saturday afternoon, we danced on the sunny grass to fabulous bands. Some young people gave us herbal highs. Their friendliness, the hot sun and the beat was bliss, manna dew to my ageing bones. There was so much sparkly love. I felt that at my grand old age of 59, I was sampling some of the rave scene we had missed. Then we all gathered on the huge lawn in front of the stately home to have our photos taken. Every year there was a colour theme. This year it was gold. I was enjoying hanging out with everyone, and marvelling at all the different costumes and gold hats and headdresses, when I noticed Jake's attention had wandered. I followed the direction of his eyes. Yes, the object of his attention was a gorgeous, young, curvaceous woman. We found out later she was a stripper named Dominique and she was doing a show at the festival.

'Hey, Jake!' I said prancing around in front of him in my tight gold shorts. Yes, I was showing off my legs again. But Jake was mesmerised by Dominique. He couldn't take his eyes off her. I felt I had lost him to her. I felt bereft. I jumped right in front of him barring his view.

'Hey Jake, remember me? I'm your wife!' He finally dragged his eyes away back to me.

'I thought I'd lost you.'

'God, sorry babe, but phew – that woman. What a gorgeous arse.'

Now my arse is pretty good- neat and compact- but hers splayed out from her waist in an enticing curve. I could see what Jake liked about it.

'But you're with me, remember?'

I dragged him off, away from the eye-catching Dominique. It was then that I noticed a hunky guy walking towards us. 'Wow.' Our eyes locked. As he walked past, he turned around.

'Nice,' he murmured, appreciating my short shorts. He walked back and sidled up to me.

'Hey, in fact, I'd like a photo with you. Do you mind?' He asked Jake who answered, laughing.

'Go ahead mate.'

'Hi gorgeous, my name is Anton,' and he gave me a playful sexy pat on the behind. Unfortunately, I have never seen Anton again. But I will adore him forever. It is almost like Central

Casting sent him along at a much-needed point in my life, as he really helped assuage the Dominique incident.

We were then distracted by a huge roar from above as half a dozen nifty, solo-propeller planes swooped into view. Now I don't like aerial displays much. I saw the Red Arrows zipping over South Devon, and they really terrified me. I was convinced that those roaring fighter jets would crash and kill us all. But at this party, this aerial display, with its cosier-looking, old-fashioned planes, was fantastic. The pilots made the planes loop, hang in mid-air, emit different coloured gases, as well as doing all that charging at each other, from great distances, and nearly crashing. Two of the planes curved a big pink love heart in the air, coming dangerously close as they completed the bottom crossover. I decided then and there, I had to meet a pilot. A bloke who could do all that must be really hot. Testosterone at its best. Daring, competent, decisive, gorgeous.

Thrillingly titillated by the Dominique/Anton/pilot display, I stood in a queue for some food. Over a loudspeaker came the languid tones of Peggy Lee, singing 'Black Coffee'. It suited my mood, especially the lines,

'Now man was born to go a lovin', But woman was born to weep and fret.'

The woman behind me in the queue rolled her eyes. 'Boy is that song dated! Pre-feminist times!'

'Don't knock it,' I said. 'I just experienced what Peggy is singing about. I just lost my husband for a full ten minutes when he was captivated by another woman. But hey, the luscious Anton saved me.' I told her the whole story. She laughed.

'Well, I am in love with one of the pilots.'

My ears zinged. 'Really? What, one of those we just saw doing those amazing stunts?'

'Yes. He is just drop dead gorgeous. Really young and inordinately handsome.'

'Where is he?' I asked, still basking in the confidence boost I had received from Anton.

'Somewhere around,' she said, drooling. 'He's wearing a yellow silk flying suit. A real Casanova, I tell you.'

That evening there was a stunning firework display, lighting up the stately home's façade. Then the dancing began in earnest. The mansion's cellars were turned into several DJ rooms and some opulent, quiet rooms where people could lounge and talk. It was a thrilling experience. Here were Jake and I at one of the best parties in the world, if not *the* best. Woohoo! This certainly beat joining the WI. The rooms were decorated with glittering fabrics galore. In every room were top DJs. Two of the DJs were Chloe and Julie, who we met at the Golden Delicious party. Poonie came up to us wearing a sexy jumpsuit with a zipped front. She always looked ravishable. Jake went up to her and toyed with the top of the zip, saying in a low voice, 'This looks like it is meant to be pulled down,' and slowly started unzipping it. I was a bit shocked at his daring – what, to flirt so outrageously with Poonie, the party queen! This could go either way. She gave him a slow, sultry look, turned to me and said with an appreciative purr, 'Doesn't wait to be asked, does he?'

'That is for sure,' I answered, rolling my eyes. And that is how a fabulous flirt relationship between Jake and Poonie started. This flirtation lasted for many years. I never felt jealous at all, as the boundaries were clear. Poonie was an important role model for me as she really owned her sexuality. She appreciated flirting with Jake as it was clearly understood by both parties that each was happily married and that the flirt would go no further. One time, Poonie was waggling her beautifully-shaped derriere enticingly, when Jake grabbed it and they had a sensual dance. She came over to us later, looking worried.

'I hope I didn't give you the wrong idea,' she said to Jake.

'Darling, you gave me exactly the right idea and I loved it.'

'Phew,' said Poonie. 'I have been in trouble before when someone I flirted with thought I was giving him a big come on. That's why it is okay to flirt with you. We both are a couple of tarts and understand each other completely.'

I kept my eyes out for the pilot. He had reached mythical proportions in my brain. Those loops in the sky were very sexy. I wanted to meet him. But how would I recognize him? I could see no one wearing a yellow flying suit anywhere. All I knew was that he was fearsomely good-looking. Still feeling flushed with the amorous attentions of Anton, I decided to take a leaf out of Jake and Poonie's book and try some flirting. They both made it look effortless.

I spotted a handsome guy in a fur jerkin. A likely candidate I thought. I had a bit of bop around him, while mustering up the courage to ask him if he was a pilot. One of the worst things about raves, especially for ageing ravers like me, is that the music is deafeningly loud, stupidly so. Anything you want to say, you must shout, at a stroke-inducing range of decibels. It felt really scary to approach him. My heart pounded; my blood raced. Did I dare find my pilot?

'Come on Eva, what have you got to lose?' I told myself to breathe. Taking Lady Macbeth's advice, I screwed my courage to the sticking place and went forward.

'Are you a pilot?' Choked voice. So awkward.

Kept on dancing; into his own groove, he obviously hadn't heard.

I tapped him, gingerly, and shouted.

'Are you a pi-lo-o- ot?'

'What?' he yelled over ear-splitting music. He looked a bit startled but bent his delicious looking head down to me.

'Are you a pilot?'

'No!' Very perplexed. 'Should I be?'

'Well, er, er, yes.' I stammered.

'Well, if you say so!' Even more puzzled.

I bottled out at this point and shuffled away, deeply embarrassed. Oh boy, that was bad. Flirt score out of 10, virtually nil. Possibly half a point for daring to approach him, and half a point for potentially good chat up line. Zero points for anything else. Totally woeful. On so many occasions since, I have thought about what I should have said. Something like;

'Well, you definitely look as gorgeous as I think a pilot should look. Phwoar.' At least I could have got across how sexy and desirable I thought he was.

Then I saw another dishy guy. Could he be a pilot? I mustered up my nerve.

'Hi, you look like a pilot,' I said in a reasonably forthright tone.

'What?' This man was really tall. About 6' 4". Bent right down, his proximity terrified me. I squeaked.

'Are you a pilot?'

'No!' He looked at me as if I were crazy and said to his mates. 'She thinks I'm a pilot.' They all sniggered. Failed again, even more miserably. I gave up.

I limped away, feeling like a silly old frump. I found Jake who had a usual gaggle of girls dancing with him. He had his Rod Stewart outfit on and looked pretty good.

'I'm so hopeless at flirting.' I whimpered.

'Well, come flirt with me,' he said. So, I did. He responded beautifully and soon I felt the queen of his life. Who needed the attentions of a gorgeous young pilot? The idea of him receded into a mythical haze. I did spend the rest of the three days with half an eye out for this being who had now assumed the proportions of Apollo. A sun god in yellow silk.

Next day I found Alicia, one of my friends from Totnes. She had a sumptuous tent and was applying makeup on her friends.

'You want me to do you?' she asked.

'Ooh, yes please,' I said. That evening was the final party which was in the main tent. I wanted to look fantastic. Alicia deftly applied eyeliner, mascara and eye shadow. I then joined Jake for a bite to eat before we headed for the party tent. I felt very exotic in my green eye shadow. But Jake looked unbelievably surly as he ate a falafel.

'What's the matter?'

'I hate your eye makeup.'

'Oh, for fuck's sake!' I exploded. 'This is the last night and I want to look exotic.'

'Well you look terrible and I hate looking at you.'

'Fuck you!' I shouted. 'Jesus, can't you just let this go and enjoy the last night here? We have had such a nice time and now you are spoiling it!'

Ah, the eye makeup issue! One of the 'problem areas' in my relationship with Jake. It is something we do not agree on. In fact, it has led to some of our biggest rows. I could not understand why he hates me wearing eye makeup so much. The trouble is the issue gets caught up with my father trip. My father did not allow me to wear any makeup and I was twenty when I ran away from home. Jake morphed into my dad that very moment. I saw Sasha's glum face and remembered my mother screaming at him, 'I hate your "I'm going to be hanged tomorrow face!"'

I threw my hands up in fury and marched off. Jake was just being totally idiotic and unreasonable. He was exactly like my father and I was fed up. Many of our friends have been caught in the crossfire. Jocasta had a go at Jake about it.

'Really Jake! It is Eva's face. She should be free to do as she likes.' He snapped her head off. 'Well, it's me who looks at her all the time!'

Well, here I was at one of the best private parties in the world and I was lurking behind a food van, feeling totally hacked off with my husband. I took a deep breath. I really did want to see things from Jake's point of view but it seemed impossible. Once in Vietnam, I had my eyelashes dyed. Unfortunately, the dye leached on to my eyelash line. Jake exploded and we nearly split up. 'You have spoiled my whole holiday,' I screamed. Now he was spoiling the best party ever. I pouted like a sulky teenager.

I wiped off some of the makeup and went back to Jake.

'Is this better?'

'No, not really,' he said. 'All I see is the gunge around your eyes and not you.'

I take another deep breath. I know that Jake gets visually caught by images and gets easily distracted. For example, we don't have paintings up on our walls at home, as he becomes visually fixated. So, I do understand that.

'But don't you understand Jake, I just want to look a bit more special sometimes.'

He looked at me sadly. 'I fear you put on that stuff because you don't feel good about the way you actually look.' That is true. I think I do look much better with eye makeup. After I had left home in 1967, the fashion at the time was to wear thick, black eyeliner, so without my father bearing down upon me, I lashed it on and soon felt naked without it. I used to dream of a time when I would be married and would have to get up before my future husband and apply eye makeup before he woke up. I had no idea that I would have the kind of husband who didn't want me to wear it at all. Now in the 21$^{st}$ century, eye makeup is again de rigeur in the fashion world. It is rare to see a woman on the front cover of any magazine without pronounced eye makeup.

'It makes me so sad,' said Jake, 'that you don't think you look beautiful just as you are.'

In a moment of clarity, I could see that Jake was not my father. I had a brainwave.

'Well if you don't like my eye makeup, lick it off.'

He was taken aback at my recapitulation and request. Then he slowly leaned forward and started licking my left eye. He did it so tenderly and so beautifully that my womb somersaulted. It was so sexy and I felt myself falling in love with him all over again. He moved to my right eye. Ooh! So sensual. Without any eye makeup left at all, and my eyes feeling well and truly licked, we headed, hand-in-hand, towards the big tent which reverberated with dazzling rhythms and began dancing happily together. After a short while, I noticed a guy nearby who was not only an incredible dancer but was also very attractive; white, crisp, open-neck shirt, black jeans, hair a bit like John Travolta in Saturday Night Fever. He snaked around the room in a mesmerising fashion, a bit like a panther waiting to pounce. He didn't seem to have a lady friend. And he seemed to be gazing at me. Me? Me, without eye makeup, who was 59 and a half! I looked behind me expecting to see some young beauty to whom he was paying attention. I looked back. His eyes were still fixed on me and he flashed a dazzling smile. God. I suddenly felt like a teenager and couldn't breathe. This guy was gorgeous- probably late 30s, dark and handsome. He swooped about the large dance floor and sometimes disappeared from view, getting me to think perhaps he was just an apparition. But no, he swooped back into view and yes, he was on to me again.

'Jake, I think there is this guy who is flirting with me- is it my imagination? That one there.' Jake appraised the situation. 'Yes, he definitely is and why shouldn't he flirt with you? You look stunning; the most lovely-looking woman here.'

Gorgeous disappeared again but then was back and swooped in for a dance around me. I was speechless and couldn't help letting out a girly shriek as he rained smouldering looks all over me. Bloody hell. I held on to Jake. This guy must know I was with someone. I didn't want to give out the message that I was available. Well, I did, but hey, I was a married woman, whose husband had just licked off her eye makeup. This did not seem to deter Gorgeous. He danced with both of us and said an easy 'Hi', to Jake. Then he swooped off again. Swoop is the adjective to describe him. He was tall and seemed to swim-dance, scanning the room as he glided through, like a dangerous shark. I dared to catch his eye. He winked. Such a predator. My insides and legs became jelly. I dragged Jake outside. 'What is it with that guy? - he really seems after me. God, I think he's so hot.'

'Well he does look like Robbie Williams,' said Jake.

'Miles better than Robbie Williams,' I breathed.

'Well just enjoy it!'

We went back inside and sure enough, there came Robbie, swooping in again. I decided to take Jake's advice and enjoy the game. So, I dared to dance with him. Meanwhile, in came Dominique looking alluring in a bejewelled headdress. We had spoken with her earlier and she had invited us to watch her striptease show. She started dancing with Jake. I didn't mind at all. The way Jake licked off my eye makeup was so intimate, so delicious, that I knew he was mine. Dominique may have had a gorgeous arse but she didn't have 27 years of shared intimacy.

Besides I had Robbie.

During the next few years, when we went back to Kimberly, this man flirted with me again. It was always on the Sunday evening and he was always alone. And he was always hot. But so mysterious. Why did he only come on one night? Why was he always alone? And why did he always flirt with only me? In fact, the flirts became really sizzling as I became more brazen. So, on the third occasion, I dared speak to him.

'It's great to see you again!'

'You too, gorgeous!'

'Where's your girlfriend?'

'I have a wife. She doesn't like raves but is happy for me to go off for one night a year. So here I am.'

We chatted a little and I introduced him to Jake. He told us he is a lawyer in the city, used to go to a lot of raves in his youth and this is how he kept his hand in.

Then we danced and flirted some more.

The last year I saw him, the heat was still on. I could see that for him I was a safe bet to flirt with, because Jake and I looked very much in love. This time he brought a male friend who said to me,

'Ah, so you're the one. He told me that there is a super gorgeous woman he flirts with every time he comes here. He is right. You are gorgeous.'

I was in heaven. So, this incredibly hot guy with film star looks came seeking me out once a year. Wow!

That night I lost Jake in the crowd. Gorgeous found me and said,

'Where's your bloke?'

'I've lost him.' I said.

'Well, let's find him, shall we?' And we did. He handed me over to Jake with a wink and that was the last I saw of him.

This man was a gift to me as an ageing woman learning how to flirt. Little did I know this was to propel me into being a rampant flirt in my 60s. That first Sunday evening I met him, I completely forgot about the pilot in the yellow flying suit. However, Lady Luck had him up her sleeve and I would be fortunate enough to meet him in the not too distant future.

Page intentionally left blank

# 8

## Meeting the Pilot—60/30 Party

When we had first moved to the West Country, there were two things that I felt I had missed out on in my life, travelling and parties. We set out to remedy the former by taking several around the world trips to exotic locations and outback 4- wheel drive adventures. Fortunately, the party scene was flourishing and I was launching into it with fervour even though I was nearly 60. Having used ayahuasca to heal a lot of the madness which was the legacy of my mother, I felt a heavy burden lift from my brow. I felt freer to have fun. My mother adored parties and certainly had not had enough to quench her desire. I took up her baton.

Jake was enjoying partying as much as I was, so we decided to throw a joint party with my son Steve. I would be 60 and he, 30 (wished it was the other way round!) He was born a month after my 30th birthday.

We would celebrate my passage into old age, in style. An all-night rave, no less. On a cold November night, Jake and I travelled to London to stay with my daughter, her husband and our new grandson. Donning some party gear, I would go and check out the Corsica Centre by attending a party there. It was under a railway arch, in a less than salubrious part of London. It was also an opportunity to practise some more flirting. Jake babysat our grandson.

So, here I was, nearly 60 and just learning how to flirt and it seemed that some rather delicious men thought I was worth flirting with. So, I wanted to squeeze in as much flirty time as I could and go to as many parties as possible before being carted off to an old people's home. I had just discovered ASOS (As Seen On Screen – Internet shopping for clothes worn by the latest celebrity). I chose a short dress to show off my legs, with a black velvet band around my neck, that velcroed at the back.

Very handy. Hid all the neck wrinkles. Plus, my fabulous hat, sprouting feathers, which sat perkily on my curly blonde head (very little grey yet- a couple of blonder streaks added). Yes, after having won my man back from the sphinx in the pink thong, I let my hair revert to its natural colour.

Feather hat in place, I arrived at the railway arch about 9.30 p.m, Saturday evening. By the standards of the young people of today, that is disgustingly early. I was the first there. I explored the venue, checking out its suitability for my 60/30 party for the following January. An important facility I wanted was a large, quiet room. All rave venues have a 'chill out' space. This usually has sofas, cushions and mattresses, where people, exhausted by jumping around like mad banshees, or coming down off some cocktail of intoxicants, can recuperate and talk. Often there is a DJ who plays 'chill out' music. For my party, I wanted a quiet 'chill out' area, with no DJ, where I could relax and chat to my friends, without shouting myself hoarse. I asked to be directed to the 'chill out' room so I could check it out while waiting for this particular party to begin. Glittery hangings adorned the walls; plush velvets draped the sofas; blue and red stars dangled from the ceiling. Not bad. I flopped on to a red velvet sofa. A couple walked in. Early too. They asked me a question. I didn't know the answer.

'Oh sorry, I thought you were one of the organisers.'

'Probably my hat,' I thought. Gave me a sophisticated air.

They sank on to my sofa, both very beautiful, very young.

'Have you been to these parties before?' asked the guy. He was wearing a coat and top hat, both in fake leopard skin. Straight from a Fellini set. Impossibly handsome.

'Ooh yes.' I said and mentioned Kimberley, the summer private party in the country.

'Oh, did you happen to watch the aerial display?'

'Yes?'

'Well, one of those planes is mine.'

'What? You …' I spluttered. 'You flew one of those planes? Don't tell me you're a pilot?'

'Yes, as a matter of fact, I am,' he said, through lips as luscious as Elvis's.

I started screaming and jumping up and down.

'You're the pilot. You're the pilot. I've found you at last.'

His girlfriend looked at me as if I was demented. She was right. I was. She was a fitting goddess for the pilot, natural blonde hair swept off her classical, Diana the Huntress face.

I hugged them both. I was deliriously happy. Glad I came to check out this venue. Rather than try to sidle away from this preposterous old woman in her preposterous hat, they seemed to like being appreciated, even if it was a tad too enthusiastically.

'I'm Flash,' introduced the pilot. 'This is my girlfriend, Sally.'

Sally was disgustingly glowing, as 20-year-olds effortlessly are.

'How old are you, Flash? You don't look a day over 22!'

'Oh, I love you,' said Flash. 'But I'm thirty.' His face drooped.

'He's been having a hard time turning thirty,' explained Sally. 'Really tough.'

'Yeah,' said Flash despondently. 'I just hate getting old.'

I snorted disbelievingly.

'You think thirty is old? Try twice that. I'll be sixty in January.'

'No way!' remonstrated Flash, falling backwards. 'You can't possibly be nearly sixty!'

'Oh, I love you too! But that's why I'm here at this party -.to suss this joint for the 60/30 bash I'm having with my son who will be the same age as you.'

'Oh, invite us.' This neatly demonstrated he was not called Flash, just because he performs amazing, aeroplane stunts.

'But I've only just met you.'

'Oh pleeee—ease.'

'I'll let you know after I've got to know you a bit better.'

'What's there to know? I think you're fab, ('and me,' piped in Sally) and you think I'm fab. So, what's the problem?'

I thought to myself. 'Yeah, what is the problem? He's my pilot.'

'Sally is really nervous about being here. I had to beg her to come. I hope this is the first of many such parties together. I'd love to bring her to your party.'

'Yes, I'm really shy,' said the Goddess. (what the hell had she got to be shy about!)

We just yakked for the next hour. Such good fun. Flash showed me photos of his plane; him in the plane, Sally in the plane, his Jack Russell in the plane. A big kid really. When Flash went for a fag, I said to Sally,

'You lucky girl. You've landed yourself a pilot. And a stunningly gorgeous one!'

'Ooh yes,' she moaned. 'He is so dreamy.'

Meanwhile, the party was filling up. Thumping music reverberated from the disco room. I couldn't sit any longer. The dance called me. Sally was too shy to come, so I took my leave.

I enter the dance floor, a little nervous. I'm relieved to see that the crowd isn't overly young. I didn't want them to all be Sally's age. A nice mix. I notice him immediately. All six feet two of him, grooving on the dance floor. Between thirty-five and forty, I guess. Obviously worked out, perhaps in a gym, but more probably in a manly, outdoor job. Handsome in a rugged way. Would make a great James Bond. I begin to dance, lapping up the lashings of testosterone in the room, as a swathe of raunchy men, both straight and gay, strut their stuff. This is a promising line-up. A healthy dollop of nice-looking guys. Mmmmm! A better pick-me-up for a post-menopausal chick than any Horny Goat, I tell you.

Marshalling up any vestiges of pheromones that might be lurking anywhere on my person, I stake out James Bond and wonder if I've still got what it takes to attract a bloke like him. The competition is stiff. Scores of stunning young women, sporting an enticing array of revealing clubbing gear, pump it out on the dance floor. I feel at a great disadvantage. I'm twice their age at least, and I've only just learnt to flirt. And I'm excruciatingly shy. But I am resolved to practise my new flirting skills. Quite an art it is, to flirt. Outrageously daring and subtle at the same time. You put out an enticing, come-get-me message, without looking like you're an old floozy who's gagging for it! Or mutton dressed as lamb, looking ridiculously cheap. I firmly dismiss the scores of put-me-downs (as many seem to pop up as there are young rivals), and dart coy, admiring looks at Mr Bond. There is a fleeting moment, too short it seems, when his eyes meet mine. And he's already glanced away. What did he see? Did he like it? Or did I miss it? Did he even notice me? I dance on in suspense. When I asked Jake about it later, he said,

'It's all it takes- an infinitesimal registering that the female is interested.'

'But he had no time to see how good my figure looked!'

'Oh, he's sussed that already, darling.'

'Really? Is that what you men are like?'

''Fraid so. Graded all the boobs and bums in the room, long ago!'

Bond is dancing among a whole bunch of other blokes. All swilling beer. Very macho. Perhaps he's gay? Then he flashes me such a look, I know he's not. Wow! Any stray pheromones that may have survived menopause, start doing wild somersaults; my knees go to jelly; ghosts of eggs tug at my ovaries. Yes, the infinitesimal glance worked. I dance on. Suddenly everywhere I look, there's some guy giving me the eye. I feel on fire. It's like something snapped and I have become the most sought- after female in the room. It reminds me of the old days when I was young and sparkling. When my ovaries bounced out eggs like there was no tomorrow.

In this miraculous, maidenly state, I enjoy many a flirty dance. The music is amazing. Sparkie is the DJ. He is hot. Well he, himself, doesn't think so. Unfortunately holds back his manhood. Met him at a party where he glumly informed me that the girl he had come with had just upped and left.

'I'm shit with women,' he said, in that endearing, deadpan way of his. 'Put me in a barrel of tits and I'd come up sucking my thumb.' All that has changed now, as he is having relationships with beautiful woman!

Sparkie is a super DJ. Knows how to whip up a storm. I want him for my 60/30 party. Probably here. Yes, as it is in a derelict part of London, you can thump away to excruciatingly loud music till 6 a.m., without engendering apoplexy in neighbours or local church groups.

So here I am. The room is rocking. Great DJ. Great music. Great guys. Great pilot! I'm on my own. Jake is babysitting my grandson. And I'm checking out the venue. Wow, aren't I lucky? I'm nearly 60, and all these blokes are coming on to me. I flash back to my 20s when I found it a drag. Always escaping to the loo, to get away from adoring males. How young I was. How I took that attention for granted. But now, I love it, even the ugly guys. It shores me up beautifully, against impending decrepitude and death. But I'm still fussy. It's James Bond, I really want. What's more, he's interested. He is strutting his manly stuff for me. I nearly swoon. I feel like a nineteenth-century maiden at a ball; my bosom is heaving prettily in my ASOS dress. I have to escape for air.

A big plus for this club is that it has an internal outside area. I get my breath back. And cool down. I fill up my water bottle from the tap in the toilet. Tastes all right for London. And it saves time queuing up at the bar. I regain normal breathing after being sizzled and fried by James Bond and make my way to the 'chill out' room. I decide to have a diversion and find the gorgeous pilot. He is still on the couch ensconced with Sally. Unfortunately, there is a DJ in there now and the music is too loud. I feel like Flash and Sally are my kids. They are in fact younger than my own children. I want to check they are okay. Flash pulls me down.

'Where have you been? We've been waiting for you to come back.'

'I've been dancing. Why don't you come and dance too?'

'Sally's a bit freaked out.'

Poor Sally is suffering from paranoia. Whatever she has imbibed, is giving her a nasty turn. Her teeth are chattering. I give her a big hug. Offer her a polo to chew.

‘I don’t want you to leave me, Flash,’ she begs, eyes as big as saucers.

‘Don’t worry, babe, I’m not going anywhere without you.’

Flash cradles her lovingly and she calms down. Yes, my pilot and his bird are now fine. I go off again. I want to check out James Bond.

The dance floor is still rocking. I have to squeeze past a bunch of blokes in the doorway. Mmmm. Very nice. Decide to go up on stage to participate in some limelight prancing. There is a raised platform at one end, where any clubber can climb up and show off. About six people are gyrating up there like pole dancers. I make to climb up. Uh oh! I know that it’s too high a step for me to execute in one agile leap. Can I make it without anybody seeing how decrepit I am? While I’m sussing out various footholds and handholds, so that I don’t give away that the body, looking so svelte in the ASOS dress, is that of a grandmother, Nick comes to my rescue. He is a friend, near my age and a veteran party-goer. He helps me up.

‘Thank you,’ I gasp gratefully. ‘I’m not a spring chicken, you know. I’ve lost my spring.’

'Tell me about it,' says Nick. 'It's not long before I'll have to come to these raves with a Zimmer frame.'

'Well, funnily enough, I've been looking at those buggies old-timers have, for the first time. Always ignored them before. Now I know the time is not so far off.'

'Well as long as my buggy has got luminous, purple wheels and carries an inbuilt sound system,' says Nick. 'I'll be happy as a sand-boy.'

Now I'm up on stage I can show off my legs. You might ask how it was possible that I lived for 50 years, convinced my legs were scrawny and shapeless? Terribly easy, I'm afraid. And what a waste. All those people who told me that my legs looked great, I had pegged as liars. They were just trying to make me feel better! So here I am, nearly sixty, showing off my legs at long last. My great role model is Marlene Dietrich. She flashed her legs until she was in her seventies! My ASOS dress (as seen on Lindsay Lohan- who the hell is she?), falls just below my hips. Up on stage, I make sure just a tantalising sliver of my backside peeks out. Black mesh tights and ankle boots complete the effect. The oomph bounces back into my spring chicken legs, and I'm off.

Sparkie is really winding up the dance floor. Most chemicals would have hit by now and the whole room is high as a kite, gripped in a love frenzy. I haven't ingested anything. I am babysitting next day and take my grandmotherly duties seriously. And ecstasy, like alcohol, can waste me. But I pick up the e vibe. It is very beautiful. It is a drug of great acceptance and heart opening. Especially in a crowd that has been clubbing together for years. Each person can just do their own thing, wear what they like, move how they like, be whoever they are. Even an aged floozy, in a silly hat, who has risked a hernia by getting up on stage.

From my vantage point, I spot James Bond, still grooving away. Still hot. He has certainly noticed my legs. His appreciation is obvious. After a spell up on stage, I decide to get nearer to Mr Bond. Fortunately, Nick is there to help. Sweetly he picks me up and lifts me down.

'Ooh, thanks.' He does it in such a way, that I feel light as a feather. 'There's nothing wrong with you, mate. You are beautifully strong.'

'All right for the time being, but only just, only just,' he sighs sadly.

I weave around the dance floor. It's even more crowded now, and the men even more attentive. One bloke looks down appreciatively,

'Nice dress.'

I turn around and flick up the back, flashing a bit of meshed flesh. He looks a bit shocked but very happy. I too am shocked at my own daring. We have a sensual dance. I'm testing my boundaries. I now know without a doubt I am sexy. And extremely happily married. I just want to master the art of flirting outrageously and NOT giving a come on. A very slippery boundary, but extremely exciting. This is what real flirting is about. Flirting keeps one alive in the moment. There seem to be no shortage of takers for this enthralling game.

I catch Bond's eye. He points me out to his mates,

'There's the girl I was telling you about!'

They all look at me appreciatively.

My chest is suddenly extremely tight. The word 'girl' has sent me into a cascading vortex. I'm so pleased I haven't imbibed any pills. Ecstasy is very bad for boundaries, as happened with Jake and Stella. Boundaries easily become irrelevant. The enticing pulse of the moment so easily takes over. I keep dancing. Bond sidles closer.

Smelling salts. Snuff. That's what I need. Desperately. Then he does such an incredible thing. A beautiful present for a woman on the edge of old age. He comes closer and flexes his arm muscle, pats it proudly and says,

'See that. I'm really strong.'

Any woman even slightly affected by the Women's Lib movement, would be so scathing. What was this macho caveman up to? Most would purse their lips and turn away in self-righteous indignation. But not this baby. Not the Women's Liberation Nightmare (WLN) of all time. Who has never changed a tyre and never will. (Why for Christ's sake? There is always a willing man who will stop and change it. Always. Well in my experience, anyway.)

Here was a man daring to be a man. So, what does WLN do? I went right up to James Bond and dared be a woman. I murmured appreciatively, felt his muscle, (the arm one of course!) and purred,

'Now, I <u>really</u> like that.'

And gave him a sexy dance.

It was so thrilling. Dancing on the edge.

I only had half an hour to go before the taxi arrived to take me home at one thirty. The party was going on till 6. But I had a plan of what I would say, in case Bond approached me and wanted more than just an exciting flirt.

'I love the fact that you are so strong and gorgeous and I really fancy you. I feel delighted and honoured that a man like you fancies me. Thank you. However, I have my very own strong and gorgeous man at home. And that's who I'm going to now.'

Mission accomplished. I had found an excellent venue and invited Flash and Sally.

On my actual birthday, Jake threw me a wonderful party at home with family and close friends. My friend in Cornwall made me a red velvet throne studded with photographs of myself. I was definitely the queen and feted as one.

Preparations for the 60-30 party were in full swing. My last ayahuasca journey in Peru inspired the theme and what I would wear. When I was manning the spaceship which symbolised my life, I was wearing an ill-fitting red and gold outfit. Now I decided to remedy that vision and set out to create a splendid red and gold costume that fitted well. This would augur a new retirement pastime- creating party outfits. What fun. Much better than settling for WI florals or joining the church bell ringers. One of the legacies passed on to me by my mother was that she sent me to sewing lessons. I ordered some red wings from America and sewed gold leaf all over them. I made a red, short, gathered cloak with gold tassels and embroidered Queen Eva on the back. I put this over a gold skimpy dress and attached red and gold hearts to the gold swirls. I threaded gold stars onto a red spiky wig. Gold shoes adorned my feet. Yes, I was determined to start my 60s as I meant to continue; wo-manning the spaceship of my life as a sassy sexy Goddess. Jake looking splendid in his outfit, encouraged me.

We invited 150 people. This was the invite.

## Party Invite

This is an invitation to an amazing party to be held at the Corsica Studios in London on January

> 27th 2007. The party is in celebration of two birthdays; Eva's 60th and Steve's 30th.
>
> The party starts at 8.30pm. There will be a fantastic cabaret at 9.00pm – including dancing girls, intriguing mime and a classy stripper (all part of the Whoopee Club). This will be followed by a live band, some amazing drinks and birthday cakes. Before midnight, the DJs will start and carry on until 6 am.
>
> The party has a colour theme of red and gold. You should take the opportunity to dress outrageously – and sexily. Expect this to be the best party of 2007!

Some of my older friends bottled out of the dress-up.

'Why?' I asked

'We feel too old and frumpy,' they said.

'But hey,' I objected. 'You guys are younger than me!''

We transported my party throne to London by taxi and set it up in the main dancing room. We hired a team of decorators to deck the place out lavishly. We also hired floor shows, including some delectable strippers.

And yes, my pilot came in his silky, gold flying suit.

'Worn especially for you,' he murmured seductively.

'Where is Sally?'

'Oh, we are through!' he said and gave me a sexy dance. Yay, at last I had found my pilot. This marked the beginning of a beautiful flirt friendship with Flash which lasted several years. Flash obviously loves older women because he is now happily married to another grandmother.

It seemed that my dire, postmenopausal predictions had failed to come true. I was getting sexier.

Page intentionally left blank

# 9

## The Saint, the Sinner and Parties!

Yes, life after 60 was great. Jake and I enjoyed many parties over the next few years and threw quite a few more. We hired fancy venues. We sold our energy efficiency business and what better way to spend some of the profits than giving a bunch of people a great time. Also, I had money and time to create lavish party outfits.

My confidence was soaring. My flirtatious star was rising, as was Jake's. He was also enjoying the attentions of many women. For a couple of old age pensioners, we were having a ball.

But I struggled to reconcile the sexy and the spiritual. My spiritual journey was still important and felt at odds with what was happening to me. I kept wondering if I should give up this new found, flirtatious hedonistic life I was leading.

I was developing a pleasant image of myself as a sensible, benevolent grandmother with a grey bun, sitting in my garden with my grandchildren. This image clashed with the flirtatious party girl who seemed to be stuck at the age of seventeen. And another part of me still hankered after a pure, saintly existence. A series of gurus I admired and had followed, reflected this.

I first encountered the Vietnamese nun, Ching Hai in 1999. She was fresh out of a cave in the Taiwanese mountains- bald and sweet and extremely shy. Some followers tracked her down and exhorted her to come out into the world. I devoured films and books about her. She was hailed as a modern embodiment of Quan Yin and taught a meditation on Light and Sound where the meditator would concentrate on the Third Eye and Third Ear. I plunged into this daily practice with great fervour. I wanted to become like Ching Hai- pure and clear and radiating oceanic love.

Then she began to change drastically. Her meditation led her from shyness to gregariousness. She transformed from a simple, bald nun to a fashion guru extraordinaire. She had (still has) a huge following in Asian countries. She designed and sold exquisite jewellery and fashionable clothes. I even hunted out a shop of hers in Hong Kong and bought a garment, hoping to be infused by her holiness. Her fashion empire brought in millions, which she promptly gave away to worthy causes. She herself changed hairstyles and clothing several times, sometimes in a single day; in some ways, she is like the Imelda Marcos of the spiritual world. She also had quite a severe eye twitch which she didn't seem bothered by at all. This endeared me to her and helped me accept my own facial twitch. If the embodiment of Quan Yin had a twitch then there was hope for me. She was perfect however she was. When she began singing and selling records, she said she was just moving with what was unfolding inside her. I was inspired. She was showing me that I need never be fixed in one manifestation of myself. I thought, 'What could I become?' If I could just really surrender to what was within me and become that. What would that be? There was a snag. Her path was tough and required two hours of meditation a day and vegetarianism verging on vegan, which meant no eggs. Now I could give up meat, but eggs? No way. There must have been many followers like me, for she miraculously concocted what she called, 'The Convenient Method.' This involved half an hour meditation a day and two days a week being a vegetarian. I could do that, so much to Jake's mirth, I went to London to be initiated in the Convenient Method.

The meditation consisted of putting one's attention on the third eye or ear and calling up holy names. I chose Francis of Assisi, Teresa of Avila, Therese de Lisieux, and two Indian holy women, Mother Meera and Anandamayi Ma.

I persevered for a few years, went to group meditations and then decided to go for full initiation. Yes, I would give up eggs. However, there was another snag. No alcohol or recreational drugs. Was I happy about this? Yes and no; my usual struggle between a spiritual path and a hedonistic path. Many traditions taught that drugs messed up the spiritual path and I noticed that drinking alcohol and smoking spliffs did cloud my meditation for a couple of days. So, I was happy to eschew these accoutrements of the devil. I went to a full initiation evening. I was asked 'Have you eaten eggs in the last three months?' Well, I had eaten some cake a few weeks before. Should I lie? A bit silly to go on a spiritual path and lie, so I confessed to the cake (eggs seemed more evil to this lot than spliffs!) I was rejected. Jake was relieved. I decided to give up Ching Hai. But I felt I needed a guiding force in my life. Something to contain me and keep me on a trajectory towards love.

Fortunately, six years of meditating on the saints had brought Therese de Lisieux into my life. Through the third eye, I felt a strong connection with her. I had also read her autobiography which was a beautiful evocation of a fairy-tale, Catholic upbringing. I found this very healing, having suffered the unholy side of Catholicism in my own childhood. Sister Therese was to become my inner guide and teacher for a while. Just before my 60th birthday, I decided to speak to her. Was such a thing possible? Wasn't it a bit weird to commune with a Catholic nun who had been dead for over a hundred years? Therese de Lisieux had lived till the age of twenty-four and died of consumption. Just before the end, she said,

'When I die, I will send down a shower of roses from the heavens; I will spend my heaven spreading roses on earth.'

So, in my morning meditation, I asked her, 'Am I really communing with you? If so please send me a sign.'

That very day I was wandering around our garden—it was late December and freezing and as I went past the side of our house, I saw it- a forlorn white rose, clinging to a trellis and being lashed by an arctic wind. I shivered and not from the cold. Spooky. Was this a sign? A few days later was my actual 60th birthday. One friend brought me a large bunch of roses. Jocasta brought me a birthday cake studded with 60 small, exquisitely-carved pink roses. My friend Alicia gave me dried roses for my bath. Others brought me more roses. I hadn't had a rose in the house for years! Jake got a letter from the cake people for my 60/30 party—it would be a swirling structure studded with 120 little rose cupcakes.

I had told no one about the deal I had made with the dead saint. I didn't want people to think me dottier than I already was. I could pass off some of the roses as coincidences, but they trooped in so spectacularly and consistently, that I wondered. Was I arrogant to even consider that this saint had singled me out and was bestowing favours upon me? It was weird, challenging stuff, but I felt Therese was helping me

Soon after my 60th birthday, I stopped off in Singapore on a flight to Australia, to fight a custody battle over my mentally-ill sister. The pious ladies of Methodist City Mission (recently commercialised) sniffed the lucrative Trust Fund my late stepfather had left Alexandra and were trying to get their so-called saintly paws on it.

I was very sad, frustrated and angry and needed support. I felt in need of a rose. Frangipanis were everywhere but no roses. I went to the loo and there, on the window sill, was a rose in a vase. Yes, my saint was with me. My other sister, Val, with whom I had a fraught relationship, decided to side with the social workers and malign my name.

I seemed to be continually in Melbourne, defending myself from attacks aiming to assassinate my character. It was heavy- I needed all the help I could get.

Eventually my criticalness of Val rose to boiling point – ranting about it didn't help- in fact, it made it worse. I was becoming more and more pinched and negative. My meditation stalled. I stopped sleeping properly. In an attempt to get unstuck, I started doing the criticalness exercise. When you feel critical- you self-inspect and find what it is in you. I used to teach it in my mind-clearing training sessions. Jake had carried it on in his Systems work with civil servants and senior police officers.

The exercise helped a bit. But I was not making much headway. Mental illness in the family had wrought its damage deeply in my relationship with Val. In desperation, I went to the writings of Therese de Lisieux, to read how she helped the nuns in her charge, face criticalness. How could I get through this criticalness which was now swamping me?

Therese's answer is 'You must soften your heart first.'

Reading those words, I realised how hard and brittle my heart had become.

'So how do I soften my heart?'

Her answer was for me, pretty unpalatable to start with.

'Pray to God for that person. Pray for the best for them'. As with all my readings of Therese and the Catholic saints, I had to wade through my history of negative trips about the Catholic Church and its effects on me. The Catechism always loomed up with pictures of creepy holy people in it, who are always praying for me. Yeuch. However, I have done countless hours of self-inspection about all that and am able to get to the essence, which in all major religions, is love. And yes, I really did need to soften my heart. So, I tried it - the 'praying' became just visualising Val as a struggling human being like myself and wanting the best for her. That was hard. 'God' became the goodness that suffuses everything including Val, and most of all myself. I cried and cried. I felt I was tackling a deeper layer around my heart which kept all other people out, not just Val. I was the little refugee girl who couldn't bear feeling inferior to all those Australian girls who I felt were looking down on me in a superior fashion. So secretly I would wish them all ill. This wish shrank my heart with its spidery webs. Throughout my life, I would build up a superior stance myself and keep this raw hurt at bay. I let the hurt be and felt my heart beginning to soften.

Then Therese said, 'Then you thank God that that person has brought you this suffering.' Bloody Hell. I realized how difficult the Convent life must be. As Therese told her nuns- this is an extremely tough path. You are on the task of dissolving your ego and surrendering totally to love.

Okay, okay. My meditation now had a deeper focus. I was not in a convent (thank God) but I was a human being, living this life on earth, experiencing its slings and arrows of fortune. Plenty to work with and difficult enough.

As well as Therese and her roses, I received help from an unexpected quarter. A top Melbourne lawyer had read my book, 'Sasha & Olga', and got in touch. She thought the book so wonderful that she had bought ten copies for friends. When she heard of my predicament with my court custody battles, she gave me sound advice, attended court and helped me defend myself. This was to become a godsend in a very stressful time, as various people in Melbourne tussled to get their hands on my mentally-ill sister's Trust Fund. Something or someone, somewhere, was looking after me.

But my sister Alexandra was deteriorating rapidly. I had finally persuaded her doctors that the drug Olanzapine was paralyzing her, but it was too late. While various bodies tried to squeeze as much out of her Trust Fund as possible, she was now in a nursing home, paraplegic and confined to a wheelchair. I felt very sad when I sat with her and her little boy Henry. She just stared wistfully into the distance as her speech became too impaired for her to even have a conversation.

It was frightening the way history was repeating itself. 'There, but for the grace of God, go I,' I thought, as I remembered my mother languishing in an Adelaide mental hospital. Of the three sisters, I had fared the best, for my sister Val could only survive on strong medication. I was grateful for my trip to Peru to face my madness and to my husband for supporting me and loving me.

During this time, I also remembered that my mother loved parties. I remembered she once threw a party and invited a Russian orchestra comprising accordion, balalaika and violin, into our living room. My stepfather's grim face contrasted with my mother's radiance and laughter. I felt more strongly that I should honour the healthy mother and nourish the party girl I was becoming. As I had realized when my father was dying- the best I could do for both my parents and the sacrifice they made to get me out of the aftermath of WW2, was to be happy, and parties were making me very happy. The party hedonist had a way to go.

I was also honouring my mother's sewing lessons by becoming a seasoned party costume maker. I had a sewing room and a party dress-up room in our house. My daughter had given birth to another child, my beautiful granddaughter. We often combined trips to London for parties and babysitting duties. If we went to an all-night party, we would arrive at my daughter's place just when the grandchildren were waking up. They seemed to be used to seeing their grandparents dressed up in glitter and feathers. Jake was also working for Scotland Yard on their Modernisation Board, so had to make sure he washed off the party glitter before he went. This failed one time when I persuaded him to dye his hair pink for a pink party.

'It will wash out,' I assured him. It didn't. I accompanied him to a lecture he was giving to senior police officers. When he got up on the podium, I breathed a sigh of relief as his hair looked fine. But then the overhead light came on and his hair became a bright pink halo. It didn't help that I had left my boa in the lift. After the lecture, a stern announcement was made over the tannoy system.

'Would the owner of a pink boa, found in the lift, please collect it from the reception desk.'

It all seemed fine and Jake's lecture was received very well. There were enough clues that their Professor had a party life, but this did not seem to dim their enthusiasm for what Jake had to teach - it was a modernisation board after all!

Yes, the party hedonist was in full swing.

The next big party Jake and I planned was our 25th wedding anniversary. Of course, the theme would be silver. We wrote on our invite:

*Costumes must be sexy and be mainly silver (plus any other colour). Failure to comply may mean you will not be admitted!*

*The very best present you can give us is to come with your favourite person, dress outrageously... and have a really good time. That's basically what we are planning to do!*

Our friend Tara had a large Queen Anne house in Oxford, the perfect party house to which Jake and I had been invited to parties before; a hot tub; a rotunda in the garden; lavish lawns. There were shows put on by friends and a flash sound and light system. Sparkie and Julie were the DJs.

I renewed my wedding vows to Jake by singing them, accompanied on my guitar. The crowd were by now looking pretty debauched. We had a couple of floor shows, including the Naked Poet, resplendent in silver glitter and not much else. We had amazing fireworks and danced deliriously until dawn.

Jake and I had so enjoyed the 60-30 party and the Silver party, we decided we loved throwing parties. We loved giving people a good time. My daughter decided to move with her husband and two children to Australia. Although this was sad, we decided to have a farewell celebration. We found a spectacular venue in Portland Place, London and it just happened that the date that worked out was Midsummer night 2009. It was exactly 30 years before that I had crawled into bed with Jake and Lara at a midsummer party at his house. So, as well as a farewell party, it was celebrating the rather nefarious beginning of our relationship.

**A Mid-summer Party**

**to**

**Celebrate our 30 years of togetherness**

**and**

**See daughter and her husband off to Australia**

**on**

**20th June 2009**

**Dress code: Sparkly, Spangly and Midsummer Night's Dream**

The venue was glitzy and sported a silver-mirrored party room with poles for pole dancers and a Jacuzzi in the corner. We had a strip show and other live entertainment. The costumes were superb and I came as Queen of the Night, wearing a black lacy see-through dress.

Yes, I was really partying and enjoying myself. I was discovering my party persona, which was flamboyant, gregarious and funny- like my mother's before she became ill. It was my way of healing all the trauma I and she had suffered, and reclaiming my right to enjoy life.

Many people our children's age and younger, loved our parties and invited us to theirs. Tara, who hosted our silver party, was one of them. She said that I was good value as a guest at her parties. When virtually everyone else was 25 years younger, this was a fantastic lift for me; better than HRT or Horny Goat. Now, of course, I had to live up to it. Did that worry me? Not one iota. I loved the challenge and turned up my party persona to full throttle. To my delight, Tara's parties were serious dress-up affairs. Much to Jake's consternation, my party dress-up room expanded to the attic. I continued flirting and received interesting feedback on my flirting skills. One man said I was easy to flirt with because I didn't need anything from him. I was so self-contained and sure of myself. I received this feedback from others too. At one Spring party, where I wore a short yellow skirt over meshed yellow tights threaded with fresh primroses, a man bumped into me on the dance floor.

'Mmmm, you can bump into me any time,' I murmured appreciatively. Soon we were in conversation and he discovered I was a grandmother.

'You are one helluva sexy grandmother,' he said.

'Can you give me some feedback on my flirting style?' I asked.

'Not too bad. What I find sexy is when a woman looks like she can take it or leave it.'

'You mean like this?' I said, walking purposefully away from him with a flick of my skirt, treating him to some meshed flesh. His eyebrows shot up in obvious appreciation.

I was pleased. Learning to flirt had increased my self-esteem and confidence.

But my hedonist persona was running riot. I felt I needed to swing the other way. Jake and I had stopped running Enlightenment Intensives, so our previously regular Pilgrim phases were becoming scarcer. How could I get back on to a spiritual path? Was it too late?

# 10

## Russian Roots

It was with great joy I discovered Anastasia, no not the doomed Tsarina – but a spokesperson for an old civilisation in the country of my ancestors who were almost wiped out by the Christians in the 9$^{th}$ century.

I had tracked down my long-lost Ukrainian relatives in 2000. They had last seen my 17-year-old mother in 1942 when she was shoved into a cattle truck to be a prisoner of the Nazis. They welcomed me joyously and told me Olga was an irrepressibly happy child who loved to dance and be the centre of attention, before tragedy struck in such a horrible way. The Nesterenko family had survived the wholesale slaughter, deliberate starvation and dreadful destruction of life that had been the lot of 20$^{th}$-century Ukraine. There seemed little in the way of hope or inspiration in this part of the world.

Through Anastasia, I discovered a different Ukrainian story- of Pagan beings who lived by love and telepathy, who strode the earth fearlessly and fought the Christian invaders with wooden swords to virtually the last of their kind. The few who survived escaped to the Siberian taiga, where they hid from more enemies. Anastasia was one of the descendants.

Anastasia had inspired a Russian entrepreneur, Vladimir Megre, to write eight books about her and what she had to teach. I found these inspiring; and an antidote for my slide into hedonism. These books described a pre-Christian time when the Kiev region of Ukraine, (where my mother was born), was inhabited by deeply spiritual people who worshipped nature as a supreme Goddess. I really needed a positive history of this part of the world which had suffered so much in recent times and had destroyed the lives of my grandparents and parents. I became an Anastasia freak and read her books avidly. They fed my spiritual hunger and reminded me that, while flirting at parties had been a gateway to shedding this heavy history, there was also more to experience on many other levels.

Anastasia expounded the importance of connection with nature and described many practical ways to do so. The tree spirits I experienced in the Amazon were still with me and from time to time reminded me of a connection I wanted, but still was unable to make. Jake was the avid gardener who orchestrated a wonderful fruit and vegetable garden. I loved eating the produce and did some occasional weeding, but not much else.

So where could I start? Geraniums. It was hard to kill a geranium. They were hardy. So, I planted a few and nervously watched them grow. I was delighted that they seemed to survive my somewhat lackadaisical attention. Our conservatory was soon full of breath-taking colours; pinks, reds, orange and white.

Another Anastasia teaching was the sucking of seeds. Anastasia maintains that the fruit cultivated from these seeds and then consumed by the individual who sucked them is capable not only of curing diseases but also of significantly retarding the ageing process. That was incentive enough for me. Jake chuckled sceptically as I chose some cucumber seeds and placed them under my tongue for nine minutes. I carefully planted a row of sucked seeds and marked them. Even my hard-nosed scientist husband was impressed by the results. My cucumbers were totally different from the ones from normal, un-sucked seeds out of the same packet. The skins were much thicker. I ate the cucumbers with relish, skin and all. Were they doing me good?

While I was delighting in my gardening experiments, I had a chance to find out. My sister Val and the Melbourne Methodist social workers took me to court again. They were trying to prove that I was a terrible guardian for Alexandra in order to appropriate her Trust Fund. I needed to develop a thicker skin to stand up to them. It was a long, stressful battle and I had a measure of success, and I swear it was the thick-skinned cucumbers which were giving me exactly what I needed.

In the Anastasia books, I was alerted to the phenomenon of Dolmens, which littered the southern Caucasus. These were stone structures, built thousands of years ago in which many holy people meditated and died, imparting their wisdom to the stone of the tomb. I was intrigued. I wanted to discover this wisdom. It was with this desire that I visited southern Russia in 2009, to visit the Dolmens to see for myself. As a prospective future pilgrim, I was encouraged to study images of the Dolmens on the Internet and connect with one of them. I chose what is called the grandfather Dolmen, which looked like a giant penny bun mushroom. I felt inexplicably comforted by the photograph of this Dolmen.

Just before I was to leave for Russia, I had discovered I had an ulcer and a hiatus hernia. All the angst of defending myself against ridiculous attacks in Melbourne had had its deleterious effects. Preparing and embarking on the journey didn't help matters. Getting a visa and internal flights on dodgy planes was fraught, as was the arrival in Krasnodar, losing my luggage and the beginning of the tour. The tour was badly organized and I was regretting coming. Why on earth was I going to talk to a bunch of 5,000-year-old stones? This was almost as bad as a dead saint sending me roses. However, the lack of organization was to be a godsend.

On the second day, we were supposed to be visiting some holy springs in a nearby forest. But the organizer Raisa and her driver made an error, and we happened to be walking in the wrong forest looking for the springs. As I turned left, my grandfather Dolmen suddenly appeared before me. I was so overwhelmed, I burst into tears. The lack of preparation, and with it the removal of inevitable expectations, transported me to another zone. I sank beside the Dolmen and sobbed and sobbed. It felt familiar in a strange way. I had an image of a mother feeding me by this very tomb. Raisa came up and whispered in my ear- the grandfather is welcoming you home and is so glad you have finally returned. At this, I sobbed even more.

'He has a message for you,' said Raisa. 'You must never fear death. Your soul is like a beautiful bird and will be waiting joyfully to break free.'

I was smitten and became Dolmen mad.

Anastasia had described the Moon Dolmen, which was the next on our tour. She claimed that this had been inhabited by one of her own foremothers. This wise being's message was that all mothers, while feeding their babies, whether at breast or bottle, should impart to the suckling infant, all the messages of love and support from a long line of grandmothers, great-grandmothers and foremothers, stretching back through time. As I sat at the Moon Dolmen, I felt the support of all my own foremothers.

This was very healing for me, as being a migrant to Australia, I had never known my grandmother, aunts nor extended family.

Anastasia also described a school in Tekos, a town in the midst of Dolmen country, with its revolutionary and spiritual methods of teaching. Tekos School was already deep in my imagination, as when I had first read about it, I had been inspired to write a Science Fiction story set there. This 10,000-word story had been accepted for an anthology of optimistic SF stories. As part of the Russian tour, a visit to Tekos School was on the agenda.

The school lived up to and beyond all my expectations and was even more awe-inspiring than in my imagination. The children (aged 12-18), designed and built their own buildings from start to finish. As well as a diversity of courses, most students excelled and passed university degree subjects within 2 years. Behind the school, on a hill, was a circle of stones and a maze where students could walk when they needed to think deeply or meditate.

On many of the walls were written wise sayings in Cyrillic, reflecting the ethos of the school's founder, Michael Schetinin. After having submitted my Sci-Fi story to the publisher, earlier that year, I thought I had made an error in writing the sayings in

English rather than in Cyrillic. However, when I was invited to the Silver House, an exquisite and magical place built by the girl students, I was shocked to see a caption written in English.

'We create our own future with our thoughts'.

This reduced me to shivers as it was exactly the caption I had written in my Sci-Fi story. Had I foreseen this? How much more magic was to unfold in my life?

It was the last day of my Russian sojourn. As it was hot, many of the party went to the beach. Not me. Nearby was a wood with three Dolmens, I had not yet visited. I wanted to soak up their wisdom before I left. One Dolmen had a flat top on which I lay and looked up at the hornbeam canopy above, relishing the peace and quiet. However, it was shady and starting to feel a bit chilly, I wished I had brought a cardigan to keep me warm. Just as I had that thought, a black cat leapt out of nowhere, immediately snuggled in on my chest and started purring loudly. I was warm in an instant.

'Wow, the power of thought!' I thought. That, coupled with the mysterious warmth emanating from the stones underneath, gave me a blissful couple of hours. I felt my oesophagus and stomach being healed.

When I returned to the UK, I wanted to write up my experiences for the Alternative Psychology magazine, 'Kindred Spirit'. I bought a copy to educate myself in its house style. Flipping through the pages, I was arrested by an image of a beautiful woman carrying a falcon on her outstretched arm. I immediately knew I wanted the peace and happiness which emanated from her. Isha was her name. I felt she was beckoning me to my next spiritual adventure. The Dolmens had led me to my next guru! My devotion to Isha nearly put an end to the irrepressible flirt I was becoming. But I had a couple of flirt assignations first.

The first, a Science Fiction conference, seemed very unpromising to start with but had a delicious surprise in its tail. My futuristic story published in 'Shine' by Solaris, was being launched. Two years earlier, I had responded to its editor's request for optimistic stories, set in the near future. Why not set it in Tekos, which I had read about in the Anastasia books? My story 'Russian Roulette 2020', described a romance between an American, web-addicted lad and a young Russian girl educated at Tekos School. She challenged him and taught him how to be more engaged in reality. The SF community was divided in its response. There were some excellent reviews which gave me 5 stars, thinking the story should be compulsory on High School curricula, and there were some dreadful reviews that gave me none, saying it was romantic, Pollyannaish claptrap. But hey, I reasoned it was good to get extreme responses, rather than dreaded neutrality. I had a great time at the book launch, talking to people about optimistic versus dystopic futures, and how important it was to create positive futures with thoughts and visions. I felt sassy and important.

Speakers at this SF conference included Iain Banks, one of my favourite authors. I was thrilled. The theme of the conference was steampunk. I didn't even know what steampunk was, but had great fun researching and getting together costumes. On the last evening, I got ready for the steampunk ball. I had decided to go as a Victorian hooker- surprise, surprise!

The dearth of men to flirt with was alarming. They were serious-looking Sci-Fi aficionados. However, I noticed a gaggle of guys in their early 20s, looking impressive in their steampunk costumes. It was immediately obvious that they took the dressing up thing to an even greater level than I ever had. Their costumes were original Victoriana. So, in hooker mode, I engaged them in conversation. Henry, wearing an original Viceroy outfit, introduced himself. I admired his epaulettes, which gathered his shoulders to an imperious height. He said he had to stiffen his whole torso to get into the costume and this really helped him in the role of Viceroy.

I asked, 'What about me, Mr Viceroy, do I pass muster in this outfit?'

He looked down at my low top and said in a toffee accent, 'Well I think your, ahem, top part could do with a little 'ahem', how can I say it, push up?' So, I left to readjust my underwear, and then returned.

He reappraised my cleavage, then put his arm through mine, saying

'That will do very nicely indeed.' We strutted around together, the Viceroy and I, and talked to the other young set in their stiff garb.

'Any other advice as a Viceroy's consort?' I asked, my impressive bosom heaving beautifully.

'Yes,' he said. 'You have to look like you own the place.' He certainly looked like he did.

'How do I do that?'

'Well, the famous stiff upper lip is what it's all about. Purse your top lip and flare your nostrils.'

I did exactly as he said and it was true; I felt I did own the place. A few of his friends came up and I admired their costumes. I engendered a blush to their post-adolescent faces, as I flashed them an 'I so own you!' look. They all wanted to have photos taken with me. I was having fun. I knew they were all fixated on my bosom, and that I had snared the Viceroy! But hey, what else was there to do in this place so empty of real flirt material?

Feeling bored, I was considering whether I should go to my hotel room and have an early night, when I spotted a half-decent looking guy in a black coat at the end of the hall. I wandered over and said, 'Mmmm, hello. Are you a Sci-fi fan or a Sci-fi writer?' Intriguingly he looked like he wore nothing under his coat.

'Neither', he said. 'I'm with the band.'

'The band!' I half-screeched. 'There's a band? You the singer?'

He started to shake his head, when from behind a curtain, walked the most appealing man I had seen in a long while. He was wearing a silver suit finished with hat and steampunk monocle.

'Wow!' I gushed. 'You look more amazing than Michael Jackson.' (He had recently died.)

'Michael who?' he deadpanned, nonchalantly. I was immediately smitten by this God in silver.

'You are a sight for sore eyes', I sighed. 'I have been stuck at this Sci-fi convention for a whole weekend, and now with you two guys, things are really looking up,'

'Oh, ignore Tom here. He raced out of the house with nothing on but a coat.'

'Yeah, I play keyboards,' said Tom clutching his coat tighter.

'And you must be the lead singer.' I am swooning.

'Yeah baby, I sure am!' He gave me a look that nearly swallowed me whole, so I quickly said.

'Hey listen. I'm very happily married. But I just love a really good flirt.'

'You're on, baby,' he said, with a wink from his un-monocled eye.

I stumbled to one of the tables set around the dance floor, while the band set up. I joined Tracey, a Sci-fi writer from Birmingham, whom I had met earlier. She, a married woman, confided that she had fallen in love with a member of her writing group and wondered if she should get off with him.

'Well, I have just met a gorgeous rock singer. There he is.' He obligingly came to the microphone and introduced himself as Mr E and the band, 'Ghostfire'.

I pulled Tracey, who was quite drunk, up to dance. A few other people took to the floor. I found the tunes surprisingly good. But then I would, seeing I had a crush on the lead singer. I gyrated in front of him, giving him a sexy dance. He responded by directing his suggestive lyrics at me.

'Hey, I swear he is singing directly to you,' said Tracey. This was so exciting. The Viceroy came up and asked me to dance. As he did, Ghostfire played their latest song, 'The Last Waltz', and the Viceroy dutifully waltzed me around the room. I felt the most beautiful woman there. As the song finished, the Viceroy bowed and led me back to the table where Tracey was casting despairing glances at the object of her affections.

'Oh Tracey,' I said 'I am in the same dilemma as you. I am seriously tempted to get off with this lead singer. He is so delicious.'

I dragged her up again to dance. Mr E started crooning.

'Oh, hasn't Mr E got the most amazingly fabulous voice?' I whispered in Tracey's ear. 'It is so deep and sexy. I would describe it as a cunt-tingler of a voice.'

As I said this, she started to laugh and then scream hysterically in disbelief. She shrieked so loudly and so deafeningly, for so long, that Mr E stopped the band and said into the microphone;

'I cannot continue until the lady who is laughing so much, shares the joke.' I froze. Oh no. Would my outrageous description of his voice be made public? Tracey shrieked even more loudly. She really was hysterical.

'Perhaps her friend, the beautiful lady in black, could share this joke?' said Mr E seductively.

'No way.' I shook my head frantically. Fortunately, Mr E decided not to press it, and continued to play. Before his last song, he announced;

'I am giving away copies of my new CD, 'The Last Waltz'. Anyone who comes backstage may also get a snog'. He looked pointedly at me. I pretty well did swoon on the spot. I dragged the still-hysterical Tracey back to the table.

'What shall I do?' I asked her. But she still looked too shocked to answer. I knew what I was going to do. I was going backstage. What happened next was anybody's guess, I was so fired up. The Viceroy and his friends came up.

'Congratulations.' Viceroy said. 'You really are the Belle of this Ball. And you really do own this place.'

'Thank you. You have been a good teacher.' Here I was, 63, and still could pull off being the most sought-after woman in the room. I remembered, ruefully, how sad I was at 50, thinking my Belle of the Ball days were well and truly over!!

'And thank you for the waltz.' With that, he bowed again and made a dignified exit.

The band finished and resolutely, this Belle of the Ball made her way backstage. Hey, she only had one life, and when else would she ever have a chance to snog a gorgeous rock singer with a cunt-tingler of a voice? I found Mr E sitting on a bench. He looked at me appreciatively as I sidled up to him. I said coyly, 'I've come for my CD.'

He rifled in a box and gave me a copy.

'By the way, what is your real name, Mr E?' I asked.

'Gary', he said. I reeled back in shock. This was the last thing I expected.

'Gary?' I shrieked (even more loudly than Tracey). 'What do you mean Gary? How can you, a gorgeous rock God, have a name like Gary?'

Gary looked quite baffled. 'It's what my parents called me,' he answered. Well, this really took the wind out of my flirt sails and probably saved me serious complications. Jake's name took on a much sexier ring in my head.

Gary looked at me hungrily.

'As for the second part of your offer, my husband and I have a rule, no kissing on the lips. So, I would like you to kiss me just here.' I pointed to my cheek. He did have rather delicious lips for someone with such a seriously unsexy moniker. So, he planted a kiss which just caught the edge of my lip. Rather delicious, but I was satisfied. I left with his CD in my hand.

I told Jake the whole story. He did get slightly worried at my graphic description of Mr E's voice, but all his worries were erased when he heard what his real name was. As he said, 'there is no way I can measure up to this youthful god of rock with the sexy voice, but with Gary as a name, I win hands down.'

I befriended Mr E on Facebook and sent him a private message describing what my friend had been hysterical about. Of course, he loved my graphic description of his singing voice and he became one of my Facebook flirt toy-boys. He eventually met a lovely young woman and wedding bells are in the air.

My flirt star was still rising. My next sojourn was as a fairy at a festival. I met Shelley Fairy, who ran the Fairy Love stalls at Kimberley, and at other great festivals like Glastonbury. She is literally the Queen of the Fairies- sells beautiful fairy costumes and loves dressing up. We got on famously.

'Oh, I'm so sad, I'm too old to be a fairy.'

'Rubbish,' she flashed her blue eyes at me. 'You'd make a great fairy.'

'Then can I work at your Fairy Love stall?'

'Of course, my beauty,' she twanged in her Aussie accent. 'Come to the next one.'

The deal was that a fairy worked four hours a day in the fairy tent, selling wares. The rest of the time was spent walking and flouncing about in all the fabulous tutus and wings Shelley provided, in order to lure buyers to the stall. What was not to like?

I fished out a tent from the barn and off I went to the Green Man festival in Wales.

I was 63 and off to be a fairy. Jake was worried.

'Why?'

'I'm not sure about this- you going off on your own?'

'Why?'

'Well judging from all your antics lately, you might get off with someone!'

I had a choice at this point. Do I see Jake as 'Daddy', who is suppressing me having fun?' Very easy to slip into.

OR

Do I see Jake being a little uneasy, as he has seen my flirting ability spiral spectacularly over the last couple of years?

I choose to go with the latter point of view. I am right.

'Yay,' whoops the inner vain flirt. 'I'm 63 and my husband is worried about letting me out of his sight.'

'Yes', said Jake. 'I'm afraid some bloke might get the wrong message and follow you back to your tent. It might get unpleasant.'

'Don't worry,' I said. 'I'll put my tent right next to Shelley Fairy's van and be within her fairy orbit.'

I had a great time, dressing up as a fairy in many different wings and glitter. The mud didn't make it easy but hey I was a fairy in wellies! But many of the blokes at this particular festival were disappointing. The only guy of any interest was a Lebanese kitchen hand at the kebab stall next to the Fairy Tent. The place was heaving with what looked like left-wing rationalist, and believe me, left-wing rationalists are prone to hide their sexiness. It can be an intellectually stifling and dull cardboard world that is devoid of any magic. I know. I used to be one in my Anarchist days. Everything was cut and dried.

Many of these men disappeared in a blur of khaki and string beneath grungy jackets and grungy face hair. Even Nonda Nesterenko gave up the ghost trying to find a trace of testosterone in this crowd. Yes, I must introduce Nonda Nesterenko, the most outrageous flirt of all, a sub-personality of mine, who has long simmered inside me, waiting to get out and spread her flirtatious wings. Nonda Nesterenko is my porn name devised from a classic method where the name of a first pet or toy is combined with mother's maiden name. As Nonda was the name of my favourite pet clown given to me by my Czech grandmother, (yes, the clown who had received many unholy drubbings), this was my first introduction to Nonda Nesterenko. She is the quintessential faded porn star, but I loved meeting her and she became a firm favourite to channel my subsequent flirtathon. But at the time (I was only 56!) I firmly put her away into the porn slot of my mind. I was still determined to be a fully-fledged, wise, old sexless crone. Decadent parts of me, like

Nonda, were frowned upon by an inner committee of how I SHOULD BE! This inner committee ran counter to who I wanted to be. Thank goodness they were losing their grip.

Will, one of my favourite flirts, helped me accept my inner Nonda Nesterenko. Will is a real outdoors man. He hunts, fishes and lives in the countryside. I was first attracted to him at one of Julie Devine's Golden Delicious parties, as he wore fur, the perfect excuse to sidle up and rub my hands through it. Will and I hit it off immediately. The banter was razor-sharp and quick. In fact, I was impressed by the raft of witticisms that came streaming out of my mouth. I had always regarded myself as not witty at all. Australian witticisms which bordered on base sarcasm had always escaped me and I never had any clever ripostes. And English witticisms always felt far too clever and sophisticated. But something about Will brought out my sparkly, witty self. And he was a great flirt. From then on, we had an easy rapport. At one party, he was looking quite dejected.

'Women trouble?' I asked.

'Sort of,' he said, 'but I'm feeling pretty sexless at the moment. Can't even dredge up a flirt.'

So, I whisked out Nonda and whipped into that persona like a medium who slips effortlessly into being a wise entity. Nonda is one of those loose, slightly faded, Russian women that you might meet in a bar, who is anybody's after a few drinks. She can make men feel a million dollars with a combination of flattery, purring, a flick of the skirt and of course the requisite ample cleavage.

'Darling' I said to Will. 'If there is even a tiny molecule of testosterone within your manly body, Nonda Nesterenko will find it and tickle it into action.' So, I did and it was.

The right word was 'molecule' for in a Facebook message Will wrote, 'Was great to hang out with you! Nonda sure can sniff out even a molecule of testosterone if there's one knocking about! And guess what? Now there are two!'

Page intentionally left blank

# 11

## Isha

Nonda and my various flirt personas were having a ball. I knew that dishy men found me attractive but I still dreaded the age thing. The crone cackled at me.

'You won't be attractive for much longer. Your flesh will become gnarled and withered. He, he, he!'

I was putting all my faith into my new guru Isha, who I counted on saving me from myself. I was convinced that it was time to suppress my flirtatious self. It was getting out of hand. In order to do so, I felt I needed a substantial spiritual practice. Her system offered it. However, it came with a plethora of snags. First off, she was Australian.

'No way can Australia produce an enlightened person,' was my uncharitable thought. 'And she is from Melbourne which has spawned some pretty horrific social workers.'

Furthermore, I discovered she had been a top horse trainer and a rock singer. 'What?' But I was fascinated. I watched a few videos and soon overcame her Australian drawl. What she promised was that I would learn to love myself. If I practised her system diligently, I would eventually look into the mirror and love what I saw. This was highly attractive to a vain woman in her early sixties, who knew a time would come when the neck wrinkles would be so hideous, I would want to top myself.

I bought her book and started practising faithfully. This was a gratitude meditation in four parts or facets. I was suspicious of the technique as it seemed to be aimed at lassoing me into a supposed evocation of Truth, by repetition. This did not fit squarely with my Enlightenment Intensive practice, which aimed at discovering my own truth. But just one look at the ugly striations on my neck, I decided if I had to bludgeon myself into loving them, then so be it. The four facets to be repeated over and over were;

Praise love for this moment in its perfection.

Thank love for my human experience in its perfection.

Love creates me in my perfection.

Ommm.

I travelled to Barcelona to see her. I wanted to meet an enlightened person in the flesh. I was not disappointed. She was in her late forties, hair dark and sleek, radiating warmth and good humour. She looked so much more wholesome than Charles Berner and smelt good too when she gave me a warm hug. At the workshop, I confronted how I had closed off my heart and sexuality in previous relationships, more profoundly than I had thought. When I returned to Jake, I felt more open to him. He reminded me we were on a path to God together. However, I had fallen hopelessly in love with Isha. I needed more of her. My path to God was forked.

I next booked to stay for two weeks in her ashram in Uruguay. Below is part of an article I wrote about the experience.

## Is the Lady Guru, Gaga?

***Eva Maria travels to Uruguay to find out***

Lady Gaga's latest offering booms out in the vast, domed tent, as 200 people await Darshan. Durga dances in, with red scarf and hair extensions, looking much younger than her 57 years. She translates into Spanish what the Lady Guru, Isha will say. Then in sweeps Isha, a statuesque vision in tight jeans and bejewelled waistcoat, swinging in time to Lady Gaga's 'Born This Way'. We all stand and jig to the catchy tune.

'If you were all expecting a serious ashram,' she addresses the audience in her Australian drawl, 'I think you've come to the wrong place. We just have too much fun here.' It is true; just earlier I had enjoyed an hour of aerobics and aero-boxing to blasting techno rave music, led by the dynamic Peruvian, Alejandro, one of Isha's band of teachers.

Isha settles on the table beside Durga, flicks back her sleek black hair and continues. 'Lady Gaga introduced this song at the Grammy Awards last night. It says it all - encapsulates all that I'm teaching here. Love yourself because you are made perfectly as you are.'

This central teaching of Isha is certainly why I have flown several thousand miles to Uruguay. I am the wrong side of sixty and am loathe to subjugate my face to a surgeon's scalpel; I want to look at myself and be able to love every wrinkle. Is that even possible? Definitely worth I try.

'Imagine looking in the mirror, and the face looking back at you is someone you truly love. Just imagine….' Isha writes on the last page of her book, *Why Walk When you can Fly*. Isha, a former singer, took the title from her favourite Mary Chapin Carpenter song. The third facet she teaches, 'Love creates me in my perfection', resonates with Lady Gaga's lyrics.

Before travelling to Uruguay, I had practised the facets and found they suited me. For someone who has tried countless meditation techniques with varying degrees of success, I look forward to doing it each day. Isha doesn't describe it as meditation, or affirmations or a mantra; it is more like polishing the facets of a diamond that represents who you think you are, until eventually who you actually are, shines out.

Isha is hardly known in the UK but travels the world teaching her system. She has taken South America by storm and has tens of thousands of students there, including many famous actors and artists. She now has several centres in South America. I stayed at one on the Costa Azul, a half an hour east of Montevideo, the capital of Uruguay. When I first walked into 'La I' as it is called, I was dazzled by the whiteness and splendour of the buildings. Isha has tastefully transformed this former Art Deco hotel into a stunning training centre and residence that can sleep up to 160 people.

The interiors are immaculately kept, with black and white marble floors and black carpets.

The band of teachers, about forty strong, ranging in age from thirty to seventy-five, also participates in a rigorous programme of spreading their message into the community. They work with the disabled, the dying, the blind and convicted criminals. It is in prisons that the Isha system has made startling progress. Prisoners and their guards learn the facets and practise them daily. This is no easy task, as many are murderers and hardened guerrilla rebels. What Isha tells them is "There's no difference between you and me – it's about choices. You have got to start making different choices. We all want the same thing and that is love.'

The L-shaped room at 'La I' where students practise the facets, is vast and laid out with thick black mattresses, one for each person. Isha believes in comfort. Students can sit or lie on their mattress with a pillow and blanket. As I suffer from a bad back, this was a godsend. I also swam at the glorious sandy beach, returning home two weeks later, sun-kissed and 2 kilos lighter.

Isha is a great animal lover and races Arabian endurance horses – an extreme equine sport that tests both the horse and rider to the limit.

I find I am beginning to love myself more. I am now admiring the cascade of smile wrinkles on my cheeks. I'm not so sure about the hoods that seem to be developing over my eyes, or those unattractive jowls, but hey I'm working on accepting them.

So, is the Lady Guru Gaga? Not at all. On the contrary, she is profoundly sane. She walks her talk and is deeply rooted in love.

I thought that the place was a palace – with its shiny marble, sea horses in aquaria, comfy mattresses, an army of spiritual helpers and translators. I was the only English person there.

However, I found myself in very badly-led groups. They were too large and unwieldy. I am a seasoned group psychotherapist. I know all about group dynamics and how to help people through emotional crises. In my view, these group leaders were dreadful amateurs. Any time a feeling came up, participants had to bang a cushion. I had banged so many cushions in the past. Did I really have to go back to the dark ages? Worse, was that any screams or shouts that came up as a result of hitting the cushion had to be stifled into the cushion. I was all for banging cushions if I had to, but to stuff the resulting screams felt like emotional barbarism. However, I put aside all my judgements and therapeutic arrogance because I loved Isha- she was a Goddess in her silks and pearls- she was a modern-day immortal- so I went along with it. I could also see that this style of therapy seemed to suit Latin Americans, whose culture repressed their emotions.

In the first couple of group sessions, participants were dealing with sexual abuse. 'Oh no,' I thought- 'I've been there-done that!' I had worked on Dave-the-farmhand trauma several times in therapy and felt I had fully resolved it. The group leader asked how I was- so I mentioned the sexual abuse. Within two minutes she had me in front of a cushion. Oh no, this felt stupid. I really didn't want to bang cushions and make stifled screams. The example of Ram Dass, one of my heroes, came to mind. When Ram Dass was in his fifties, he had been asked to attend a primal scream group. The group urged him to lie on a mattress and start screaming. Even though he really thought he didn't need to do that, he surrendered and went along with the instruction. He got a lot out of it despite his misgivings. So, I decided to follow his example. I thought – perhaps there is more I can get out of this- so relived the whole scene again- bashing the pillow and then shouting into it. It felt a bit of a charade but hey, if Ram Dass could do it, so could I. It felt okay. Afterwards, other participants made comments. Roberto described a time his eight-year-old sister had been sexually molested when he was a boy of ten. His father had woken him out of bed, told him to get dressed and come with him. He vividly remembered the gun his father took down from a cupboard. Out they went to find his sister's molester. He described the thrill and the fear. The group ended and we all went to bed. I found myself haunted by Roberto's story. Next day in the meditation it kept coming up and with it came many tears. I went to one of the assistants for help. It was then that a question struck me like a thunderbolt.

'Where was **my** father?' I loved the fact that Roberto's father went out with a gun.

'Why didn't my father find Dave, the farm-hand, and sort him out?'

I was overwhelmed by profound grief for the father we had fled in Czechoslovakia only months earlier. I felt intensely bereft of a father, my real father. I had buried that grief much more deeply than the sexual abuse. The absence of a father to protect me at a time I needed protection, opened up wells of pain deep in my heart.

That evening I shared this with the group and did some more stifled wailing and beating of breast and cushion. I told Roberto how grateful I was for his story and asked him if he would be my surrogate dad for a while. He was glad to oblige.

Next day was the second to last day and we were told that Isha would be in our group that evening. I was beside myself with happiness. I had been put in the second group because I had done an introductory group in Barcelona. Below us in hierarchy was the baby group and above us were two more advanced groups. We felt honoured that the great Isha would be attending our very lower level group.

The group started and I put myself next to Isha- I wanted to breathe in her fragrant, enlightened flesh and soak up her vibes. Vito, a participant, began by relaying a conversation he had had at lunch with Eduardo, another participant, who always seemed disdainful of group proceedings. Apparently, Eduardo had spoken disparagingly of another group member. This was translated by Durga, Isha's translator. I wasn't really taking much notice of the conversation as I was busy imbibing Isha's divine air, but I did notice Vito looking at me uncomfortably.

Then Eduardo drawled 'yes I was talking about Eva.' My ears pricked up.

'Yes,' continued Eduardo. 'I was telling Vito, I really think Eva shouldn't be here at all. She should be in therapy. I came here for spiritual upliftment, not having to listen to all her woes and bad sexual history. I have enough of people's troubles where I live. I didn't come here to hear more crap.'' He said this in a superior, sardonic kind of voice while Durga translated.

I couldn't believe what I was hearing. Something deep within me snapped. A fury like the fire of seven dragons erupted within me. I screamed at the top of my voice,

'How fucking dare you!' The air stilled. Everyone was shocked. The translator didn't even translate. The meaning of fury is very clear. Eduardo blanched as I let him have it.

'You don't know shit about spiritual upliftment. You wouldn't know a true feeling if it fell out of your arse and bit you! This IS the place to deal with bad sexual history, as you call it. How dare you put your arrogant, stupid shit on me.' Silence and shock. I then resumed my normal voice, and calmly said. 'Okay Eduardo, you can continue – I have expressed what I needed to.'

By this time, Isha had gathered herself and turned to me saying, 'Strictly speaking, you should really scream into a cushion.'

'Oh!' I gulped. In my fury, I had totally forgotten the rules, which as I was to discover was a good thing.

Isha then ushered the trembling Eduardo outside, to work with one of the helpers. Isha turned back to me and said, 'You don't belong in this group.' With a wave of her beautiful arm, she ordered me in the direction of the top group.

'Oh,' I thought, moving very reluctantly. I really wanted to stay with my group and continue sitting by her. But hey, she was the Queen; she had given her orders; I had been elevated up the hierarchy, despite flagrantly breaking the rules. So out I went. On the way via the bathroom, I looked in the mirror. I looked stunning- alive, electric, beautiful. Love really had created me in my perfection. Something deep within me had clicked together. I walked into the top group which was run by the leader of the Isha community in Mexico.

'I'm sorry to interrupt, but Isha sent me to your group.'

'Are you the person who screamed?' she asked.

'Yes.' I said.

All faces were ashen and turned to me in awe. I sat down. Many in the group were crying. My outburst had reminded them of their mothers screaming at them when they were children. One woman was in the middle of a deep piece of work as a result. When she finished, the leader invited me to share what had been happening. I told the whole story with the help of another translator. The group was mesmerised. As I spoke, I saw what a gift Eduardo had given me. He, with his damning judgements of me, had unwittingly facilitated the feelings of rage I had buried, for being a victim of the unsavoury attentions of Dave, the farm-hand. The abject humiliation I had felt then and couldn't express was triggered by Eduardo, and I let him have it, lock, stock and three smoking barrels. The people in this group were on my wavelength immediately and were incredibly supportive. They applauded my empowerment. The fact that I had broken the rules by screaming was ignored and secretly admired. At the end of the evening, I went back to my own group where I was feted like a heroine. My screams had shifted everybody and it was the best group they had ever had. Eduardo had cried for the first time in thirty years and had opened up like a flower. He apologised to me and we had a warm, healing hug.

I looked into his wet eyes and said 'Thank you for your gift.'

'And thank you for yours,' he replied.

I spent the rest of the time in Uruguay floating on clouds. Durga, Isha's translator, told me she admired what I had done the previous evening. Isha's attitude towards me had shifted and she was giving me the approval I so craved from a mother figure. My own crazy mother had not given me consistent mothering. I rode a horse Western style and loved it. Isha galloped past and said I had a 'good seat'. I glowed with the praise. I wanted to stay and practise Western riding. Ride Arabian steeds. I wanted to be initiated by Isha. I wanted to bask in her fragrance. I had become her devoted disciple. I would give up partying and do something useful, like work in prisons! I would put Nonda Nesterenko into the granny attic where she belonged and give her some crochet to do. I would give up drugs and alcohol and imagined myself as a leading light in Isha's ashram. An enlightened being sitting at the Queen's feet. I was blasted by discipleship fervour.

I flew home to Jake.

Jake was far from happy. He was not at all keen that I wanted to be initiated in Isha's path and saw me demeaning myself to do so. This entailed among other things, giving up drugs and alcohol. And did he hear me right? I was going to give up parties and flirting!

We had a major fight that lasted for days.

'You want to be subservient to a guru?' Jake snorted disbelievingly.

'Yes. Isha is amazing,' I answered. 'Does such important work.'

'But I thought we were to be guiding lights for each other,' answered Jake. 'Remember our connection on Machu Picchu?'

'But I need Isha as a teacher.'

We were not making any headway. Jake reminded me that we were on a relationship path together. He did not want to lose me to a guru. He asked me to spend an evening with him, really checking it out with the help of a joint- something we had used many times before to sort out thorny issues. After much opposition (I had wanted to eschew drugs), I finally agreed.

I had been given a secret mantra in Uruguay. I felt flattered and strange about this. One supposedly had to acquire a certain level of understanding and surrender before being given the next step. This could be seen as a clever form of flattery. Secrecy was one of the factors that led to the dramatic unravelling of Charles Berner's ashram. He was having secret assignations with women followers who must not tell their husbands. These women were flattered into thinking they had advanced to the heart level and were therefore suitable sexual love partners for the enlightened guru.

I wasn't supposed to tell anybody about my secret mantra. Not even my husband. This did not sit right with me. It felt like a division between us and as I had vowed not to keep secrets from Jake, I decided to tell him. We arranged an evening in front of a fire to sort it all out.

What Jake hated most was the way he felt I was putting myself down.

'I don't like the way you put Isha up on a pedestal as if she is better than you.'

'But she is better than me- she is more enlightened.'

'Crap!' he yelled. He wasn't having it. I found my devotion to Isha wavering and I opened myself to the truth of all that Jake was saying.

Jake was right. I did demean myself in relation to Isha. Totally. I had found in her, a perfect, beautiful mother. And when I really boiled it down, I wanted to be like her- in essence, I even wanted to BE her! I was blinded by her. As her glow wore off, I could see ingredients in her system endemic to all ashrams. The disciples are encouraged to develop their consciousness, and at some point, a select few reach a stage of enlightenment which is verified by the guru. This was the case in Isha's ashram. It was a beautifully-run hierarchy.

Gradually I saw sense, and with some relief, felt I could let Isha go. But the time I spent with her had been extremely valuable. As the dust settled, I noticed things had shifted energetically between Jake and me. I felt more open-hearted towards him. What Barcelona had done for me was to face the pain of closing down in my former relationships, and what Uruguay had done for me was to heal the grief of having to say goodbye to my real father. As a result, I had closed my heart to men on an unconscious level. I now could see that my relationship with Jake must come first- NOT my relationship with Isha.

I had scrambled from the Isha pool, a little more emotionally whole. I had healed more of my hurt from preverbal times when

I had been torn away from loving grandparents, and especially my real father. I had involuntarily closed a part of my heart, never wanting to experience that wrenching pain of loss again. Jake had always complained that I was still closed off to him at a deeper level. And this had been true. I couldn't bear the intensity of our intimacy. I would flinch away from him involuntarily. After finally uncovering and facing the loss of my real father, I could now receive Jake's intensity. There was now somewhere for it to go.  I was surrendering to him on a deeper level. Now, I could embrace the relationship path where the love between me and Jake could flush out the gremlins that kept intimacy at bay.

I had fond memories of Isha's ashram and her devoted band of teachers who had helped me so much. But that was not my spiritual path. In the end, Isha was still the Queen Bee and always would be.

'How can **you** be the Queen Bee of your own life?' challenged Jake.

How could I be the Queen Bee of my own life?

That was an excellent question and one that required my full attention.

# 12

# Becoming My Own Queen Bee and Owning My Russian Bar Girl

I had to get rid of some of the fixed attitudes in my brain, for starters.

I had always compartmentalised my mind into seemingly impermeable categories. There was my sexy, flirty self who could be bad, there was my drug-taking, hedonistic self, which was very bad, and then there was my saintly, spiritual self, definitely very good and something I should be aspiring to. I needed to question the categories of behaviour I had been taught were "right" and "wrong".

With Isha, I was attempting to suppress my sexy, hedonistic personality and develop my saintly self who, in my mind, had a long way to go to reach Isha's level. I was trying to transcend the desire for drugs and flirting and become pure as a saintly nun. Despite all my Isha meditations, even the 'Love creates me in my perfection', I still couldn't look in the mirror and really love myself as I was. Should I go back to Ching Hai- let the true me emerge? But that path also had strict rules. Where should I go?

It was deeply wired into my brain that I needed a guru- that I was not enlightened enough; that I needed a strong set of spiritual rules to manage my unruly, chaotic nature. This now struck me as crazy, as I had spent my life battling with crazy rules. My mother's rules were mad- a result of being mangled by Stalin and then Hitler- and being made to feel the lowest of the low on the earth- first as a Ukrainian peasant who Stalin had a good crack at starving to death in the 1930s, and then to Hitler, who treated Ukrainian peasants as slaves of the Reich. Then she went to Australia and experienced another set of weird rules that put her at the bottom of society's heap, slightly more elevated than the hapless Aborigine.

I had been desperately searching for sane rules to live by- always looking for a new guru whom I could follow and become worthy or a system where I was special in the eyes of the guru. I elevated Ching Hai and Isha way above myself. Fortunately, Charles Berner's limitations became very obvious and he fell off his perch with a resounding splatter. I began to see clearly that there are plenty of gurus who were happy to feed off my subservience, and glory in my worship of them. I needed to really take note of the lesson I had learnt from ayahuasca- that I should be in charge of my own spaceship. I didn't need to confine myself to the limitations and rules of a guru. I could honour the teachings and good works of gurus like Isha and Ching Hai without needing to bow to them.

'Why go anywhere but within?' I had spent countless hours on Enlightenment Intensives asking myself the questions 'Who Am I?' and 'What am I?' I knew how to go within. And since Peru, I was not afraid of the scary, mad ghosts who might want to ensnare me in their grip.

So, I continued to meditate, surrendering deeper and deeper to whatever was my truth. It was probably really obvious to everyone but me, that the unvarnished truth was that I was not accepting huge parts of myself.

My mother was a great flirt- she was beautiful and sexy- but that side of her was never allowed to flower during the hardships of World War 2. She had great hopes for a new life in Australia. Unfortunately, she ended up in Adelaide, which in the 1950s was ruled by a puritanical Premier, a farmer who suppressed frivolity and believed all good citizens should be in bed by 10 pm. Sir Thomas Playford ruled, unopposed, for 37 years. No dancing or drinking alcohol after 6 pm was allowed. This suited my hard-working stepfather but was a disaster for my fun-loving mother. She grew to hate Adelaide and my stepfather's work ethic and became more and more unhappy. She eventually slipped into insanity and became a dribbling, drooling wreck. I always thought I had only imbibed my mother's craziness- but what about her flirtatious beauty? A small voice inside me whispered,

'You owe it to your mother to really own the party, good-time girl inside you. I could hear Ching Hai asking, 'who are **you** destined to be? Discover that and become it.'

Stop trying to be a saint!' I felt the blessing from the arch Saint of all, Therese. Her roses were after all, earthy, sexy and voluptuous.

Even though the life of a nun appealed to me enormously, I am not that kind of a nun. I am a sensual being who dances in the divine light of my husband's eyes. And he must be strong and amazing to be able to earth me as I can get flighty, over-excited, exuberant and chase after young men. I also was becoming more accepting of drug-taking as a part of my spiritual path. It seemed that the more I was with Isha, the more I wanted to give up drugs and alcohol, to become 'pure'. In her school and most spiritual schools, that was the way. I couldn't commit totally to a drug-free path because it meant denying the enormous benefit that taking drugs, consciously, had given me. Marijuana was like a herbal, magical blessing that had helped Jake and me see a deeper layer of what was happening, including highlighting my subservience to Isha. It illuminated certain aspects of our relationship and helped us achieve a refreshing clarity. Ayahuasca helped me overcome my fear of being subsumed by mental illness. Ecstasy had helped me tell the truth and unearth lies conveniently submerged in the substrata of my mind. Hallucinogens like Psilocybin and Ayahuasca had plunged me into a world of huge, unlimited potential and given me glimpses of the amazing person I could become, for example, the Serpent Queen and the driver of my spaceship, clothed in a sexy costume.

All this drug exploration had been balanced by fervent adherence to several drug-free spiritual paths, the most important being my dance with Enlightenment Intensives. I think I could lay claim to being one of a handful of people on the planet who (as well as leading them), had sat through the most Enlightenment Intensives as a participant. Two 6-week EIs, several two-week ones and many 3-day ones, I sat face to face with myself from 6 am to midnight. And that is a lot of self-exploration and self-challenging. And I had to do it. My upbringing at the hands of a mad woman was deeply stressful. I wanted to do it as I knew there was a lot more to life than just what had been meted out to me. And I did not want to be ruled by my unconscious. So, I had sat, day after day, uncovering the layers of my mind, battling through what felt like iron casings of judgements, festering pools of negativity, dense liquid fogs of self-loathing and rolling mists of boredom and fruitlessness. Several times I would be blessed and pierce through to a Truth-truth with a capital T- which blasted through all my illusions with a blinding clarity. Often it was just a glimpse of what Sister Therese was swallowed by at the age of 15, or what St Francis was illumined with when he loved a leper, or what Rumi experienced in the light of the moon. These experiences were REAL, not airy fairy. In those fleeting moments, there was a clarity and light that strengthened my core and dissolved the deep sense of unworthiness, a lot of which was my mother's heavy burden: starved into submission by Stalin, used as an expendable slave by Hitler and rejected by my real father's family. I didn't have to carry her burden.

So, the path ahead was very simple really- just accept myself totally- all of me! To be as real as possible more of the time. To capitalise on the direct experiences I had had, to shore myself against the mother madness layers. Easier said than done. I concentrated harder on the positives my mother had given me. She had been sexy and fun before she became ill. What did I have? – a budding flirt- a Nonda Nesterenko- a pulsing serpent queen- I was all these things and I disparaged them as unsavoury, unsaintly and unenlightened.

Paradoxically, all the meditations I had followed were about accepting what I am. What if I REALLY accepted this part of me? As I delved further, I saw that what I am in essence is a Russian Bar Girl; a younger version of Nonda Nesterenko. What I mean by a Russian Bar Girl is based on the women from Russia and Ukraine, who use their sexiness to pick up a man, usually in a bar. For example, one woman from Moscow researched all the men who owned yachts in France and where they had drinks. She put on her most gorgeous outfits to find herself a rich billionaire (which she easily did). My own Russian Bar Girl did not need to be like that. I had my man. But the serpent queen wants to lure ALL attractive men. She is voracious. My recent flirting experiments gave me great confidence that I could pull any man.

But hey, I was 64. This seemed a ridiculous age to accept that I was a Russian Bar Girl. Those beauties from Moscow and Ukraine were young, fresh-faced, springy. What chance did I have? Jake was very supportive as I expressed my misgivings.

'Hey, it is you when you shine who is irresistible.'

'You think I am a Russian Bar Girl?'

'Absolutely. Totally gorgeous. There is an eternally young woman in you.'

So, I experimented. By now I had a fairly extensive party wardrobe, so once a week I dressed up as a different Russian Bar Girl, looking as sexy as I dared; perhaps a Natasha in a white fur hat and coat and nothing underneath, or a Ludmilla in leather shorts and a jewelled bustier, or a Galina in thigh high boots and sparkling mini dress. Jake loved it.

'When are you going to give me a sexy dance?

Funnily enough, in our 30 years together, I had always been too shy to do a private sexy dance for Jake.

'I'm too shy. And isn't it far too late?'

'No way. I have been waiting patiently for years.'

So that's what I started to do. It was so liberating. I found myself daring to be sexier and sexier. Jake put on some great music and the dance would stem from what I was wearing, whether it be a short, swishy skirt with boots and pearls, or very tight jeans. It was such fun and gave me great preening opportunities where I would try on different outfits and decide which ones were the most titillating.

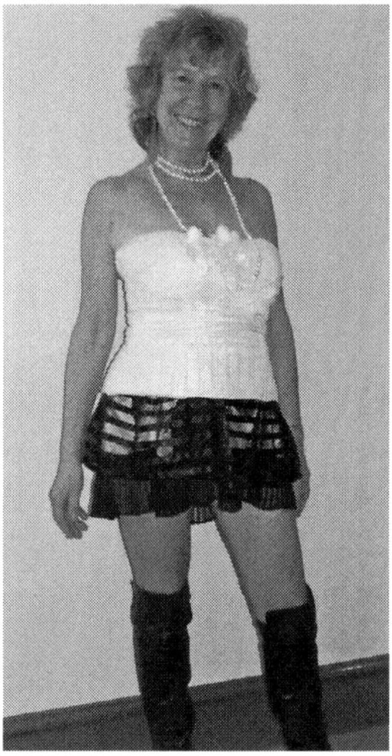

I also closely watched other women and took tips from what they did to make themselves more alluring, whether it was the way they moved their hips or let the strap slip off their shoulders. Yes, I was embracing Channel 1, the physical dimension Ram Dass referred to, big time.

I continued to meet resistance within myself in which I was judging that this was too shallow and too much like a whore. Deep within me, my Catechism Christ looked on in disapproval. Would I ever be rid of this introjected spectre? He was faintly hologrammed across my inner psyche with the message that to really enjoy sex was BAD. I continued to meditate on accepting myself as I actually was. It felt that every time I did so, a cleansing energy swept through all my cells and the hologram became fainter and the spectre of condemnation faded into the background. The more I let myself sink into pleasure, the more lovely it was. Jake helped counteract any niggling doubts, for the sexier I let myself be, the more encouraging and responsive he became. We were egging each other on. As I dared to let out my femininity, Jake reciprocated by turning up the heat on his masculinity. Phew! Electric. And it was helpful that I had made the breakthrough about my real father in Isha's ashram, to open myself more deeply to his loving. The very nature of our relationship path meant there was nowhere to hide. And I was sick of hiding. Why hide the truth?

We continued going to parties together. We discovered something rather interesting. Even more people hit on us.

'I told you, darling,' said Jake. 'It's your confidence that works. You shine out. You are a Russian Bar Girl. But just remember you are MY Russian Bar Girl!'

We also discovered that the more attention Jake paid me, the more attractive he became to other women. They loved his sexy claiming of me. The reverse was also true. As I said to Jake, 'you are so good for my street cred. If I am with you, men seem to think I must be okay to be able to keep a man like you.'

The yearly Kimberley festival was a great place to experiment with my emerging Russian Bar Girl. There were plenty of women there who liked flirting. Poonie was the greatest flirt of all and she encouraged me, both by her example and commenting favourably on any outfit that she saw me in. 'Ooh!' she said when I wore a revealing, cut out top on the last day. 'That's a sexy day 4 outfit- I usually give up by the last day but I think I'll take a leaf out of your book next year.' She was a shining example of a happily married woman who loved having fun flirts and did not judge herself being any less, because of it. She continued to flirt outrageously with Jake and they enjoyed the fact they could safely do so. The year the Kimberley colour was red, she arranged for a dozen women to dress up in a skimpy nurse's outfit, to load up our plastic syringes with wine, then smuggle ourselves into an ambulance from which we all burst forth to join the crowd waiting for a group photo. Each nurse then administered to the gaggle of men waiting to be administered to. My husband was one of them. Here is the delectable Poonie acting sexy nurse with Jake.

I also discovered it was easy- much easier than I thought- to be a Russian Bar Girl in my 60s- to own my inner 'Nonda'- to bring her out into the sun- to let her strut her stuff – and to ignore the inner, suffering Christ who was fading fast.

Sporting a variety of sexy outfits, I went up to several men and said,

'I really want you to tell me the truth. Do I look like mutton dressed as lamb?'

It was a unanimous 'no.' I could see by the look on their faces that they were pretty wowed by me.

'Are you sure you aren't just being patronising or trying to make an old woman feel good?'

'Old??? No way, you are hot!' I enjoyed some wonderful flirts. And there was always the divine Robbie on a Sunday evening and luscious Flash, who was always up for a flirt.

Jocasta and Vincent had a son who was in his late teens. He loved practising to flirt with me and we had good fun with the game. I saw him at Kimberley with a handsome friend so I flirted with him too. I asked him how old he was, expecting him to be in his early 20s.

'Forty.' he said.

'Forty!' I shrieked. 'You can't possibly be forty! That's far too old to be my toy-boy!'

He looked dejected.

'How old do I have to be to be your toy-boy?'

'Well under 40,' I said.

I had inadvertently stumbled onto one of the best chat-up lines ever, for a Russian Bar Girl in her sixties, which basically goes as follows,

'Mmm. I do like the look of you. How old are you?'

Whatever age they say, my answer is always.

'Ooh, I'm so sorry but you are too old to be my toy-boy.'

It works every time. I am followed by a coterie of adoring young men.

The other thing I discovered was that men love to be appreciated. If I saw a hunky guy, I would let him know. This was so different from when I was young. I would studiously avoid beautiful men, thinking I shouldn't let them see that I was interested. This was the social etiquette of the time! Is it still?

Not for the new me.

I went up to one particularly attractive guy on the dance floor. Mid-twenties, I would guess.

'Wow, you look just divine!' I said.

He gulped.

'This is my wife, Tessa.' She happened to be dancing opposite him.

Without missing a beat, I turned to her and said,

'Congratulations on landing such a sexy husband.'

I then danced with them both. His wife loved my forthrightness and we had some great conversations. She became a bit of a fan. Another development I was noticing, was that I was building up a following of younger women who said I inspired them and they wanted to be like me when they were in their sixties. At another party, I saw Tessa's husband looking captivating in a tight, white, tank top and I nearly swooned.

'You know you are by far the hottest guy here! Phew!'

'Thank you,' he answered. 'Coming from a woman like you, that is a real compliment.'

What I was learning was that men love compliments but the compliments have to be real, not gamey. My emerging RBG was not afraid to show the effect that some men had on her. And the effect was often pretty powerful and I would say something like- 'Phew, I need a fan – you are so hot!' And men love being seen and appreciated. There was a black guy in a very fine, dapper outfit, dancing in a really cool manner. So, I said, 'Ooh, I really like the look of you.' He was visibly shocked,

'Wow I don't know what to say,' he said. 'You have dumbfounded me. I don't know how to respond.' He looked up at the ceiling looking perplexed. Then said – 'It is like a gift what you just gave me. Like receiving a delicious bar of chocolate. It makes me feel really good. Thank you.'

I love putting men into roles. Sluggy, who is a great friend of my witty Will, reminds me of a swashbuckler so that is what I call him. He loves it, as it is unique to him. Another friend becomes Igor the Cossack, riding his horse bareback.

Then there are the accoutrements of a Russian Bar Girl. These include hats with veils and long gloves. These are particularly handy at a party with buffet. RBG can go up to an attractive young man and say,

'Would you mind feeding me that little croquette?' I murmur, showing my gloves. 'I can't pick it up.' When he obliges, he then must raise my veil to pop the delicacy into my mouth. This lifting of the veil is like removing a barrier and very sexy. A veil is always enticing anyway, as it covers my face in an interesting criss-cross of shadows which deflect from my wrinkles.

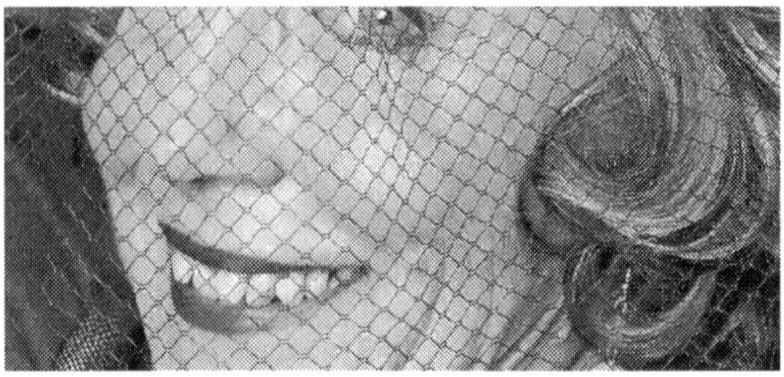

Julie Devine, who introduced me to the party world at Golden Delicious, loves my flirting abilities and likes to hang around with me and watch. 'I'm amazed', she says 'that when you see a sexy guy you don't hesitate and just go straight in.'

'Well,' I say. 'it is a lot easier for me as I feel very safe in my relationship with Jake. And also, if I don't get a response, I just move on. Plenty more guys out there who will respond.'

Jake and I went to Ibiza and enjoyed clubbing at Pacha and acquiring tans for our next party. We were throwing this one for our kids, three of whom had turned 40. The colour theme was purple and silver. At a swish venue in Paddington, we hired two burlesque acts, a magician, a beat bopper, several DJs and 'Hot Flush'. Hot Flush was an ensemble of party friends (which included Poonie and Julie), where women of a certain age (young by my standards), took lessons from Hot Gossip dancer, Ali Hierlehy, and danced on stage. I would have joined them if I lived in London. Their show was electric and fun. Afterwards, I went up to thank them.

'It is you who we should thank,' they said. 'You are our role model and inspiration. Look at you!'

So, what was a Russian Bar Girl wearing to her daughter's $40^{th}$? Very skimpy silver shorts, a purple, sequinned top, silver boots, the requisite neck frill and a riot of purple feathers in a fascinator.

s

I deliberated at length whether I should bare my Ibiza-tanned legs. I am glad I did. I was 64 and the flesh was still sticking attractively to my bones. My daughter looked sensational and the party was a brilliant celebration. Our kids loved it, their friends rating it as the best party they had been to.

The party frenzy continued at Kimberley in July. The theme was blue. Our son and wife joined us. As well as Prince Harry and his entourage.

We celebrated our next wedding anniversary in Venice.

Ben, who had organized all the amazing Kimberley events, had now launched a series of House of Honey (HOH) parties. They are full-on dress-up affairs with top DJs banging it out in a warehouse in West London.  Lorca became my party buddy when Jake preferred to stay at home. Lorca, my best girlfriend, is in her 40s and stunning. The party was to be gold, Ali Baba theme. I rifled through my burgeoning party outfits and exotic materials (which had now spilled out to the top of our barn) and made a fabulous Ali Baba outfit, looking spectacular in fine, gold, see-thru harem pants and glittery gold top with gold tassels and a sumptuous hat.  The flirtatious Nonda was in full swing.  I met Andy and his wife Suzy. I had admired Andy for a while and told him.

'Thank God we have been introduced. I've had my eye on you for ages.' I turned to Suzy. 'You are lovely too. And happily, you look like the kind of woman who can keep such a sexy husband. He needs a woman like you to keep him in the nest.'

She was instantly on my wavelength. We watched Andy have a dance with Mary who had recently been dumped. Mary is one of the most beautifully slinky, sexy women I know. How could anyone dump her?

I said to Suzy, 'I see you do what I do- lend your husband out for a sexy dance.'

'Yes, Mary really needs it right now.'

I spotted Jem, the 19-year-old godson of friends. When he was 16, he had asked me to teach him to flirt, so we have a little flirt game when we see each other at parties, and I give him feedback. He is always so effusive, so I said to him, 'Jem, if you want to be a successful flirt, you have to be a bit cooler.' He said, 'But Eva, I am always so thrilled to see you, I don't want to suppress that.' So sweet. He then caught me up with his love life. Pretty disastrous and he still hadn't got laid.

'You have to be proud of being a man and not be afraid to show it. It will happen soon enough!'

As I was flashing my gold tassels about, a guy started dancing near me- well not dancing- undulating in a fairly unpleasant manner- then started twirling me around. I guess he was late 20s and very uncoordinated. I was reminded of all the dances I had been to as a young woman and being borne down upon by nerdy guys and having to escape to the toilet to get away from them. Instead, I stopped him mid-twirl and said,

'Stop, I don't want you to do that'. He looked a bit miffed but undulated off in another direction.

I then got up on to a dais to dance up higher than the throng- a great way to show off. I was enjoying myself when Undulating Man jumped up and insinuated himself near me, saying, 'I'm sorry I offended you earlier and am I invading your space now? If you really don't want me here, I will go….'

This was said, not in just an apologetic manner but also in a wheedling and whiny way. I couldn't stand it so I interrupted him.

'Stop it! You are disgusting! If you want to dance up here, just do it and stop snivelling and whining!' He looked shocked. I continued,

'Stop apologising for yourself. It is a total turn off.'

'So, you want me to go then?'

'Shut up! Stop asking for permission. Be bold. Be a man!'

He looked rather uncertain. 'How do I do that?'

'Do you really want to know?' I hadn't a clue what I would say.

'Yes,' he said sheepishly.

'When you dance, dance from your cock!' A shock to me as well as him.

'Oh,' he said, visibly blanching.

'Look like you own yourself! Stop seeking approval. Women hate a man who seeks their approval.'

He took what I said to heart and began to dance in a different way. Looking absorbed by trying to dance from his nether regions, he moved away of his own volition.

Then on came the belly dancers. So beautiful. So young!!!! I couldn't believe they were so good at it at such a young age. I had practised belly dancing in the past and appreciated the difficulty of shimmying the breasts while keeping the hips still, and then shimmying the hips while keeping the top still. When they finished, I went up to one of them and told her how good she was. She blushed prettily and I asked her how old she was. '19!'

Oh dear, I remembered a Californian actress in her 40s who was eschewing facelifts, declaring, 'What's the point? Every year there's a fresh influx of gorgeous 19-year-olds in their 1000s. There's just no way I can compete with that.'

I slumped in a chair. My bones ached. I felt glum. Old. Jem came up and sat beside me. I said, 'Oh Jem, I feel so old compared to those fresh, vibrating, young things. Who am I kidding? I still always want to be the Belle of the Ball- I just have to give it up.'

Jem looked at me so earnestly, 'Oh Eva, please don't compare yourself to them. You are just so beautiful.'

'You are sweet Jem, but I think you have me up on a pedestal as I have been teaching you how to flirt.'

'But really Eva, I mean it. You are fab.'

I felt his sincerity. He wasn't just trying to make an old woman feel better. So what if I was his flirting guru? Young men need that. In fact, it was within a month or two that Jem got laid and then went travelling in South America with a beautiful girl, having a ball!

Meanwhile, I noticed Undulating Man dancing, what looked like, from his cock. He had stopped trying to twirl women around. He looked good. I tried to catch his eye but he studiously ignored me. I was even more impressed. So, I went and danced in front of him. He finally looked at me and I gave him the thumbs up saying, 'Next party I see you at, I expect you to be pursued by a bunch of women.'

A couple of our young friends were celebrating their birthdays in the hotel in Wales where Jake and I had our first Golden Delicious party. Chloe, our intrepid DJ, and Mikey Tiger, a great friend, were turning 30 and Jake a mere 67. It was great to share a Libran celebration. Mikey, a human rights lawyer, is in a long-term relationship with Andy, a successful actor, and they both flirt outrageously with me. It was a fabulous two-day party and everyone dressed up. Mikey had invited a large group of his friends, both gay and straight, who arrived by bus.

One of them was a rather delicious man in a blue wig. I pounced.

'Mmmm, I like the look of you,' I said. 'Please tell me you're not gay.'

'No, definitely not,' he said, looking flattered and possibly thinking 'hey this party promises to be good.'

'Oh, and you're Italian as well? I love Italian men,' I purred

'I am Federico and I have come to this party from Italy. I met Mikey at law school.'

'Oh no, you're not over thirty, are you?' The killer question.

'Well – er- yes,' he said. '

'Oh damn, that rules you out as a toy-boy. My toy-boys have to be under 30.'

His face fell.

'But I am only just 30 and I am also a real lawyer.' (Of course, he meant fully qualified.)

It was so funny. And I had to put him straight.

'I must tell you that I am happily married to Jake. I just love flirting.'

'Will Jak mind?' He couldn't rhyme it with cake.

'No, Jake flirts outrageously too.' I pointed out Jake who was doing just that.

So that was the start of my friendship with Federico who couldn't take his eyes off me all evening and was a bit crestfallen when he saw how close I was to Jake.

Isha's influence was fading rapidly. I had embraced a new guru of my own making – my own Russian Bar Girl.

# 13

## Fall from Grace

Although the Russian Bar Girl was in her element, I seemed to be veering rapidly towards vanity and frivolity. I was becoming a total flirt and I loving every minute of it. But what about Jake, whom I wanted to accompany on a path to God? Jake was now in his late sixties and was working extremely hard in our house and organic garden, preparing for a time when his body would not be as strong. He was making non-slip paths and creating systems which would require less maintenance when we were in our 70s and 80s. How was this fitting in with me spending hours preening, making party outfits and flirting with lots of guys? Obviously not well. Something was hugely out of balance.

It now felt imperative to redress some of the imbalances in our relationship, and the imbalances within myself. I still had a way to go before I could claim my own power and become the woman I really wanted to be, which was spiritual as well as sexy. How was I to find a balance between my sexuality and spirituality? Was it possible?

I got some help from a surprising, if long and painful direction. It started with innocuously-sounding compost heaps!

Jake was building and creating a second polytunnel to extend the growing season of our mouth-watering vegetables. This did nothing to reduce the need for compost heaps. We had eleven in all, plus two large leaf mould bins. I knew that I had to do more in the garden and had to get myself stronger, so I could help Jake as his body declined in strength. Jake had always been the strong able one, the one who looked after me. And he did it really well. I wanted to stop being the weak one who needed looking after. So, I decided to empty three of the compost heaps and transport the contents to the second polytunnel. A noble desire! I launched into the task with great determination, drawing on the strength of my female Ukrainian forebears who could scythe a hayfield as well as any man. I dug up the dark crumbly earth, heaved it into a wheelbarrow and pushed it up the hill. This was all well and good for the first couple of days and then it started to rain. No, I wasn't going to let that stop me. I loved getting wet. So, did the ground. The crumbly earth turned heavy and the ground over which I pushed the wheelbarrow, sodden and slippery.

I kept going, determined to finish emptying the three compost bins. I dug, turned and heaved; I slipped, slid and tottered.

'You should stop,' said Jake. 'You mustn't overdo it.'

But hey, I am Eva, who, whenever she throws herself into something, does it with gusto.

A few days later I found it hard to get out of bed. My back started to hurt. Had I overdone it?

It was early December. House of Honey was putting on a Christmas party with the theme, Barbarella.

'Are you sure we should go?' said Jake, seeing my back get stiffer and stiffer.

'Of course, we should go.' I said. As well as emptying compost bins, my party girl persona had been designing and making my Barbarella costume for weeks. Furthermore, Federico was bringing over a bunch of young Italian friends. Nonda Barbarella didn't want to miss that!!

I researched Barbarella outfits and studied every one that Jane Fonda wore. There were many Barbarella costumes for sale on the Internet. None of them were right. None fitted the way I wanted to present myself- they were too hard- too metallic- too many straight lines. I wanted something softer. So, I cut the arms off my silver body suit and sewed on fluff and feathers instead. I made a silver jewelled belt that sat on my hips just covering my tummy and splayed out with feathers at the back. Then I extended the silver platform boots I wore to my 25th wedding anniversary, to thigh height and covered them in silver and black fabric. Then came the concoction for my head - a flurry of white and silver feathers – To top it all off, I unzipped the front of the silver jumpsuit to reveal my ample chest swathed in a fluffy, silver, push-up bra. I didn't realize that all this frippery plus the platforms would lead to a total revolution in my life- painful but necessary. Fluffy Barbarella looked magnificent but was in for a great shock.

Jake wore silver trousers matching his silvery grey hair and looked fabulous as ever. We went with a bunch of friends and had a great time getting ready and sashaying about in our outfits.

People had really made huge efforts with the Barbarella theme and everyone looked amazing. I sat near a woman who had perfected the whole Barbarella outfit, her hair in a bright pink wig, to bring out the pink in the bands around the boots and skirt. She looked sensational and I told her so.

'You know,' she said, 'I agree with you that I look pretty amazing and it took me weeks getting this together. But then I see you! I researched all the outfits online and I saw nothing like yours- where did you get it?'

'Well, I made it and like you, spent weeks doing so.'

'You made it? Wow!'

'Well, I wanted to be fluffy Barbarella- and this is what happened.'

'Well, I tell you I'm pretty determined to win the best fancy-dress prize, but you know what? I think you should win it- and if you do, I don't mind at all.'

'Well, that is very gracious of you.'

'And by the way, are you a yoga teacher?'

'No,' I said. 'I've done yoga, but not for ages.'

'Well, how did you get such a pert, neat bottom?'

'Because I massage it!' chirped in Jake, helpfully.

I danced like an idiot in my platforms, ignoring the persistent ache in my lower spine. Digging and twisting in mud had caused it to feel very tender indeed.

'You really shouldn't wear those platforms if your back is bad,' warned Jake.

Did fluffy Barbarella take any notice? She who preened in front of the mirror for weeks and spent a lot of ingenuity and sewing skill extending the top of the platforms to make them thigh high?

Of course not. The outfit would not be complete without them. And they made me feel so tall and fabulous.

So, there I was, jigging away.

'You should really cover your chest too, you know'- the air outside was icy as we were in an open warehouse in early December.

'No, I can't yet,' I said. 'I still have to find my Italians and show my fluffy boobs off.'

Jake rolled his eyes. He was surprisingly patient with my outrageous flirtatious behaviour and was great at supporting the emerging Russian Bar Girl I was manifesting. So, there I was in my platforms, pert bottom and fluffy tits, looking for 'my Italians.' This involved going up and down several levels of DJ rooms, bars and chill out areas. I also had to negotiate outside iron stairs which were a challenge for my increasing rickety gait, as well as exposing my chest to blasts of cold air that ruffled my furry tits and froze them.

I looked for my Italians everywhere. Mikey Tiger said they were around and looking for me.

But alas, the time came to leave and I hadn't seen them. Oh well.

'Your chest is freezing,' said Jake, as I stumbled wearily into a taxi. I was beat.

That was early December. Two weeks later I could hardly walk and my cold chest had developed into a severe attack of bronchitis. The coughing made my back worse. I couldn't move.

'Oh no!' I was in a panic. My daughter and family were arriving at Heathrow and I was going to pick them up, spend the first couple of days sightseeing in London before heading back to a Xmas at home.

I couldn't do it. I got worse. Various chiropractors and osteopaths couldn't click me back.

I had to give up going to the airport.

'Please fix me before Xmas' I begged the practitioners. 'I have all my family here'.

The bronchitis got worse. Jake was so worried, he begged me to have antibiotics as he was afraid I might develop pneumonia. I reluctantly took them. But I couldn't fix my back.

'You have sciatica and it will take months to heal,' announced my chiropractor.

'What????'

'Well, was it worth it?' asked Jake as I perused the photos from the Barbarella party.  Up to that point, I felt it had been, but the next three months really shook that conviction to the core.

Xmas saw me lying down- my birthday also lying down. And then I couldn't walk or climb the stairs. Jake built me a little crawl way from my downstairs bed to the loo.

During the day when the pain eased, I kept contact with friends on email and Facebook; and dabbled in some Facebook flirting. One was with Federico who said he and his Italian friends had missed seeing me at the Barbarella party. I found that RBG was beginning to define a new role for herself! It was the continuation of helping the sons of my friends in their flirting abilities and helping Undulating man. I was enjoying what I felt was a calling, to help men embrace their masculinity. Federico told me in a message he wanted to kiss all the women at the party

 I told Jake that you wanted to kiss all the pretty ladies at the party- Jake's s response was 'I wanted to shag them all!'

 He's made a good point indeed!

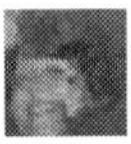 Does that mean you wanted to shag all the women?

 Noooooooo.....

 Really? Well, I tell you what, when you start to blend the naughty boy with the good boy, the girls will come flocking.

 What do you mean??

 Oh, come on Federico you are an Italian- you know what I mean. I remember an Italian businessman I met at a conference. When he looked me up and down, he undressed me with his eyes. It was so hot! Then he went on his way. It was a delicious moment. If I wasn't with Jake I would have gone after him. He had lead in his pencil!!

 Well, some women allegedly complain that Italians are sleazy and too horny etc, especially in the UK we do not have a great reputation, do we?

But thanks for supporting us!

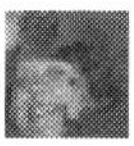 You are right Italians do have a bad press in this country. The Italian who undressed me with his eyes was not in the slightest sleazy- if he was, I would have hated it. So that is not what I mean.

I was involved in the beginning of the Women's Liberation Movement. Then it was a movement between both men and women to bring back the female principle into the world. But what happened was that many women became more masculine and many men became emasculated. Today with many men it has gone too far. I think they try too hard to please women and be good boys and have lost what makes them essentially male. I think many women give out a double message to men- they want a nice caring soft man but also want a sexy hard man. The ideal man, of course, has both these sides and I think it is tough for a man to get it right.

 I totally agree with you, Eva

I am indeed like a pendulum and find it always hard to let women understand how much I like them without appearing massively horny.

The fact that Italians do have a reputation abroad obviously influences me.

Anyway, I will be attending the Valentines HOH party and will bring a few friends again. See you then. x

 I am on my back in pain, so can't write too much. I loved your response and it was great to hear that you can be massively horny. Any red-blooded man worth his salt is. Jake said 'what's

wrong with being massively horny?' You shouldn't deny such an essentially male thing about yourself. Just learn how to bring it more into how you are.

I really hope I am well enough to come to the Valentines HOH party.

I LOVE Italian men especially you Federico and your friends.

 Ah ok! Thank you.

There will be a few going to the Valentines Party

 When I was a migrant kid in really boring conservative Adelaide, the Italian migrants arrived in the mid-50s- they transformed the place- they opened exotic ice cream parlours, and restaurants, served alcohol in china cups (it was forbidden) and encouraged people to dance (dancing was forbidden) I love Italians whatever you say!

I am not sure I will be well enough to come to the HOH party.

 Aww thank you, Eva

I really appreciate your words and it's good that you have met some Italians back in those days. I think we generally know how to enjoy life

This also means that there's a total mess in politics and lots of corruption, but that's an aside issue.

BTW I am bringing LOTS of hunky flirty friends to the next HOH party including, Dominic, Eugenio and Francesco, all looking forward to meeting you.

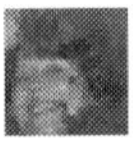 I am SOOOO happy! You are gorgeous!

Hope to see you at the party.

I really wanted to go. As well as the bevy of hunky Italians, my lovely friend Poonie would be there. As she was an excellent masseuse, she also offered to massage my back saying sciatica was a speciality for her. I even bought a fantastic sexy red dress from ASOS.

'No way are you going to another party,' pronounced Jake

'Oh, we could just go in a taxi.'

'No. I am the one who has had to look after you after the last party. And you want to go again? Your sciatica hasn't healed. It is still the middle of winter and you want to bare your chest again!'

'I will wear flat shoes.'

'No.'

Unbeknownst to us, we were headed for a major crisis. Would our relationship survive?

Jake had been a saint. He cooked for 13 people over the Xmas period and then for another dozen for my 66$^{th}$ birthday. I had to lie at the table like a diva to eat a 9-course feast, having gobbled two Ibuprofen beforehand.

Jake cooked me all my meals and looked after me hand and foot. He channelled the intensity of his love into taking care of me. It was very beautiful.

But there was nothing he could do to ease my pain at night. From my bed downstairs, I could continually crawl to the kitchen and replenish ice packs and heated pads. Although I gobbled painkillers, these did not seem to ease the agony. I spent a lot of time in Internet chat rooms and I was definitely not alone. It seemed that thousands of people were suffering with sciatica.

I decided to spend the long, agonising nights more productively. What was my body trying to tell me? I had said offhandedly to a friend, 'It feels like there are seven tigers attacking my spine.'

I had been a psychotherapist for over thirty years and had lots of therapeutic techniques in my kit bag and I had helped many other people. What could I use to help myself? So that night I started the process of confronting the seven tigers and finding out why I was in so much pain. I decided to use an inner guide active meditation that I had borrowed from the Jungian tradition.

In the middle of the night, as the pain seared through my spine and down my left leg, I asked,

Tell me, Tiger, why are you attacking me so viciously?

Tiger 1- Aah, finally you are paying attention!  I'm sick of you ignoring me. Flying about like you don't have a body. I'm here- I am your SPINE!  I am your core tiger and will claw at you until you take notice!

Me: Oh! (He was furious- so I asked the next part of the process) What do you want from me and my life in order to be my friend and ally?

Tiger 1- Well, let me see. There are many things, but let us be practical as you have got yourself into such a terrible state. Every time you stand up, I want you to straighten up slowly and take a couple of deep breaths and say I love my spine.

Me: Okay. I am willing to try.

Tiger 1- No, I didn't ask you to try! You must just do it!

Me: Okay. What will you give me in return? (the third part of the negotiation)

Tiger 1- I will give you back some core strength and make sure you are more rooted to the ground.

Over the next few days I mostly remembered to do this and every time I did, it helped

As I put my attention on the pain a few nights later, it seemed to be concentrated in my coccyx. When Jake and I had stayed at Iguazu Falls on our way to Machu Picchu, I became drunk on limoncello and had a bad fall, during which I smashed my face and hurt my coccyx badly. Was that now playing up too? So, I named Tiger 2, Limoncello Tiger.

Tiger 2- Limoncello Tiger. You know I'm sick of you making a joke about the time you had a big fall at the greatest waterfall in the world.

Me- Well it was funny in one way and everyone laughs when I tell it. So, stop being such a grumpy bugger.

Tiger 2- Well tell me that funny story again (through ironic sabre teeth).

Me - I was lying by the pool, tipsy on limoncello at the 5-Star hotel opposite Iguazu Falls, looking up at the glorious stars, when I thought it would be lovely to go for a swim. So, I rushed off to get some towels and tripped over a low wall.

Tiger 2- And you think that is funny?

Me- Well yes, the limoncello had made me drunk.

Tiger 2- YOU MISSED THE WHOLE POINT!

(Wow this tiger was scary) Do you know what you really did, you ignoramus?

Me - No, (small voice).

Tiger 2- You RUSHED to get the towels. The alcohol made you even less in control of your speedy, destructive nature. If you weren't rushing to get the towels you wouldn't have had that terrible fall and you wouldn't be suffering so much now. WOULD YOU? (Roaring)

Me - No (Even smaller voice).

Tiger 2 - Good, I hope we are now on the same page.

Me- What do you want from me and my life in order to be my friend and ally?

Tiger 2- I want you to make a real and proper commitment to slowing down. Tomorrow night at supper, I want you and Jake to each have a glass of limoncello and make a toast to you slowing down. After that I want Jake to put a drop of limoncello on your coccyx and then for him to lick it off. Can you do that?

Me –Yes (I was sure Jake would agree). And what will you give me in return?

Tiger 2- Well, I want to see and feel that you have made this commitment and I will let you know. However, while Jake licks your coccyx, I will take away my claws and do a healing lick from the inside.

We did as Limoncello Tiger asked. The sorting out of what toast to make, was very instructive and led me to committing myself to be in charge of the person who wants to rush- not to stop rushing, because that would have been too hard and impossible, because I am by nature, very zippy and quick. Jake was very up for carrying out the next instruction (of course!). Fortunately, or unfortunately, the limoncello went everywhere and much licking had to be done. What with the inner licking as well, we had rather a lovely time…!

In the third tiger confrontation, I felt the tiger twisted deeply around my spine. I named him the twisted tiger.

Tiger 3- Yes you are right. I'm twisted around your spine and your legs. I feel caged in. You are caging me in. You are strangling my essence.

Me- No, you are strangling me! I am in agony.

T3- Okay, we are strangling each other. I feel you have been mangling me your whole life. You have always sat winding your legs tightly together. I feel like a piece of wound up spaghetti. Let's call a truce and see if we can help each other.

Me- I mangled you because I was always so terrified- I felt I had to wind myself up tightly to hold everything in.

T3 - You always never breathed properly. And now I've had enough. I feel crippled and twisted and in great pain.

Me- I'm so sorry. (Tears)

T3 - Well, you have hurt yourself as much as you have hurt me. And now you really can't hide that you are crippled inside.

Me- Yes, the Beatles song. I am now so crippled. I can't walk or use the stairs. I can't even do exercises. I have to pee in a bucket and crawl to the loo.

I think it's too late. I have destroyed you and me.

T3- Yes, you have injured yourself quite severely. But you are slowing down which is good.

Me- Well, I'm being forced to slow down with all this pain. Please help me.

What do you want from me and my life in order to be my friend and ally?

T3- I want you to allow me to unfurl inside you. You are always trying to force everything. You have to give me air. Space

Me- I don't know how to stop forcing. My mother force-fed me- forced me to go to sleep- beat me if I didn't. My digestion is fucked. My sleeping is fucked. (sobbing)

T3- gently licks the tears from my face.

T3- I know sweetheart. I was there.

Me- You were there?

T3- Yes, through everything- the good, the bad, the ugly. I was there.

Me- Oh, that reminds me of an ayahuasca trip where I was told that I was never, ever alone.

T3- That's right. That was me- always with you.

Me- Well that helps me feel better already. So, what can I do to stop forcing? I don't know how to be if I'm not being forced or I'm not forcing. When I try to breathe into the pain, I can feel it tearing me apart- the epitome of forcer and forced. I feel bad for trying to force my son Steve to be a certain way- to interfere and not accept him as he actually is.

T3- Each time you feel a stabbing pain just say 'I forgive myself'.

Me- I've done that sort of thing before. I don't believe in it. It's just fancy therapy.

T3- Well, just try it again. Start by saying sorry to yourself and then work towards forgiving yourself.

Me- Okay, I will try it tonight as the pain always gets bad at night. And what will you give me in return?

T3- That will be revealed eventually. Meantime, I will wrap my warm body around you, protect you and help you fall into a soothing sleep.

Next night, the pain was excruciating and I was flooded by images of being a bad mother. I felt so sorry for what I had done to my children and cried and cried.

Me- Oh, Twisted Tiger, this is so hard. I am unable to forgive myself. I also feel really sorry for myself. I feel I can't help the way I am. And it feels terrible to say that. The Therapy mafia will strike me down for being such a victim. I feel helpless. Please help me.

T3- I'm here, sweetheart. I was there when you were severely punished by your crazy mother. That's the way it was. You were never a bad child- you tried bloody hard to be a good child at the mercy of a raving lunatic. Now you are confusing being punished, with calmly and clearly looking at the things you need to forgive yourself for.

Me- Yes, I feel I fall into a pit of self-loathing so easily. I can see I have to differentiate between how I was made to feel as a child, and actions I did when I was older. (And yes, Therapy Mafia, I tell you I was made to feel humiliated and feel shit as a kid. I refuse to say I chose to feel it. BULLSHIT! I felt forced by fancy, American Gestalt Therapists to run before I could walk.)

T3- Now I am here. And you don't have to beat yourself up again and again. You really couldn't help it. You have faced this stuff many times before. The purpose of facing this stuff now is to forgive and accept yourself, on an even deeper level.

I am here as your inner protector. The truth is you were unskilled as a mother, as you had never been properly mothered.

So, keep the inner inspection going. Core Tiger and Limoncello tiger are also delighted you are facing this stuff.

Next couple of nights I stayed with it. Tried different painkillers. Still, the pain was worst at night. And I soooo needed a good sleep. Every time the pain was severe, I said 'I forgive myself'. But I wasn't connecting. Then a shift happened. What was I forgiving my SELF for? Being a shit mother? Feeling bad for my kids? And I realized I felt sorry to myself for the mother I could have been. For the fierce mother inside me who felt unfulfilled. For the one who wanted to build a beautiful nest and family for my children. Instead, I had dragged them through two divorces. I had missed out terribly. A lot of sadness and weeping. My twisted tiger murmured to me and squirmed deep inside. I felt deep sorrow towards my deep animal self- the one who wanted to lick and nurture my cubs.

Me- I'm so sorry. (Much weeping).

T3- Your animal self forgives you.

I stayed with this for a couple of days. My youngest son came to visit and I curbed the desire to control his life. I could see that my fierce mother energy was wanting to control because it had been suppressed, was coming out now and it was not appropriate. He was nearly 36. I had to let my last cub go. Let him be the tiger he had grown into.

I started to knit a baby blanket for my next grandchild. (which was to be born shortly to Jake's oldest son and his wife). And as I knitted, I felt I wanted this blanket to be kept for my great-grandchildren (whom I would probably not live to see). That felt comforting. The twisted tiger was unfurling into a lovely old tiger, and was purring in satisfaction. I felt some deep animal part of me was being nourished as I knitted designs into the blanket. I also comforted myself with the fact that my daughter was being the mother I could have been. She adores being with her children and is fiercely protective of them. It is beautiful to see.

That evening I rested in front of the fire with the thought, 'Oh no, now it is the turn of Tiger number 4- Oh no, not more shit to face!!! What the hell would he be like? And then ANOTHER 3 tigers!''

A voice deep inside said 'just relax and allow the new mother energy to unfurl. Enjoy it. Enjoy knitting.'

It was Twisted Tiger unfurling inside me, and he gave me a huge surprise.

T3- I haven't finished with you yet. Here is what I have to give you in return.

And there appeared Tiger number 4 AND Tiger number 5. But not how I had imagined they would be.

T3- As I am softening and unfurling, you have now given room to Tiger number 4, who is the Mother Tiger, and crushed tightly below her, right at the root of your spine is Tiger number 5- little cub Tiger.

Mother Tiger 4- 'I am the deep animal mother inside you, whom you have kept imprisoned by the hurt of your own mother's actions towards you, and the guilt of your actions towards your children.

Me- (I was gulping in wonder!) What do you want from me and my life to be my friend and ally?'

Tiger 4- I want you to help me nurture this tiny, wet, bedraggled creature which is the baby you. Every time you feel pain in the root of your spine, just know she is crying and in pain and needs you to love her. Be gentle with her, caress her. She has been twisted deeply within your spine and now you have allowed her to come into the light. So, the good animal mother in you can love her back to health.

I was gobsmacked by this turn of events. It was so beautiful and unexpected. It felt like a tangible practical way to love the deeply suppressed, unlovable me. I had been doing the Isha meditation 'Love creates me in my perfection' for 3 years. Now I had a new image to hold in my mind. A little tiny runt of a tiger which is me, and I and Mother Tiger can lick her and give her the nurture that my own mother couldn't. I weep for Olga, a terrified 22-year-old homeless refugee, condemned and ostracised for being pregnant unlawfully. She did her best, but hers was a dark, lonely world.

Tiger 4- Yes, Olga was terrified and felt totally unloved. She couldn't cope and had a nervous collapse after you were born. Probably postnatal depression.

Me- Yes, apparently my father's mother looked after me and wanted Olga to disappear.

I stayed with this a few days, feeling the runt me being nurtured. One night I had a dream of a baby girl with blue eyes who smiled for the first time. She was stunning and I knew that it was me and the way I had first smiled at my mother. That smile was just manna dew for this poor beleaguered woman.

T4- Yes, she fell totally in love with you and despite her illness, was determined that your grandmother shouldn't keep you and that she would escape with you to freedom. At huge personal cost and great fear, she ran away with you and fled Communist Czechoslovakia. You eventually made your way to Australia. But the happiness she sought eluded her and she became mentally ill. You, once her saviour, became the reason in her mind that she was miserable. She saw you as the root of all her problems. The good mother loved you and did her best, but the mad mother blamed you and was cruel.

So, now you have to let me, the good mother inside you, nurture you.

Me- Yes, I find that helpful. How can I nurture myself?

T4- Well when you feel pain, that is the result of you discarding yourself, not taking care of yourself, rushing about, throwing food down your throat, etc. So, all the more reason to heed Limoncello tiger. Slow down. Let the healing happen.

I spent a few days trying to do just this. Each time I felt pain, I let the mother tiger lick the runt cub and suckle it. Cub Tiger nestled into Mother Tiger's furry chest and became a little fluffier. As Cub Tiger grew, I started to negotiate with her.

Me- 'What do you want from me and my life in order to be my friend and ally?'

Cub Tiger 5: I want you to be tidier.

Me- Oh no- I have tried so hard with that one and have failed.

T5- Well, start with your knitting basket. I have noticed you are getting into a big tangle with all your wools while you're knitting a baby blanket for your great-grandchildren.

She was right. So, I started. And it was really difficult. All was a huge jumble and I couldn't find my scissors or tape measure. As I was knitting in intarsia style, the wools were totally tangled.

Me- I just can't seem to do it. My back hurts and I can't find my glasses.

T5- Just slow down. What is happening as you look at the mess?

Me- I feel hopeless. I feel I cannot sort it out. It is too much.

T5- Do you always feel like this when there is a mess?

Me- Yes. I just can't cope. So, I just give up and shove piles of mess into cupboards, and stuff all my drawers full of rubbish and can never find things. I've worked and worked on this in therapy and have never been able to make any significant headway.

T5- Let yourself feel this despair and how you feel you can never resolve this issue.

Me- (deep crying- loads of it).

T5- Yes just sink into it.

Me- I am remembering this dream I had on a 6-week Enlightenment Intensive. I was a baby in my father's garden and I was very sad as I knew my grandmother hated my mother and wanted her to go away.

T5- Yes, that is just how it was. Really painful, really sad.

Me- I so desperately wanted it sorted out as I loved them all deeply. My love wasn't enough to keep them all together.

Deep wracking sobs.

T5 and T4- Hey, you couldn't sort it out. It was too big. Your grandmother hated your mother because she was a Ukrainian peasant and a servant in her house – not good enough for her son. The grandmother was the wife of a wealthy factory owner and hated how the Communist party took away their riches. Your mother became the butt of all that was wrong. But she had also fallen in love with you and wanted to keep you.

Me- But my love, my smile wasn't enough to want them to stay together.

T5 and T4- No, unfortunately it wasn't. You have a wonderful smile that radiates your love, but it wasn't enough. You were born out of the ashes of World War 2. It was a dark, tragic time. And all those people suffered terribly. You couldn't save them.

Me- It's true, but I so wanted to. (much sobbing)

T5 and T4- However you **can** sort out your knitting basket. Do it.

So, I did. I found my glasses, got into a comfy position, wound up all the balls of wool and eventually I had a tidy basket. I felt a great sense of achievement.

Me- It was so dreadfully tangled. It took ages.

T5 and T4- But that is all part of it. You must give yourself time! As Limoncello Tiger says, you are always rushing. It takes time to sort things out, slowly and methodically. So, every time you tidy something up- go slow and know you can sort it out. And know that each bit is much easier than sorting out the havoc that WW2 wreaked in your family's life. Anyway, you wrote a beautiful book about how you helped heal your stepfather.

Me- And what will you give me in return if I become more tidy?

T5 and T4- Grace. When everything is tidy, you will relax. You will not be setting up the scenario, over and over again, of trying to keep your first family together. You will let go all that fraught energy and allow grace to inhabit your body.

It's now February $7^{th}$ 2013.

I'm getting better but it is still not over. I can move around a bit now and walk. It is still not too easy going up the stairs. I still have pain. There are two more tigers to go. What's coming up next it seems is Fire Tiger. I have been having terrible night sweats, several times a night and a few in the day too. My blood pressure has gone right up. And the inflammation along my sciatic nerves is burning. And I have a hot itching in my vaginal area.

Me- Hey you, you are burning me alive. Because of you I can't sleep and have to keep changing my pyjamas and throwing covers off and on.

T6- Oh, quit moaning, you victim you. You just don't seem to get it! You just don't get how serious this is. You are still wanting to go to the Valentine's HOH party. Thank God I have Jake on my side. He needs to put his foot down with you. Oh yes, you do an occasional stretch for Tiger number 1 and shilly-shally around with Tiger number 2. But I'm a deeper version of those tigers. I'm trying to protect you! Your sciatic nerve runs through the core of your body. It's a NERVE! And being a nerve, extremely sensitive. You, yes you, have damaged it. So, I am making sure you realize this and start taking REAL responsibility.

Me- OK, OK, OK! What do you want from me and my life in order to be my friend and ally?

T6- Pay attention to what you are doing.

Me: What do you mean?

T6- Pay attention to what you are doing! In every moment. You have spent your whole life running from your body; trying to escape it. Instead, you live in a very elaborate operetta that you conduct inside your head that keeps you out of the now.

Me- Oi, that's a bit harsh!

T6- Well, tell me a time when you have been inside your physical body.

Me- When I gave birth.

T6- And what was that like?

Me- It was amazing. I was gripped by a physicality which was so total. And when I have sex, now. Although I see what you mean, for in the past, I often lived in a fantasy world during sex as well.

T6- Good. Yes, giving birth really brought you into the present. All your meditation has been a vehicle for bringing you into the present. But you are so stubborn. You are convinced that you can control the future instead of being in the here and now.

Me- I'm trying to be in the here and now.

T6- Rubbish. So here is what I want you to do. Today, I want you to pay attention to what you are doing. Observe how you do that and report back to me at the end of the day.

So that is what I did.

T6- Well, how was it?

Me- I was Crap! So many times, I lost the plot. For example, I would be taking the lid off some cream or potion and then not know where I put it. I lost my glasses 3 times. I bent over and picked up my laptop and wrenched my back a bit.

T6- Yes that HURT! The pain you feel is as a result of you not paying attention to your physical reality. Yes, you have a very vivid, wonderful imagination; but at the expense of your physical self. So, continue. Adopt Aldous Huxley's parrot. 'Pay attention. Pay attention'. And don't beat yourself up each time you fail. Just observe. Me and your sciatic nerve are happy that you are taking me seriously. Pay attention and report back.

17th February:

It is a long process, but Fire Tiger has given me an indication that if I can make some progress in my physical attention, Tiger number 7 will appear. Tiger 7 is Kundalini Tiger!

However, he would not make its appearance until well over 2 years later.

Suffice to say, I did not go to the House of Honey Valentine's party. I did not get to flirt with the sexy Italians. The red dress hung forlornly from the back of the door. Little did I know that it would be worn, but in totally different circumstances.

My work with the tigers may have been over for the time being, but worse was to come.

My symptoms of sleeplessness, thrush and hot flushes were getting worse. Tests at the doctors showed that my sugar had skyrocketed to a dangerous level. I had diabetes.

Jake had been a saint for weeks but when diagnosed with diabetes, our relationship went through a severe crisis. I now became totally obsessed with getting my sugar down. As the weeks rolled on and I didn't seem to be improving, cracks began to form in my relationship with Jake. A part of my nature is to become obsessed, as I had in my 50s about my wrinkles. And deeply obsessed I had become, again. With sciatica, and now with diabetes. As I became more obsessed, I became more withdrawn and selfish. I was unavailable to Jake and was increasingly taking him for granted. I got lazier and lazier.

We had a couple of rows and I sobbed that 'I couldn't help it.' He blew up. Things became more strained between us. We had more rows.

Then one evening, Jake just disappeared. I had come downstairs from my bed in the spare room and he was gone. What? He always cooked me supper, but there was no sign of activity in the kitchen. I staggered out the front. The electric car had gone. 'Oh no, he has left me,' was my first thought. 'But he would have taken the other car if he had.' 'So, he must have gone to our village for a meal. 'What?' What about me? What can I eat? The fish hadn't been defrosted. So, I boiled some quinoa. I had also read that cayenne pepper was excellent for diabetes, so smothered the quinoa with it. It was hot. I swallowed loads thinking it was doing me good. I felt bereft and also angry. I thought- 'perhaps we should split up- I can't live with a man who can't take the heat when I am ill - I am 66 – I am likely to get more bouts of illness as I get older. After all this – have we now found out that we cannot be together in old age?'

Jake came back. He looked grim. His thoughts had been mirroring mine but in a different way.

'I've had it,' he said. 'I cannot continue in such a lopsided relationship.'

We had reached an impasse in which we floated uncomfortably for a few days. My own discomfort was compounded by the cayenne pepper which had scored a painful trail through my intestines. 'Was this the end of the road?' I found myself wondering, 'Where would I live?' 'You can have the house,' Jake answered my thoughts.

Even though that was rather horrifying, I felt strangely comforted.

Slowly, we started unravelling the impasse.

Yes, Jake had felt very ignored and taken for granted. Looking after me for four months, hand and foot, had clearly illuminated the lopsided nature of our relationship.

He couldn't be Superman any longer.

Yes, I had been lazy and selfish.

Yes, I had treated him like a slave.

He was fed up with calling the shots, being in charge.

He recognized and acknowledged that the sciatica had been brought on by me trying to take more responsibility in the garden.

But that had failed miserably. Now I was as useful in the garden as a worn-out pair of old socks.

And now I had diabetes!

Something had to change.

Help came from a surprising quarter, my pancreas.

My acupuncturist gave me a healing visualisation on my pancreas.

During the process, I was accosted by seven witchlike dervishes, all clothed in scarlet dresses which splayed out in blood red tatters around them as they swirled angrily around me. In the visualisation, I was staked out on a smoking pile of wood like a witch. They danced around me, screaming.

'How dare you ignore us. We are fed up. Your six tigers have confronted you heavily and you are still ignoring your body. Your 7th Tiger has disappeared in disgust. We have had it and are going to burn you alive.'

'Oh no, not seven more angry entities to deal with!' My body was becoming an unmanageable zoo. I was not in control at all. Was I ever in control? I decided to address them en masse. I couldn't bear to confront all of them individually. And was it true that Kundalini Tiger had disappeared in disgust?

'What do you want from me and my life in order to be my friends and allies?' I whimpered to the bevy of scary beings with demonic faces.

'Stop being so lazy!' They screamed.

'I've been laid low!'

'No excuse! You obviously haven't been laid low enough yet! Look what you have done to your husband. Taking him for granted. Look what you have done to your body. You throw sugary food down your throat- getting away with the bare minimum of effort. You are a lazy slob.'

'So, what can I do?'

'Right now, we demand you commit yourself to a task that you have been putting off and complete it.'

I immediately thought of the big mess at the back of my bed. It was a wide shelf, full of books and papers that I hadn't touched for at least five years. It was dusty and mouldy with papers stuck together with bits of sticky throat sweets. It was disgusting and I kept ignoring it.

'Just like you are ignoring us! Tidy it up now!'

'But my back still hurts. I am so tired. I haven't slept properly for weeks.' I had been suffering from classic diabetes symptoms; having to pee every half hour, hot flushes, thrush, losing weight.

'You are always so full of excuses. Tidy up that mess NOW! And don't you dare ask what you will get in return. Just do it!'

So very reluctantly and knowing that I would be burnt alive if I didn't, I started tackling the mess. It took all day – sorting through and throwing out old papers and chucking old magazines and books I would never read. As I ploughed through the detritus, I remembered the lesson from Tigers 4 and 5- that while I couldn't sort out the mess created for my family in the aftermath of WW2, I could at least tackle this corner of my own making. As I came to the last grungy corner, under a mouldy apple core, I found it. My next step. A book called 'The Miracle of Hsin Tao'.

I opened it curiously. I didn't even remember having bought it. The book contained many time-lapse photographs of simple movements which were part of an ancient meditation technique, called Hsin Tao. It had been designed for older Shaolin monks who had become badly hunched while transcribing holy books. I knew immediately this was what was next on my path. The Isha meditation was fizzling out since I had brought Isha down off the pedestal on which I had placed her. I needed a new daily practice that did not involve elevating a guru up high, and here it was staring right at me. A quick email search informed me that I had bought the book from Amazon nearly five years earlier. I had no recollection of why I had made the purchase and in my lazy way, had just chucked it into the corner behind my bed; which now looked pristine. I gazed at the clean area and breathed a sigh of relief. I felt peaceful. It reminded me of the message I had received from Tiger number six- that if I made an effort and was tidy, I would achieve grace. It seemed that the pancreatic dervishes had calmed right down and were giving me a second chance.

No more sugar! I had had a haemoglobin blood test which showed my sugar level was double what it should be. The doctor wanted to put me on the drug, Metformin. After devouring information about Diabetes 2, and the side effects of Metformin, I refused to take it saying I would bring the sugar level down by diet and exercise. I bought a blood glucose monitor.

I eliminated sugar immediately and cut down drastically on carbohydrates. It was tofu, spinach and almonds for breakfast, not the usual sugary cake. And I started exercising. This was difficult as my sciatica was still gripping me, so I began bouncing on a mini trampoline, a piece of advice I received from my good friend Jimena. My sugar levels plummeted to manageable proportions.

And I began practising Hsin Tao. This involved learning some simple Tai Chi-type movements. I had tried Tai Chi in the past but could never get the hang of the form. I never remembered what came next. I was a bit daunted by the various Hsin Tao movements and gave myself two weeks to learn them. I practised diligently and had remembered most of it by the first week. One of the immediate benefits was that the standing movement, a simple undulation back and forth, was supremely beneficial for my spine.

So here I was constantly reinventing myself and utilising all the skills I could find to lead to a better life.

Page intentionally left blank

# 14

## Road to Recovery

But what about my relationship with Jake?

Sciatica and diabetes were a great gift to us. The tigers and dervishes challenged my laziness, my obsessiveness- my willingness to let Jake take all the responsibility, my willingness to stay weak, my willingness to just go with the flow. I finally knew what my tigers had been banging on about. This is what being awake, aware, real and spiritual was all about- responsibility.

It was a deep blindness and it nearly led to the end of the line with Jake.

After a lot of talking and negotiation, we felt we had entered a new stage of our relationship. I vowed to take more notice of where Jake was at, to take care of him. This required me to heed the Tiger's message, 'Slow down'. Jake had been saying it for years but I did not listen. The inner tigers had become my spiritual teachers. The old relationship was ended. On his side, Jake vowed to show me his vulnerability and not slip into Superman. To celebrate the beginning of the new relationship, I wore my red ASOS dress. Instead of titillating a bunch of Italians, Jake benefitted from a sinewy, sexy dance, my spine much improved by the Hsin Tao meditation.

We also decided to spend some time apart. We had always done so in the past but that had slipped. Our rule used to be, one hour a day, one day a week, one week a year. It had worked well. We both needed time alone. I went and stayed with Julie Devine for a couple of days and went to a party at my friend Jimena's house.

Chloe was compering and DJing with Julie. They were both happy that I could hobble to a party. They gave me a chair and looked after me beautifully. I felt a bit like an old lady. I really thought my flirting days were over. Oh well. I managed to get up and dance, knowing the exercise would be good for my blood sugar levels. As I started moving my stiff body, I glimpsed him; a lovely man who started dancing appreciatively, near me. I had seen this guy before a few times at parties and we had cast a flirtatious eye over each other. He is one of those men who just oozes sex appeal, effortlessly.

'Wow!' I said. 'Hello, I'm very pleased to see you.'

'Yes,' he said. 'And me you. I know who you are- the famous Eva Maria- hello, I am Bruce.'

'I am so glad you are here. I really thought my days of being a flirtatious woman were over. I have had several months of serious illness and thought I was done for.'

'Well, you look pretty good to me!' The way he looked me up and down, I knew he meant it. I felt new juice coursing through my lower spine and legs. I said,

'I think you might have made it into the top 10 on my toy-boy list.' (another favourite line of mine which always seemed to work)

'Top 10!' His face fell. 'That is insulting. I want to be at the top.'

That was definitely the right answer.

I went up to Bruce's pretty girlfriend and said,

'Thank you so much. Your boyfriend has given me back the confidence in being a sexy woman. I thought I had lost that forever.'

So, I returned home happy.

I was still a Russian Bar Girl.

I then had some crushing news from my friend Poonie. Although our friendship had started as a party and flirt relationship, that had changed when we found a depth in each other where we resonated. She had read and loved my book 'Sasha and Olga'. We had many soul-searching chats. Her husband, Greg, was looking for a GP practice outside London and was pursuing a vacancy in a village near where we lived. Consequently, we spent a few times together and I looked forward to becoming even closer to Poonie. But it was not to be. Greg landed a job in Guernsey instead, and the family moved there. I was disappointed as I wanted to deepen our relationship further. We enjoyed seeing each other at parties and kept up a fruitful correspondence. When I developed severe sciatica, she invited me to Guernsey as she said sciatica was one of her specialities, in her practice as a masseuse. I was seriously considering going to visit when I got the following message.

**March 22, 2013 9:38 pm**

 Lovely one, This a brief message to tell you that I have had a very challenging time of it in the last month (a few friends know) but I have been diagnosed with a Stage 4 systemic cancer four weeks ago and already have started chemo in the hope that I might buy some time. Boo! Sorry to be the bearer of grim news...always horrid to tell friends about it as I know they will worry...but not all bad. It is the journey I have to take and I will do it the best I know how. I send you and Jake much love and hope we see each other soon, Poonie xxx

Oh Poonie, I burst into tears reading your message. You darling, darling woman. What a diagnosis to bear! And after you were so supportive with me and my sciatica. I really hope the chemo helps. Thank you for letting me know- I feel very honoured. Eva xxxxxxx

Her courage from then on was stupendous, as she fought for her life. Greg made sure she got the best medical treatment and she underwent further bouts of chemotherapy and radiation, to buy time. Her youngest son was still only ten and she wanted to be around for as long as possible. I sent her two books, one about surviving chemo, and the other on a radically alternative fasting cure. But she was embarking on the conventional route so I wanted to support her that way.

**April 2, 2013 7:18 pm**

Darling, I have sent you a couple of books that should arrive soon- different ends of the spectrum of dealing with cancer. Love you to bits!

 Thank you, my dear. I have one week in 3 it seems when my brain can actually read! The rest of the time it can't focus. The most challenging thing for me, more than any pain, is the chemo-fog brain. I find it so difficult my mind compromised...sure makes you appreciate things! Love to you and Jake xxx

I'm so sorry sweetheart. If you can't read that's fine. Just see the books as messages of love in cardboard packages. That must be so hard not to be able to have a sharp mind. So, you've taken the chemo by the horns! 'Anatomy of Hope', one of the books is all about chemo and people's responses to it. Love you heaps!

**April 4, 2013 11:30 pm**

 Xxx you are an angel xxx

**April 15, 2013 12:47 pm**

 Hi my darling, wanted to say thank you very much for the book. I have started reading it and it looks very good. Will definitely be passing it on to the good doctor! Love you xxx

April 25, 2013 9:32 am

Thinking of you, sweetness. Sending you strength and love.

I had a beautiful dream about you last night. It has got me to think about you a lot. You are probably in some heavy phase of your chemo. Sending you lots of love and delicious healing for whatever you're going through. Huge amounts of love.

**May 21, 2013 4:50 pm**

 Beautiful dreams.... yes, please! Am in the heaviest, deepest and murkiest waters but I have a lifeline made of the thoughts and dreams of friends. This is strong and golden and I am clinging on for all I am worth. Love to you sweet one xxx

**May 25, 2013 10:07 am**

Oh, you are such a beauty! I now have a vision of you being carried into a patch of sun in a wood full of bluebells by some men (oiled and gorgeous of course)! Love your sexiness and passion.

**May 26, 2013 6:05 pm**

 hee hee...yes please! xxx

**June 23, 2013 1:08 am**

Dreamt about you (AGAIN) last night. You were strong and wise and teaching me how not to be afraid. Thank you. I am in Australia having a magic time with my grandchildren.

If you have the energy let me know how you are. Chemo finished?

Look forward to seeing you at the Give festival!

**June 23, 2013 10:48 pm**

 Hi my lovely, things going ok here. Chemo finishes on 8th July, I hope. That will be 5 months worth...it's been a long tricky time! Then it is a week of tests and scans and then my operation is scheduled for the 1st August. I've been told to expect a long recovery but I am going to absolutely try my best to get to 'Give' even if just for a day. Friends have given me their house for the weekend so I don't have to try and rough it. I hope you are having a fabulous time in Oz...granny Eva...brilliant! Bet you are the best granny ever! Huge love to you my darling and hope it won't be long before I see you and Jake xxxxx

**June 25, 2013 5:07 am**

Oh, such hopeful news!!!! But what a gruelling time for you! You are amazing in your fight for life. It's great you are giving yourself some rewards. I'm dragging Jake to Give- he really doesn't want to go ('my days of camping out and staying up all night are over!! I want to stay home and harvest vegetables!')

However, I said you must come and see Poonie!! So, it may be the last time for us that we come to such an event. We feel we are moving into a new and wonderful stage in our life - a golden ripe Autumn. Kimberley and Give have been amazing for us. We really felt loved, supported and acknowledged as a couple, by all of you. Yes I love being a granny and I am a much better grandmother, than mother I tell you. I was telling my family at the dinner table how all your friends meditate every morning at eleven and send you healing- when Cassidy (7) interrupted and said 'Oh no that's when my lunch time is - otherwise I would meditate then too!' So sweet. My biggest wish for you is for you to enjoy being a grandmother in the future. Love to Greg and Finn. And keep that strength and hope burning! You are such a beautiful being. But I'll stop now in case I become the raving old loony hippy that I am!

**June 25, 2013 11:21 am**

 In case I become' !!!!!! Honey, I hate to break it to you, but your secret is out......bolting horses and stable doors spring to mind! I love you for it. Also, the loan of this house (5 bedrooms) does come with the offer that our friends can also stay so if you need a quiet space, especially if it is poor weather, then please come and stay. Big love xxx

In Australia I was loving being a grandmother and embracing this aspect of who I was.

Taking my granddaughter to school, reminded me of going to school when I was little. How scared I was being in an alien culture. I watched her vitality- so much energy; like watching a mini-me and how I could have been if things had been different. I felt blessed to witness it, to see the incredibly sweet vital little girl I might have been- I had buried her under pain and fear.

The Hsin Tao meditation was now a way of life and I did it religiously every day. While I practised, I could feel vitality seeping through my bones, coming back home. I was so grateful for the sciatica and the diabetes- such wake-up calls; to really look after myself, slow down and stop throwing myself away- to really learn to accept myself. I felt my drivenness to flirt had been a way to be recognized for my vitality, trying to recover what I had lost. Except for the menopausal blip, my sexuality was always something I could access- even though it was often a seesaw between the frigid little girl and the raunchy, serpent sexpot. I felt that the more I re-owned my inner sweetness, the more I could see a way forward to becoming a sweet, vibrant old lady.

In Australia, I also had to deal with my sister Val, who was still giving me a hard time. As well as hating me, she was refusing to expedite business on our father's estate. To deal with the despair I felt over the intractableness of my sister's position, I focussed on her during my meditation. Feeling hopeless, I began to think I would never get anywhere- then the healing energy started flowing through and I felt calmer. Then came the words- 'Heal your inner Val.' So, I had an inner dialogue with Val who continued to be resentful of me getting any share from my father's will. She was still punishing me for leaving home when I was 20, leaving her and Alexandra without a mother. 'Val, stop punishing me!' I cried. This felt good- and then the times I was punished came up, and the terror of the strap hanging on the back of the door- it was horrible- I could feel the flinches, the pain and the terror all locked deep in my body and especially my spine. I felt the tigers with me- it was good to let my chi heal it- it felt like a strong but invisible spider's web weaving through my muscles- I cried a lot and started to feel a lot calmer. I felt more empathetic to Val and imagined a conversation where I said, 'I understand how you feel about the money but you know what, I am not going to be controlled by your craziness any more. My father wanted me to have a share. And I won't be punished by you.'

I took my grandchildren to see their great grandmother in Adelaide, my first husband's mother. She and I continued a deep love relationship even though I was no longer married to her son. She was my wonderful second mother. At 92 she was frail and beginning to fade. Perhaps this was the last time. Before I went, she said 'Eva, one of the best things that has happened in my life, is meeting you.'

Beautiful Lilian died soon after. Life was a series of saying goodbyes and hellos. The great grandmothers and great aunts and uncles had all died. I was now in the front line. Shouldn't I now take on the mantle of being the Babushka? Should I just put RBG to bed? Had she had enough of an outing?

I then flew with my Aussie family to Malaysia and we all met up with Jake for a fabulous beach holiday. Jake and I had a beautiful healing time together after all the trauma of the last few months.

After our return we had two parties, Give and our 30th wedding anniversary. My sciatica was healing fast, I was controlling my diabetes and feeling more in charge of my life.

Poonie's brother, Ben, who had been running the Kimberley 3-day festivals, had now found another venue and called his parties 'Give'. Giving had always been the main theme in the past. All party-goers were encouraged to bring gifts. There were strawberries dipped in chocolate, orange quarters, heart-shaped sweets and many other delicious titbits. The next Give was coming up after our return from Malaysia. I wanted to see Poonie who, after several rounds of punishing chemo, was determined to go.

It was lovely to see Poonie, who sported a shaved head and had to be hugged gingerly.

Jake and I continued to reconnect to our love for each other. Many people came up to us and said how much they loved our togetherness and obvious passion as a couple. And this time was special as it was the run-up to celebrating 30 years of our marriage, the following September.

I was 66 and recovering from serious health shocks. Even though Babushka was now in the front line, did the Russian Bar Girl have any buzz left?

Andy and Suzy, whom I had met at the Gold party, had set up a flamboyant camp with large gazebo and comfy armchairs. We visited them and described the crisis we had been through.

Jake reiterated how he always did everything as Superman, and I was a lazy princess.

'Yep, similar to our relationship,' quipped Andy. 'I do everything and Suzy does very little.'

Suzy flushed. 'That's so not true. I do so much and even do DIY.' Her indignance faded as she saw Andy was teasing.

'Boy, I could really feel my defensiveness rising,' she said, playfully swiping at her husband.

Andy gave Suzy a sexy squeeze saying, 'She is my best friend and she's really hot, even after 20 years and 3 kids.

'Aah, you know what makes you hottest of all Andy,' I said, 'is that you really love and cherish your woman. And it is great to flirt with a happily married man. It is the safest way- you can let out your flirty self and know it is completely safe.'

This led to a discussion about what married people do with their sexuality.

'I don't think you can be into your sexuality without being attracted to and attracting other sexy people,' said Jake. 'I adore

Eva and think she is really sexy but so are so many other women. I can't be a horny guy with her, and then turn it off.'

'For me, it's a balancing act,' I said, 'between feeling very safe with Jake and being glad that other women still find him sexy.'

'And I have to keep you on your toes,' quipped Jake.

The colour theme was purple and my Russian Bar Girl had fun with costumes. She discovered bustles and fans. I had always admired how Poonie worked a bustle, so I incorporated one into my Saturday night costume. I had also seen a young girl using a fan at the Friday night burlesque show, so looked forward to wielding my purple fan as well. The bustle had an unexpected benefit in that Jake could fondle my behind without being seen. A delicious man nearby started giving me the eye. Phew! It was then I saw the benefit of a fan. It is to cool down when the heat is on! Especially when a man floors you with just a look.

While I fanned myself furiously, I murmured to Jake,

'That guy is really giving me the eye, but I am really into you.'

Mr Delicious danced past and bumped into me purposefully.

'Ooh, sorry,' he murmured giving me that look again.

'Bump into me any time,' I purred. It just came out of that Russian Bar Girl's mouth, even with Jake right there.

'I can't believe that happened with you standing right there', I said to Jake.

'Oh, don't worry darling. He spoke to me at the bar, saying– "I know she's your woman, mate. Respect! She is gorgeous".'

I could feel the life coming back into my coccyx, sitting so perkily beneath my bustle.

On the Saturday night, Jake and I were dancing when Jake said,

'Wow, look behind you! On the podium.'

He pointed to a sexy woman in silver shorts.

'She's a mate of yours.'

'What do you mean?'

'She is another Bar Girl like you. Look at the way she works the room. She certainly has my full attention.'

I was impressed- she was classy. I joined her on the podium. Jake went up to silver shorts and said, 'You are so gorgeous.'

'Tell me more,' she purred, leaning down.

'Well, you are so sexy and really pretty, just like my wife,' and pointed at me. I danced up and said, 'My husband believes I am a mate of yours- in that we are both Bar Girls.'

She laughed and agreed, perkily.

We danced on. I was mesmerised by the way she moved her hips.

'Are you a stripper?' I asked.

'No, not at all,' she laughed. 'I'm a yoga teacher. I love the way you and your husband are so together. I have been watching you dance with him. You are one helluva sexy woman.'

Phew, that was high praise from a fellow Bar Girl.'

'Yes, we have been together 34 years.'

'Wow. I think if that's what a relationship is like way down the years, I have something to really look forward to.' Then she turned to me and said,

'Do you think I'm too old to have a second chance at love? I am 46.'

'Of course not,' I said. 'You are stunning.'

'But I had the kind of close intimacy you have, with my husband of twenty years. We had two kids but now have been divorced for 4 years. He went off with a younger woman and now has two children with her as well.'

'Oh no,' I said, wondering what crazy idiot of a man had run off away from her.

'I'm feeling fine about it all and have got over it. But now I want another man.'

'Looking like you look, you certainly stand a good chance.'

I watched as a gorgeous young man flirted with her.

I heard him murmur.

'You look so hot and I am smitten.'

It looked pretty steamy and there was snogging going on. After about 20 minutes, he left looking dejected.

'What happened?' I asked.

'I had to tell him I wanted a man, not a boy."'

I was so impressed.

'IT WAS REALLY TEMPTING. We could have had a lovely time but it's not what I want. I want what you and your husband have.'

I never saw silver shorts again but I dearly hope she found the man she was looking for.

OUR 30$^{th}$ wedding anniversary was coming up. We hired a beautiful boutique hotel and wrote this invite;

We would like to celebrate our 30$^{th}$ wedding anniversary by celebrating intimate relationships and invite you to share your understanding and experience of intimate relationships. We anticipate starting this process sometime Saturday afternoon and continuing through the leisurely dinner on Saturday evening.

We emphasise that this is an invitation; no obligation. We are writing about it at this stage so that if you want to contribute you have time to think about what it is that you would like to share.

Last year, whilst visiting Ibiza, two new friends, B and L, raised the question: "What is it that gets you through the really difficult times - the times that you hate the other person and are seriously thinking of quitting the relationship?" This might be a useful starting point– it certainly set us thinking. Here is what we came up with:

Eva's first answer was "a strong sexual attraction". One of the reasons this has worked for us is that we are well-suited sexually. It is also obvious that we make an effort to continue to look good for each other, despite the ravages of old age!

Jake's first answer was "a solid commitment". When we married, thirty years ago, we made a vow to face our stuff in any argument that arose, and only consider quitting the relationship *after* facing whatever we had to face. It also meant that our relationship might not survive any given row, but the decision about whether to part company would only be made when we had both faced up to the issues that were causing so much hurt and distress.

When we thought more about what had kept us together a deeper principle emerged, namely our profound willingness to prioritise truth over everything else. This principle arose as a result of our involvement with Enlightenment Intensives which have the sole aim of facilitating participants to discover, for themselves, what is absolutely true for them. We often credit the first EI in which we both participated (in 1980) as helping us to really come together as two adults wishing to become more real together; up to that point we were often both acting out parent-child dynamics with each other. As well as discovering who we actually were on that Intensive, we also saw clearly that it is always better to know the truth than to keep it hidden. And if the truth was that we were better off not being together, then the sooner we knew that the better. Sometimes our willingness to be completely honest with each other struck other people as brutal – we would say things that might normally cause injury. But we had discovered that the greater injury was caused by *not saying* what was going on – because *not saying* broke the intimate contact of the relationship.

Another way of expressing this principle is that we both value being real over everything else. In an argument, it is all too easy to fall into a trap of maintaining a particular story about what happened, usually a victim story of what the other did to me. The reality is often that, having been hurt, I now really hate the other person – and voicing this can bring enough reality into the row to break the stories that are being maintained. We know that this prioritising truth has helped us out of many difficult and nasty rows. We also think it is why we have been successful using other processes to develop our relationship – including the conscious use of drugs.

A delightful, and unforeseen, outcome of this is that our relationship is now the main vehicle for our spiritual development. We disagree with the many spiritual teachers who assert that relationships keep one apart from the Divine or Enlightenment, and are learning how to become ever more real and present with each other.

We look forward to hearing what has helped your intimate relationship.

Jake and Eva

These were all wonderful words but were dramatically put to the test the night before the party. Jake and I had a big fight. I had been to Paris with my daughter and bought a fabulous black and silver dress, which I wanted to wear as a surprise. Jake got the wrong end of the stick and thought I was excluding him. He also wanted me to wear a dress he had bought for me. I blew up at him.

'Well, I'm not going. You can bloody well go on your own!' I was furious. 'And just tell everyone that we didn't quite make it to 30 years!' Yes, I hated him. This was the reality.

The next couple of hours were grim. Like on my second ayahuasca journey in Peru, I felt I was writhing in a deep bucket of snakes. I took a deep breath and listened to Jake's point of view. Fortunately, we did sort out the wrangle, enough to go. When it came to sharing, I was first and just told the truth about what had been happening to us. I finished with, 'which dress I will wear to the dinner will depend on my husband's approval. I will try on both and see which one he likes best.' Jake chose the black and silver dress.

Our friends loved how real we both were and how it was obvious that even though our relationship still had its ups and downs, we were getting better at resolving our crises. The level of deep sharing was wonderful and our 30th wedding anniversary was truly a celebration of long-term commitment in a relationship.

I wrote to everyone afterwards

Oh, you guys, you are so fabulous. There was in A's and L's words such a mix of 'frivolity, sweet silliness, depth and the divine'. And I love the fact that many people have been propelled into a new direction or have experienced a shift. I think the thing I would want to get across most (if I haven't already), is that our own relationship keeps changing and shifting more and more- these often include a crisis of some sort and usually confronting some cherished belief or attitude, but as a result our relationship gets better and better- often surprisingly. I thought retirement was a winding down- it's more of a winding-up!! And all of you are so inspiring especially when you share your difficulties, What I loved so much on the weekend was the flirty fun you all were willing to partake in and seemed so good at ('sacred party power' as M described it). I feel I have a bunch of delightful loonies to play with. Hallelujah!

# 15

## Getting Old

I was perusing the photos of the wedding anniversary and saw that, in some, I looked really old. How depressing.

But not only that, I was beginning to feel old inside my body. This was different from my spirit which feels ageless- or my wrinkles – this was ageing in my joints, sinews and bones. When I tuned into my body, I could feel it ageing. I hadn't been able to spring up for a few years, but now I felt more heaviness in my back and legs as I lifted myself out of a chair. Yes, time was having its effect. The positive side was that I was forced to slow down, to take note of what was occurring in my body and carry myself to the new position. This was a timely reminder of the tiger lessons. When I stayed in Lorca's attic, she helped me up and down stairs a few times and supplied me with comfy cushions and blankets. I felt the vigour of her young body and knew that she had no idea of the feel of wear and tear- and took her vitality for granted. The sweet oblivion of youth. I felt sad that my strength was going so fast. I wanted to hang on to its sweetness.

When I took my next-door neighbour's dog for a walk, I noticed how creaky my joints were, especially climbing over stiles. I cried. This with neck wrinkles and droopy jowls was too much. I was 66 and three quarters; nearly 67; which meant late 60s- or nearly 70. I walked along, sobbing, before sitting on a log with the dog. He is a Cairn and he looked at me with his big brown eyes. Around each eye was a whorl of fur with grey flecks. Yes, he was going grey and looked really beautiful. Then I gasped as I noticed all the trees around me. They were all gnarled and wrinkled and utterly full of swirling energy. The trees seemed to be appraising me lovingly. I was reminded of the tree spirits in Peru. And it *really* looked like one of them winked at me. It seemed to say,

'Hey, just stop it. See your neck as a branch that connects your head to your body. It will be a beautiful gnarled branch that holds your head up proudly. So just stop your snivelling.'

I took the dog home to my neighbour who is 87. She has a really gnarled neck with lots of turkey folds. Does she care? Not one iota. And she always has twinkling eyes and shines with love. She's also a great hugger. Unusual for a British woman of her generation, whose husband was head of the Hong Kong Police in the 1950s. She is always delighted to see me. I told her my ageing problems and she just scoffed. I look really young to her, just as people in their 40s look so young to me.

I went with trepidation to Andy's 41st birthday party. Was I really too old to go?

He and Suzy were younger than my kids. So, would all his friends. What was I doing going to such a party?

'Oh, you don't have too many party times left!' whined my inner party animal, gazing at her wrinkles.

'For goodness' sake' said Mrs WI. 'You are 66- stay home and make chutney from all those green tomatoes!'

As Suzy introduced me to her friends, I said, 'I'm not sure why I've come to a party where everyone is my daughter's age.'

'Don't be silly,' they said. 'Age doesn't matter a fig to us and welcomed me warmly.'

Stuart had a terrible cold. 'Man flu,' he croaked. 'Better not hug you, though I'd like to.'

'By the way Stu how old are you?'

'41.'

'Oh no you are just too old to be my toy-boy. I like them under 40.'

'Oh no, I am only just a year out,' he moaned. 'Dammit.'

'But I am under 40.' Carl swaggered over. 'I'm only 36!'

'Ooh' I said 'Great'

So I was off doing what I did best. Flirt.

Andy is blessed with some great DJ mates so the music was fantastic. The energy I received from dancing and flirting was reviving my ageing sinews.

One of the DJs, Justin Cookee, was with his new love Michelle, a voluptuous and gorgeous Canadian. I turned to Michelle who was dancing nearby,

'I know it is early days with you and Justin- but in a few years' time, I suggest you put him into a sexy role. It certainly keeps my marriage to Jake alive.'

'Really?' Michelle's eyes widened. 'Well, what was your latest role?

'Oh, it was last night- I was Aphrodite and he was Apollo.'

'Really?' she said.

'Well he was feeling a bit poorly and wanted a massage, and showing his vulnerability asked me if that was okay.

'Hey,' I responded. 'How could it not be okay when you have the ability to make me feel like Aphrodite- the sexiest woman on the planet. And you are my Apollo. Needless to say, the massage led to the joining of Apollo and Aphrodite.'

'That is awesome,' said Michelle.

I came back from the party feeling rejuvenated. Parties like our 30th anniversary and with friends like Andy and Suzy seemed the way to go as I slipped into old age. I could have long-term flirts among my friends, especially those who were crazy about their wives. We could dance on a dangerous edge but never step over the line. The boundaries were crystal clear. And I was developing some great flirting relationships that were safe. Vincent and I, for example, have fun acting out roles. If I envisage him as a warrior on horseback, he will oblige me with a comment like, 'I'm ready for you baby- I have had a 2-seater saddle specially made.'

The men I flirt with never seem to want me to stop. My neck wrinkles and falling face don't seem to put them off. Flirting is like an electric charge that lights up my sexuality; I imbibe the sweet nectar of youth - firing up the synapses one more time- reminding me of the sweet fruit I once had in abundance and took for granted. It's almost like I'm a flirt vampire who sucks up the juice and recharges my batteries.

I realized I was becoming addicted. The Bar Girl needed a flirt from a bad boy, like a heroin addict needs a next fix. I was like a vampire who needed blood, the younger the better. I was 66 and this was getting out of hand. When would it stop? And it wasn't like I wasn't getting it at home. I was getting plenty. My guy was the best bad boy of all. In fact, I kept saying this might have to stop for as I get older, my body might not be able to take it. All that delicious loving! 'Oh yes it will,' Jake would say in a deep, naughty voice and again I would turn to putty in his arms. One of the things I was developing was a taste for a really strong squeeze. I was Jake's squeeze and the harder he squeezed me the more I melted. It often felt that this was the squeeze I had been waiting for my whole life. Then he would do this 'romantic hero in a movie' thing- where he looks down at me, licks his lips and gazing intently at my lips, coming slowly enticingly closer. So yummy. Then withdraws and says 'nah'. By then I am jumping him avidly. But hey, I don't want to give away too many of our intimate secrets. What happens between Jake and me is so intimate and so private. To keep the juice going in any relationship, this fire dance is always alight, simmering low often, but able to be ignited at any time. When Jake and I lose that, we know we are in trouble. But even this was not enough- the Bar Girl was insatiable- she wanted this simmering thing happening with a few blokes. Was I the ultimate bad girl- well, bad, old, wrinkly woman, more to the point? I kept thinking that the old scraggy neck would finish it off for good. But it hasn't happened yet. The men who I simmer with always seem to be up for a bit of stoking of the fire. Perhaps there are not enough flirtatious women out there.

Next Babushka had a date with her grandchildren in Australia. I would return just before the next HOH Xmas party so I put my costume together before I left.

In Australia, I connected with my Chinese Hsin Tao master, who taught me some more exercises and also treated me for diabetes. Unfortunately, while I was away, the virus that had been plaguing Jake got worse and he was quite ill. The upshot was that he said he would not be well enough to go to the HOH party when I returned. I went through a crisis- my inner party girl really wanted to go to the party, but my husband was ill and needed me at home to look after him. My daughter was very supportive and accepting of my party persona.

After much inner torment, I decided not to go to the party and to stay home with Jake. But what of my amazing costume? I posted it on Facebook saying this is what I would have worn if I was at the party.

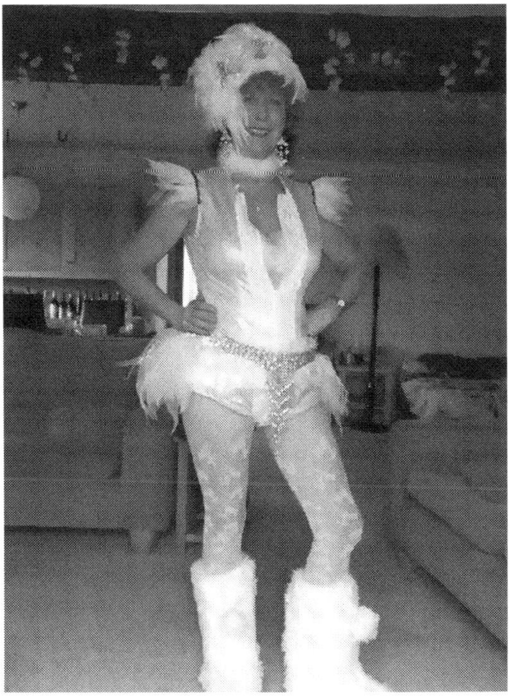

Amazingly, I won a prize for best outfit. And I didn't even go!! It felt like a reward from the universe for doing the right thing and staying home and looking after my husband.

The prize was tickets to the Valentine's February party. I looked forward to making the costumes for both of us, which were lavish King and Queen of Hearts costumes.

Jake was appreciative that I had put him first and said he would throw me a party for my $67^{th}$ birthday at home. We invited a few party friends and had a great time. They clubbed together to present me with a session in a photographic studio in London. It took me four months to get the courage. Well, I thought, 'what have I got to lose?' So, I chose four sexy outfits and off I went. I was unhappy with all the makeup that got plastered on me as I felt it aged me. However, I was delighted with the resulting images. I felt I could let go and just get old. The photos were out there and I was still looking good.

So now I felt in transition, witnessing within me a battle between the Russian Bar Girl and the Russian Babushka. The latter is always homely, possibly plump with soft folds everywhere. Grandchildren love to nestle into these folds. This is love. Eventually, I must say goodbye to the Russian Bar Girl and that feels desperately sad. I just love the male-female sexy dance. It has been so good and the years since my late 50s have been the best of all.

The best things are so hard to let go.

However, I have a husband who seems to love all bits of me, whether crinkling, unfolding, pigmenting, drooping and er... creping. Yes, creping. I was at a swimming pool with my grandchildren when I first noticed this additional assault on my rapidly diminishing youth. Creping. I remembered seeing a 70-year old ballerina on television speaking about ageing.

'There's nothing you can do about this,' she said, showing her arm to the camera. 'You can have facelifts, eye lifts, botox, but there is nothing you can do about this creping. And you know what? It is really okay. My body has served me well.'

I wish I had her acceptance.

Creping is when your skin starts to get pixilated; the space between the pores, fill with tiny lines. Next stop parchment. I had also noticed that my face was developing more age spots and my neck was noticeably loosening. Even though I was with my grandchildren and loved them snuggling into my folds, I panicked.

I took a bus into central Sydney and hunted down skin rejuvenation centres.

'What can I do?' I asked an immaculately made-up woman. 'I don't want a facelift or botox.' She took me through a staggering array of treatments with staggering price tags to match. Fraxel laser, either full blast or in stages, Thermage, microdermabrasion, amongst others.

'Have you had these done yourself?'

'Ooh, yes,' she said. 'All of them.'

'How many times?'

'About a dozen.'

'Any good?'

'Oh yes I had dreadful pigmentation of my skin and it has got rid of it.'

'But has it made you look younger?'

'Very much so.'

'Do you mind me asking how old you are?'

'Why don't you guess?' she said confidently.

I looked closely. Her skin was immaculate but that was also down to extremely good and expensive makeup.

'Well you are probably a lot older,' I said. 'But you look about 44.'

She was not well pleased. 'I am 48.' She said curtly.

'Oh', I thought to myself. 'Spending $1500 on one laser treatment, just to get rid of some age spots didn't seem worth it.'

I decided to be brave and asked her, 'how old do you think I am?'

I think she was sizing me up for revenge.

'Oh, I would say, mid-50s,' she said, looking a bit wary of insulting me.

'Well, I'm 67.' She looked visibly shocked.

At the second skin centre, I talked to Natalya, a very attractive woman with a Russian accent. She recommended Fraxel laser and was very realistic about it.

'It will clear and freshen your skin, but don't hope for a miracle.'

I liked her approach and the price, $499.

'Have you done it?'

'But of course. I had to in order to experience it for myself, before doing it with other people.'

'So how old do you think I am?' I asked, thinking I would get in first this time.

'I would say, early 50s.'

'I am 67.'

She was surprised. 'Your eyes are so alive and you look full of energy.'

'So how old do you think I am?' she asked. I was liking this game and thought, 'ahh there are so many skin rejuvenation parlours and I could spend all my time playing age guessing games.'

'Ooh about 34,' I said looking into her pretty face, framed by dark, wavy hair.

She looked happy. 'I am 44. But it is my genes.'

'Mine too,' I said. My parents are from Eastern Europe and so my genetics are programmed for scorching summers and freezing cold winters.'

'Well, I am Russian.'

I liked this girl. I was now seriously thinking of doing the Fraxel thing. The downside as she explained, was that my skin would stay very red for a few days. I thought of taking my grandchildren to school with a bright red face. 'Was that a good idea?'

So here I was in a dilemma. Shall I? Shan't I?

In my meditation next morning, I asked Therese. No answer came. I asked again next morning. In the silence, the battle sharpened. 'Did I really want to fry my skin? For a little possible tightening?' I felt my face and felt love for it. I felt it was a silly question to ask of a divine mother. This body I was in, was so ephemeral. I thought of my name- mother of all life, mother of God. Yes, quite a trip but so beautiful. But then an image of a Russian Bar Girl swung by. She looked like Natalya and was wearing a sleeveless white fur coat with only knickers underneath. I thought of Vincent's 50$^{th}$ I had been invited to shortly after returning home. Mmmm, I thought. I could look really good- slightly younger face with my body tanned by the Australian sun.

'Hey this body is ephemeral,' said the Russian Bar Girl, flipping up the hem of the coat and stroking her tighter neck with the furry collar. 'What is a little laser work in the grand scheme of things?'

Oh, if only the Fraxel woman was not Russian and so beautiful. I would love her to work on my face and neck.

The jury was still out.

I didn't dare tell Jake. I had mentioned the crepey thing to him in an email. He said, 'If you keep going on about looking old, I will have all the locks changed. AND YOU WON'T BE ABLE TO RETURN. So just stop it!'

I decided against the Fraxel- I really did not want a red face for the next few days.

So, what has the ageing RBG got left?

Well, the best thing is our weekly parties a-deux.

Jake cooks an amazing meal and we dress up. A fire is lit and all the flower lights are turned on, transforming our lounge into a fairy palace. I always put on Russian Bar Girl clothes and make a grand entrance. I have a whole cupboard of such clothes, which are flimsy, sexy and daring. And I frequently add to the collection by scouring thrift shops in whatever location I am in. Sydney is fantastic and I always return to the UK with a pile of RBG finds. An Australian friend (in her 40s!) said she felt she and her husband weren't having enough sex. I asked her,

'Are you dressing sexily for dinner?' and showed her my latest acquisition- a faux fur waistcoat with a lacy back. 'This may look like total frippery but it is what I will be wearing on top of some skimpy shorts, on my next dinner date with Jake.'

'God, will you get through dinner?'

'Probably not.'

'Well, the idea is certainly worth a try.'

And then there are my hats and fascinators. I have about 100 such items. Jake takes great pride in the fact that he is a crusher of these hats and all of them look a little battered. But that is the sign of a good evening. And yes, I always do a sexy dance for him. That was a huge breakthrough for me, seeing I had been too shy to dance or strip in front of him in the past. But now the Russian Bar Girl had taken over. She is not shy at all. She allows the sexy Serpent Queen to come out in all her sinewy and luscious glory.

What is brilliant about having parties at home is that it is not too far to go to bed. We are old now and home comforts are of prime importance.

I went to Vincent's 50th birthday party. There were some of my usual flirts there. I was horrified to see that one of them had got fat. That was the end of him. However, I found that I did not feel like flirting. What? First of all, I put it down to what I was wearing. Mindful of the fact that I could catch nasty colds at parties when I was letting all my bits hang out, I dressed up warm; black lace tights and body with a black and gold dress on top. But I felt like a suffragette. But it was not that. Jake also was paying a lot of attention to me, which was lovely, but even if he went away somewhere, the flirt thing wasn't happening. I went into the dance tent and saw 3 or 4 of my old flirts. They wanted me to flirt with them. I saw clearly how flirting was a 2-way process. Men genuinely love me flirting with them because they know I mean it. I love their maleness. And also, they feel they can express their sexy selves with me and I won't accuse them of being an inappropriate sexual predator. I escaped from the dance room fast. I did not want to respond to anyone. I found Jake.

'Guess what? I think I have caught up with you. I don't feel the need or desire to flirt.' I put this down to several reasons. I now know I am sexy and hot even though I am a 67-year-old grandmother. It is partly because my husband thinks I am beautiful and tells me so every day. The energy between us is smoking; very similar to the energy between people when they first fall in love. I was confident in my sexual allure and did not need to prove it.

So, feeling rather smug, thinking I was over the flirt thing, I suddenly spotted two new guys I hadn't noticed before. I went up to one of them;

'Mmm, where did **you** come from?'

He looked startled and said guiltily, (I found out later he was a gate crasher,)

'Oh, er, London.'

That line hadn't worked so tried another.

'How old are you?'

'er…27.'

I was so amazed I forgot the usual follow up, and just gushed,

'Ooh, I just love 27,' and had a great flirt. I happily dumped my suffragette dress and changed into a short, flouncy skirt. And was delighted to do so. I swished my skirt and really got into it. I felt like a seventeen-year-old cavorting with a new boyfriend.

No, I had not given up flirting!

I found Jake and told him the sequence and how I hadn't got a good response from the line, 'Where did **you** come from?' Jake replied, 'well to be fair, it is a bit difficult to respond to that.'

'Really?' I said. 'Let me try it on you then.' I disappear and come back to him and say. 'So where did **you** come from?' Jake doesn't miss a beat and answers in a husky voice,

'It's not where I come from honey – it's where you and I are going to, that you should think about.' Phew! He never fails that man!

I was disappointed I hadn't given up flirting with young men, hoping that I would naturally want to give up. I didn't want total wrinkledom to be what stopped me. But it seemed the time had not yet arrived. Would it ever?

It seemed I was still well and truly stuck in the superficial dimension of Channel One. In fact, I think I must be the Queen of Channel One. 1 really have to own that and accept this part of myself. That is in essence what a Russian Bar Girl is.

Page intentionally left blank

# 16

## The Party Is Over

However, my Channel One, light-hearted existence was to be shattered when Cancer made its brutal entry into our lives. It was already there with darling Poonie, who was braving her Stage-4 diagnosis and experiencing life with her husband and family to the full. She was harbouring some hope with a new type of cancer treatment.

Jake had been suffering from a virus for months and the doctor sent him for a lung X-Ray. This showed up a small shadow. With further investigation, there seemed to be a growth in his right lung. I was in Australia when Jake told me that he might have lung cancer. We both looked up survival rates. They were grim. Not many people did survive. I faced the possibility that I might not spend a glorious old age with Jake. What would I do? I felt devastated.

Jake's specialist recommended he should have the growth out in case it was cancer. I contacted Poonie and Greg who checked and approved of our doctors, hospitals and plans.

Poonie was so gracious in her reply as she faced her own long battle with cancer.

I think what you guys are asking for is longevity and I will pray for that my darling ones along with swift, minimally invasive treatment. I am sure I will see you both back on the dance floor! But the positive outcome is to realise whatever life may offer up, you and Jake have been privileged to know true bliss. The only outcome is love. Loving you xxxx

Poonie's life had been transformed by her suffering. She had come to terms with what she was facing. She experienced some profound spiritual transformations and rested in a place of deep love. And she was able to happily acknowledge that Jake and I had reached a blissful state. She had become more spiritual as well as sexy.

After many discussions, we decided that Jake should go for the operation which was keyhole surgery, during which a piece of his lung was sent to the lab. If it was cancerous then he would have a third of his lung out, while still on the operating table. I was convinced that it could not be cancer and awaited the lab results nervously. I was shocked. It was cancer and he had a third of his lung removed. Fortunately, the cancer was caught at an early stage and had not spread. The recovery took a long time, but Jake and I were grateful that he had survived lung cancer. It made sense of a vivid dream he had had a couple of years earlier. In the dream, one of us was dying and we were saying goodbye to each other. The upshot of the dream was that Jake decided he wanted to spend as much quality time together as we could. The lung cancer was a big reminder and we renewed the commitment to live in as much love together as we possibly could. Poonie had recognized it in us when she had written,

'You and Jake have been privileged to know true bliss. The only outcome is love.' Things were getting worse for Poonie.

At the beginning of 2014, she declared that in this year she would have her summer of love. She was determined to be at several events- the first at an evening, where her fellow Hot Flush troupe were dancing and raising money for a cancer charity, then a Golden Delicious party on a boat and thirdly, to be in charge of the healing area at the annual Give Festival in July. She was also undergoing some experimental radiotherapy. She shone at the Hot Flush event, taking to the stage and presenting the cancer society with money raised, and she accompanied Greg to the Golden Delicious boat party, where he played a mean set. But her future was closing in.

On May 17th Greg made her a picnic on the beach and they posted some happy photos of the occasion.

However, the very next day her lungs collapsed and she was in Guernsey hospital. Despite the seriousness of her condition, she still found the energy to write to me, to support Jake's entry into hospital for the keyhole surgery.

**May 19th, 9:53 am**

 I think that sounds very positive regardless of cancer or not (although, of course, not would be fantastic!) I am very glad that you have a concise plan with all possible permutations explained. You are in good hands and I feel very happy about

that. You've got a while to go yet, Jake!!! As for me, I am currently in big trouble. I'm in hospital in Guernsey. Unable to breathe unassisted and with an ever-worsening condition that they are, as yet, unable to fathom. The London team here are liaising with all the results in the hope that they can understand it but I have to admit I am terrified at the moment. Just collapsed in the shower and turned blue half an hour ago. Even on an oxygen mask. That's just the truth of it and I've not really thought to tell friends until I know what's likely. Don't really want a flurry of worry! Still, ever holding hope in my heart that I may enjoy some brief respite in a summer meadow with the people I love and, if not, well, I have been privileged to know such exquisite beauty, time and time again. I'll always shout for just one more tune but it is gluttony, not need. I send you both love from the bottom of my heart and strength to keep you well. Poonie xxx

**May 19th, 11:50 am**

Oh, Poonie darling. I am praying for you to pull through this current crisis- I am so moved by what you have written- it is so REAL- both your terror and the exquisite beauty you are experiencing. That is life in a nutshell as I see it- the profound challenge (acutely physical in your case) and the amazing beauty.

I love you from the bottom of my heart too and have a vision of you smiling radiantly in a field soon.

Jake sends his sincerest love.

**May 25th, 2:38 pm**

Hello, lovely one. Hope you are recovering. Thanks for the lovely message on my timeline. I see you as my divine elder on the Cancer-fighting front. Jake says he has had a fabulous life, and if death is around the corner he has fulfilled all his dreams. We are having a lovely bank holiday weekend luxuriating in our love for each other. Hope you are out of hospital and doing the same with your fab family. Love and strength to the whirling dervish inside you. And btw love the photo of stunning you with your stunning mother.

**May 25th, 7:39 pm**

 I am glad you are having a beautiful time my darlings. I'm afraid that I have rapidly deteriorated and am definitely at end game in hospital in Guernscy unable to breathe unassisted or indeed do anything more than, literally 3 steps. This is not information I want you to share. I know I am loved and I can't field the whole text/FB/ email thing at all now. But I felt I

wanted you both to know as I hold you very dear and perhaps it explains my message earlier. I hope to get home with the palliative nurses this week if I can hold out. I'd rather be looking at the sea than a linoleum floor! My body is done (and it is extraordinary when it starts to close down!!!) but my spirit is clear and bright and preparing to go. It is with a heart full of love and gratitude for a life well lived and all my blessings. I will not correspond again in all likeliness as I am just focusing on my boys and have very little energy left. Of course, there may be a miraculous turnabout and I'll have embarrassed myself...tee hee! ....but I think not. Please know that I love you both, Poonie xxx

**May 26th, 9:04 am**

Darling woman, what a blessing your touching words are to me. Your humility and clarity in the face of death astounds me and humbles me. And is teaching me, preparing me for my own. Thank you. I appreciate how you have always acknowledged and encouraged my sexuality - how you have acknowledged Jake in the same way. I have loved our magic conversations especially the one at Julie Devine's party- you and Greg were one of the first people we met at Golden Delicious who welcomed us warmly into a fun party world beyond our wildest dreams. If there is a miraculous turnaround I will love to see you again-however f I don't meet you in the flesh I will do everything possible to connect with you again- on the other side (whatever dimension that is in!). I hope you get to see the sea and that you have more lovely precious time with your boys. All our love.

**May 26th, 8:57 pm**

 Perfect x

**Saturday 11:07 am**

Poonie had put up this message on her Facebook timeline

'Gratitude is the attitude...it will set you free! Yippee!'

She made it to her and Greg's 10th wedding anniversary. I sent her scented roses. She was teaching me how to die. I wanted her to have a little of Therese de Lisieux, who lived a life of total gratitude and wanted to spend her heaven strewing roses upon the earth.

 Your flowers arrived and made my heart sing, my spirit soar and fuels further this 'love bukaki' I kneel before. How blessed am I? How blessed are we? Love abounding xxx

Oh, my darling. I am soaring with you. Every morning when I meditate, you come pouring in. In fact, many times a day you come pouring in. Your spirit is definitely not confined to Guernsey. I am gobsmacked by you and your surrender. Inspiring. Feeling really blessed. Love love love

Beautiful Poonie died 3 days later on June 3rd in the arms of her family. On June 1st her last Facebook entry was the following poem. Bee is her brother, Ben.

**June 1, 2014**

This is a little poem that Bee wrote many years ago and I thought you all may like it;

Glistening small, sitting on a rock, Gazing out to sea, happy to be me. Wearing a frown, Now I'm a rivulet, trickling down,. Perhaps I'll drown......PLOP! Now I'm the ocean.

Page intentionally left blank

# 17

## A Tribute to Poonie

Ben had found a new venue for Give which was in the beautiful grounds of a stately home. Jake was still recovering from a major operation. After checking with him that he didn't need me to stay home and look after him, he was happy for me to go with Lorca.

This was a lovely gift from him as he knew I would take the opportunity to take my Russian Bar Girl out and flaunt her un-

Fraxelled, 67-year-old self. In the corner of my mind sat a cackling crone with a gnarled neck. I told her,

'Just shut up. This might be the last time I can still get away with flirting- really flirting.'

'Oh, you are always saying that- but you keep flouncing around like a demented floozy. Act your age!'

'Well I have a really good excuse this time as the biggest tribute I can give to Poonie's memory is to have a really good flirtatious time.'

'Pfwwt. Always excuses!' She grimaced and retreated in disgust.

Give Festival 2014 was dedicated to the memory of Poonie. During the weeks before her death, Poonie had made cakes and gifts for everyone who attended. Several hundred lovingly-made presents. The party was a bittersweet affair with many tributes to Poonie, including a magnificent shrine and a beautiful song sung by my friend Charlotte. We were all sad that our party Queen was no longer with us in the flesh.

I felt bereft that my role model was gone, but I was sure she was looking down upon me and approving of my outfits and my roving eye.

I had met Sam, the rigger, several years before at Kimberley. He came to Julie Devine's tent looking rather manly with his tool belt. I said – 'Mmmm a rigger! – I *do* like a rigger.' He gave me an appreciative look. On the first evening, I lost my bag and in it was the key to my hotel room. I wandered about feeling really tired, wondering what to do if I couldn't find it. I bumped into Sam.

'Hello,' he said, 'you okay?'

'No, I've lost my bag and if I don't find it soon, I'm going to have to find a guy with a tent, and sleep with him.' I looked at him meaningfully.

Sam's jaw dropped.

'Are you serious?'

'Well, no, not really- I am happily married and I wouldn't do that.'

'So, if it isn't even an option, why are you saying it?'

'Oh, just because I wouldn't do it, I do like to think about it.'

'You are such a bad girl, Eva.'

That was a real compliment! Suffice to say, I did find my keys and the temptation dissolved.

I met the lovely Bruce who saved me at the party when I was recovering from sciatica.

We had some fun banter and dancing. I told him I was writing a book about flirting during my previous ten years, and asked him if he minded being in it.

'No, I don't', he said. 'In fact, I've just finished writing my book- a kid's book - about global warming and saving the planet.' Then he gave me such a great compliment.

'I can see you have a really good man. You are the sexiest, happiest woman I have ever met. Your man must keep you that way.'

'Yes,' I said. 'You are right. Jake is really amazing in every way'. Then I gave Bruce another dance. He was really appreciative.

'You have now reached the top of my toy-boy list,' I said, reminding him of the time I had met him the year before, and said he was in my top ten. He said 'Well you are rapidly rising to the top of my list of sexy older babes.'

Simon is a great old flirty friend of mine. He is always surrounded by a bevy of gorgeous young women who congregate in his huge party tent, a veritable den of iniquity. I gave him a dance too. He said 'Wow, you have still got it, babe.' That meant a lot coming from a guy like him.

I had a frisson with a dangerous, what I call, 'bad' boy. I had to tell him in no uncertain terms I was happily married. Unfortunately, I do like the bad boy from the wrong side of town. And the further trouble is that that kind of bad boy always responds to me, even if I am way old enough to be his mother. As my lovely friend Sluggy says- I epitomise youthfulness- the naughty 17-year-old within me bursts out of me demanding 'I am ready to have my wicked way with you.'

After a serious crisis in confidence, I found that at age 67, I could still attract young guys. That was great for my ego. But I felt sad, as I knew that really the time would have to come when my flirting days were over. I couldn't pull off being seventeen forever- especially now I was fifty years on. I would be 70 in two and a half years' time. I'd had a brilliant innings and the last few years had been great.

I went home to Jake. I have one sexy man, and he really is the ultimate bad boy. And he adores me. He has found the balance between being desirable, being attracted to other women and confining his sexuality to just me. And I have found the perfect man to tame the wild capricious, flirtatious side of me with a roving eye for every hot guy on the planet.

Jake's health had improved enough for us to throw his 70$^{th}$ birthday party at home. Our women friends organized a special treat for him where he sat in the middle of the room, and they all took a turn at giving him a sexy dance.

This suited Jake, as he said 'I find looking at women keeps something alive.'

'Well, that's the same for me and flirting with guys. I find their sexiness towards me thrilling, and it keeps my libido ticking over. And I find I am getting more turned on to you as a result.'

And it is true for both of us. We are delighting in each other. And the sexier we are together, the more attractive we are to other people. So, it is a wonderful positive feedback loop- win, win, win, all the way!

But how much longer can it go on? I feel I have to move on from the Russian Bar Girl. I feel I must grow a new persona that is more befitting of a grandmother approaching her 70s. I said to Jake,

'I have to stop flirting as I am getting too old.'

'Why?'

'Do you think it's attractive for someone with big wrinkles on their neck to flirt? Have you seen a 91-year-old woman looking sexy?'

'Well, you could be the first.'

Now that is a challenge. Mind you, Marlene Dietrich looked great right into her 70s.

'Just because you are getting older and have wrinkles doesn't mean you will stop liking guys.'

'That is so true- I think I will always be on the look-out for attractive men. I just don't want to be inappropriate like some old women and men who are downright embarrassing.'

I had seen a clip circulating on Facebook, which showed a woman about 80 flirting with a much younger man- thrusting her hips at him suggestively. I wrote underneath the clip. 'Anyone seeing me do that when I am 80, could you just please shoot me.'

'What!!' replied Sluggy. 'Never. You, darling, wrote the book on flirting with younger men.'

That was very prescient of him because now I have!!!

Jake added, 'you don't know how lovely you are and until you really own how sexy and gorgeous you are, you will always be looking for acknowledgement from other men.'

This was so true. It was not dissimilar to the Isha syndrome- as long as I kept her up on a pedestal, I was denying my inner beauty. As long as I was looking for acknowledgement from men, I wasn't at peace with my own allure. Was this what was leading my desire to pull attractive young men? Was this true? How much further did I have to go? A constant struggle.

I was pleased that Jake was coming with me to the next HOH Christmas party.

The theme was Green Fairy Absinthe; a challenge. I made a top for Jake out of a t-shirt which was given to him by a flirtatious girl in Australia, who was promoting Absinthe. It had a picture of a willowy green fairy on the front and back. I cut off the arms and sewed on some black and green feathers. Jake looked dashing in it. I enjoyed making the costumes, as it was fulfilling a very creative side of me.

Ben, of HOH, posted up on Facebook that he hoped we were getting on with our costumes. Claudie is a brilliant party dresser and designs and wears some amazing party outfits and we always corresponded about what we were concocting.

**Eva Maria:** I am working on my costume! Such fun. Green feathers everywhere!

 **Claudie**: I see your green feathers and raise you my green leather dress, cosplay wig and knee-high red platform boots, (I'm going for green punk fairy)

 **Eva Maria**: Wow! Fantastic. Well, I raise you a green catsuit with green sequin belt and green tail feathers- furry, feathery green wings. Green spurred boots. Headdress still in my imagination. I think I'm going for a Bohemian, sexpot, feather-bird fairy?????

 Claudie: Bloody hell, Eva, I think you win, on description alone!! I LOVE the sound of that! xx

 **Eva Maria**: I have won before, so it's your turn!!!

I loved my outfit and walked into the party feeling every inch the sexy feather-bird fairy. A young woman came up to me

gushing at how great I looked. When she heard I was nearly 68 she was in awe.

'When you walked into that party you were the most stunning woman in the room. So confident, so sexy, so beautiful. You outshone all the younger women there!' Yes, I had gathered another fan- the beautiful JoJo. Another young woman who was inspired by me. I also found I loved having sexy dances with her and other women.

Tony Roseman the photographer snapped Jake and me a few times and came over and said,

'I just love seeing you two together- how long?'

'Oh, over 35 years.'

'Wow,' he said, 'That is what I really want – a relationship like yours.'

I became Tony's friend on FB. I wrote. 'How come a lovely man like you is single?'

'Oh, because I have been hurt a few times- don't want to take the risk again.'

'Well if I wasn't happily married and 25 years younger, I would be first in line.'

He liked that so I wrote ‘but you can be one of my toy-boy flirts.’

Such fun.

# 18

## Kundalini Tiger

I remembered Tiger number 6 saying, Tiger number 7 is Kundalini Tiger! He won't come till you are ready.

I waited patiently- meditating and doing the lessons the Tigers taught me. I continued being in control of my diabetes, with good food and exercise. Both Jake and I were keeping our sides of the agreement we had made. I stepped up with being more responsible and less lazy. He showed his vulnerability more and slipped into Superman less. Our intimacy deepened.

But still no Kundalini tiger. Perhaps I was not enlightened enough. I gave up waiting.

He appeared in Spring 2015. And in a surprising way. The previous Autumn, I had found 100s of psilocybin mushrooms. I felt they were calling me to take a trip. I hadn't had psilocybin for over 20 years. Ayahuasca had helped me face my madness and I felt I was finished with psychedelics. This time I was attracted in a new way to these mushrooms with their beautiful, creamy liberty caps. They seemed to be calling me. The springiness of their very long stems felt like they would do my back good. I was reminded of the Anastasia teaching that plants in one's own garden had great power to heal, and these were growing all around us in our fields.

On Easter Sunday, Jake and I decided to take a small dose in a psilocin tea- something we had never tried before. Because I was so susceptible, I had half of a small dose (the equivalent of 7 mushrooms). As I sipped the tea, I set my intention to heal my back. Within ten minutes I was gripped by an intense energy travelling up my spine. It was so powerful, my spine started pulsing.

'Wow!' I said to Jake, excitedly. 'It's working! I think I am imbibing the springiness of the stems.' Then I couldn't speak any more as I was engulfed by what I recognized as kundalini energy. I had experienced this phenomenon a few times on Enlightenment Intensives and it felt like I was plugged in into the power of the universe; energy pulsated like waves throughout my body.

Out of the blue, Kundalini Tiger had gripped me totally and I felt expanded by his presence. It went on for about an hour and I surrendered to the purifying energy as much as I could. Jake told me later that the whole room was vibrating.

The tiger acknowledged me for all the work I had done and had decided that at last, I was ready for him.

'Ready for what?' I thought with some alarm, as a searing heat travelled up my spine and hovered at chest level. I felt a tiger claw enter my heart into a deep, tight spot. It was excruciatingly painful. This place felt like it demanded release and purification, which is what kundalini energy does. It was the part I had closed down when as a child I couldn't bear losing my mother to insanity. Grim images of the mental hospital assailed me- me, the stalwart young girl closing down the horror I felt as I saw my mother foaming at the mouth in a straightjacket- or screaming at the doors of the closed wards as I left. 'Don't leave me here- they are killing me. Don't go'. I howled in despair for what seemed hours, letting that frozen helplessness, guilt and agony out. As the effects of the psilocin wore off, I stayed with it and spent the next couple of days wailing. It was a heavy purge and every time I thought of my mother rotting away in that hell for the last 17 years of her life, tears just gushed from my eyes. I remembered the young woman, Olga, her radiant smile lighting up her heart-shaped face, who so longed for happiness and love. The pain was so sharp, so unbearable. Kundalini tiger stayed with me, deeming me ready at last to face that heart-shattering pain. I finally emerged, my heart feeling much softer and less constricted.

I was so deeply affected by this experience, that I wanted to try and see a real tiger in the wild. The opportunity came up the following month, as I was planning to travel to Australia to see my Sydney family.

I arrived at Jimmy Corbett's safari lodge after a 7-hour taxi ride from Delhi airport. The manageress, Rati, welcomed me warmly. After a delicious diabetic dinner of chicken, organic vegetables from the garden and a buckwheat pancake filled with soft cheese, I relaxed with a gin, soda water and lemon. Perfect.

I was up at 5 a.m. for a dawn safari. Rati packed me buckwheat and cheese and unsweetened tea for a snack. I was in a jeep with a tax collector from West India and his serious-looking camera. There were spotted deer, black partridges, peacocks and a menacing wild bull elephant. There are only ten tigers in this part of the national park. Would we be lucky enough to spot one? There was a flurry of excitement as the jeep turned into a riverbed. There was the tiger, moving majestically in the undergrowth at the edge of the river. So exciting. I tingled all over as we returned to a great breakfast. After jungle walks and a swim, I was due for another safari at dawn the next day.

That night I couldn't sleep. Jungle cats on the roof and scare shots for elephants didn't help. I fell asleep at about 4 a.m., typical of the insomnia that had plagued me all my life. I had one of those ghastly awake-asleep dreams. I dreamt I was really tired and everyone was ignoring me. I felt useless and chaotic and desperate. And still, they ignored me. At the alarm, I felt jangled, bereft and abandoned. I needed my tiger allies. 'Just go with it, dear one,' they answered. On the way, in the privacy of the front of the jeep, what came up under the pain of my mother disappearing into insanity, was the anguish I felt about her hitting me when I couldn't sleep. How could she be so unkind to me? I felt dreadful and thought it served her right that she ended up in a mental hospital. Fortunately, I was able to cry as the driver and people in the back could not see me. For the next hour (which was the time it took to get into the safari park) I allowed myself to feel all of it, especially the injustice of it. I wanted a warm, kind mother who soothed me or sang lullabies, not bash me.

I was distracted by a burst of activity among the queue of jeeps- a tigress had just been glimpsed ahead. Apparently, her two cubs were hiding nearby while she foraged for food. I cried again, and wished I had a beautiful tigress as a mother.

The queue of jeeps moved forward. I settled back and continued to face my anguish. I missed my grandmother terribly. I wish I had known her. I wanted her to cradle me and soothe me. I remembered the Russian words for ‘I am very tired’. 'Ya ochin ustalaya babushka’. She spoke back to me and said my mother was a disturbed, unhappy woman, and she was sad that I had to suffer at her hands. Like my inner tiger mother, she would have loved to protect me from her. I even put on a babushka scarf as I sank into sadness.

Then the jeep turned a corner and stopped among other jeeps quietly waiting for the tiger that had been glimpsed earlier. In one of the jeeps were two handsome Indian men, both about 30, with a very large camera. I had spotted them the day before and one had flashed me a captivating smile as we went past each other; one of those delightful brief encounters. Now there he was again! And I was in my babushka scarf, with a blotchy face!! Oh no! My abject misery vanished as quickly as it took me to divest myself of my scarf. This guy was striking and looking straight at me. It reminded me of my first Enlightenment Intensive when I was bawling my eyes out, didn't hear the bell, and the only seat left was in front of an attractive man. His touch of sympathy had sent a sexual charge through me which jolted me into direct experience. I went from total misery to total bliss in a second. Here was a similar experience, but this time with just a look.

All jeeps were silent as we waited for the elusive tiger. The charge between this man and me was electric. I was reminded that I was a lot more than just a sad little girl in need of a babushka. I was female incarnate. Sexual energy buzzed through me from head to toe. Not quite kundalini, but sexual energy none the less. Wow. I had not expected this. I almost couldn't contain it. We were there for about 15 sizzling minutes. The spell was broken as the tiger rustled through the brush. We caught just the back of her. A fleeting glimpse, but a definite tiger sighting. I was quite relieved when our driver decided to move on. I smiled as we drove past. He winked back. What a gift this man had been! And with it the sighting of a real, live tiger! I was high for the rest of the day. I felt a little more healed. Puzzling about this later, I saw the importance of sexual energy and how my pursuit of it seemed to do me good. I am glad I live with a husband who helps me feel vibrant and sexy. I think sexual energy was really important to my mother, and when she didn't have it fulfilled, it contributed to her craziness, and inappropriate angst towards me.

I told Rati, the manageress, about my journey with the seven tigers. She was fascinated and before I left, she gave me a holy seed to wear next to my heart to help heal it; and a mantra; such a beautiful gift. She also packed me boxes of food for the return taxi journey. It was good to slip into a bed on my Business Class flight to Sydney.

Before I drifted into sleep, I pondered my learning from the tiger safari. Kundalini Tiger had helped me face even deeper agony of losing my mother to madness; this safari had brought up my fury of being shredded by her madness. Having always been so overwhelmed and heartbroken by her insanity, I hadn't had the room or capacity to express my anger, resentment, irritation at how badly she was treating me; how she was falling short of being an adequate mother. I had bought her trip that I was the reason for her all her unhappiness and misery; it was all my fault. This safari had shown me and given me the wherewithal to stick up for the child who was the victim of her extreme and crazy treatment of me. She not only beat me when I couldn't sleep, but beat me when I didn't eat. So, I am beset by severe digestive and sleep problems. Surprisingly, and unexpectedly, sexual energy had helped towards healing the trauma. I felt blessed.

On the flight, I read one of my 'Course in Miracles' lessons (something I had followed for years), which asked 'What is your function? What is your way of bringing light into the world?' As I was flying all the way to Australia to be with my grandchildren, being a devoted grandmother was at the top of the list. A few days later we were on a car trip, my daughter driving and my son-in-law navigating.

'Daddy's good at navigating,' said my grandson.

'And I'm terrible at navigating but good at driving,' said my daughter.

Ensconced in the back between my grandchildren, I said,

'Unfortunately, I'm pretty bad at driving and even worse at navigating.'

At which my 7-year-old granddaughter said, 'but you are very good at being a Baba.'

And yes. I am. I love it. I am a much better grandmother than I was a mother. I am so much calmer and more patient. I was brought up by a woman driven insane by the horrible circumstances of her life. I managed with a lot of therapy and a lot of help, not to impose as much wackiness on my own children. My grandchildren are the proof of the 'awareness' pudding. My daughter is fantastic with her offspring who are growing into balanced, happy human beings. I have also enjoyed being a fellow grandparent with my previous husbands. My daughter's dad and I have a lovely connection regarding our grandchildren. We both recognize we are much better grandparents than we were parents.

I also bring light into the world by letting out my flirtatious self, which honours the good part of my mother. I am REALLY good at flirting. I am REALLY good at parties. I am REALLY good at dressing up for parties. Do I stop all this because I am 68? No. So, what have I to contribute? Loving my sexy self- being the woman I am in all its glory. Loving my body and daring to flaunt it. Daring to wear hot-pants- plunging necklines – feather shrugs and swirly skirts. And to 'dare' is the word to overcome ageism and misogyny which was demonstrated in widespread disapproval in social media when Susan Sarandon exposed her décolletage at the age of 69 at a film awards ceremony. I was gratified to see Helen Mirren on TV after her 70th birthday, tartly refuting the interviewer's remark, 'You don't look 70!'

'Of course, I look 70- I have good hair, good makeup and good clothes and I look 70.' And she did. And 70 looked beautiful. I found that inspiring. It means I can look my age and still be beautiful. I also began to really see that I could be 70, have wrinkles and still be sexy. That was another strong inner voice- you cannot be wrinkly and still look sexy.

I will continue to flaunt my assets and be an example to other women. I have Poonie, as my great role model.

*Poonie's sister Femi, found an after-party message from Poonie, which she posted on Facebook soon after Poonie's death*

'Femi..... You were spellbindingly beautiful. I just love to watch you dance. A whole other league of sexiness and grace and ownership I can only ever play at! (Fooled lots of 'em in my time though... not being modest) Respect sister!'

This was quintessential Party Queen Poonie, who was always so generous in her encouragement and praise of other women's sexuality. I was pleased that I could emulate Poonie and do this for many of my younger women friends. I commented on what a friend of mine had worn to my 30th wedding anniversary, a long ethnic skirt.

'You look so feminine and very sexy- just like a gypsy. Very mysterious and unique.'

'You know what, Eva, it is you. You help me bring out my inner sexiness- I feel I have the space to expand my sexual self around you.'

Many friends come to me for sartorial advice and for loans of clothes. A friend, who works in responsible positions in the civil service, wanted to know how to dress more sexily. I gave her a red suit in which she looked fantastic, but she didn't wear it.

'The fact is, Eva, I am not you.' That was certainly true. Not everyone is channelling a Russian Bar Girl. (what a relief!) My friend was inspired to discover for herself what she looked good in, and what she could dare wear. She is much more sophisticated than I have ever been, and she looks lovely. I was hoping I was passing on what Poonie had given me in spades; the confidence to be my beautiful, sexy self. And every woman is unique. For me this deep self -acceptance is profoundly spiritual. Thank you, Poonie.

What else I have to contribute is to dare acknowledge a man's ability to be a man, which involves him expressing his potent self. If I recognize this sexy potency, I want to acknowledge it. The fact I am NOT going to follow through, as all these men know I am happily married - they feel safe enough to allow that frisson between us. I think many men have been knocked sideways by part of the Women's Lib movement. Because male sexuality has been so warped over the centuries and has been siphoned into warmongering and Corporate takeover, many men have tried to suppress their maleness so as not to be offensive – a little like my Italian friend Federico. I see my function as honouring the real man - the sexy, but loving man, in his magnificence- separate from all the other warped male sexuality stuff.  The 'me too' campaign of 2017 has empowered some women to stand up to sexual abuse- and as it took me a lifetime to express my own rage at being sexually abused as a child, this has been essential. But I fear in many ways, it may have also gone too far and often amplifies the 'woman as victim' story. Even though I have been flirting outrageously, I have never ever felt any man overstep the mark. I like the healthy, consensual, sexual dance between men and women and want to support that.

I returned from Australia and the tiger safari, feeling more whole. I went to Poonie's Pink Ball in commemoration of Poonie, to raise money for the cancer charity she supported. Looking pretty hot in a pink outfit, I saw Tony Roseman, who immediately asked,

'Where's Jake?'

'Oh, he's not here'

'Oh, so tonight, darling, could be our night!' he said giving me a wolfish look. He introduced me to friends saying – 'if this gorgeous woman wasn't married, I'd be all over her.'

He repeated this to Jake at the Give festival, a month later.

'You and half the guys at this festival,' quipped Jake, not missing a beat.

'Yes, you're certainly right there,' said Tony.

I felt acknowledged by this exchange and liked the fact that Jake was staking his claim. And I liked that Tony was very upfront- and not secretive. Later Tony said to me,

'Darling you are my Bar Girl- you make me feel like a sexy, hot man.'

'That is what we Bar Girls do.' I demurred. 'That is our job.'

Tony spent the rest of the festival flirting with all the women and having a ball.

When I introduced Bruce to Jake, he said, 'Your wife is so gorgeous- you are one lucky man.'

'Oh no,' said Jake giving me a playful pat. 'She's the lucky one.'

It seems that flirting with other people, strengthens what is between us.

I hugged Bruce warmly. It felt like a beautiful completion of a flirt which started when I was suffering severely from sciatica. And Bruce, like Tony, is an unabashed flirt. So, I feel I have become what a Bar Girl is, in a safe way. I have fulfilled the hunger expressing what I am in essence. A sexy, Bar Girl.

At Give 2015, I felt I had reached the apotheosis of my party girl persona as well. The colour theme was pink and I really had fun creating outfits. On the first evening, Allegra, Poonie's mother, admired my pink catsuit and called me a 'Sex Goddess'. Like her daughter she is so generous with her praise. Next afternoon for the photo session I wore

a short, pink, sequin dress with an elaborate headdress. With the help of Jake's engineering skills, I had created a Mardi Gras-type headdress full of sparkles and pink feathers. Allegra dubbed me 'Star of the Show'.

As Julie Devine said after the weekend, 'You were more radiant and beautiful than ever'.

So, at age 68 I had made it as the hottest ticket in town. Allegra's comments that I was a 'Sex Goddess' and 'Star of the Show', was like a crowning. I was still Belle of the Ball.

Poonie would have been proud! She was such a pristine Sex Goddess. She owned her flirtatious self but did not step over the boundary of her committed and loving relationship. She, like me, did not want to suppress her flirtatious beauty. I remember early on in our friendship, I was debating whether the hot-pants I was wearing were too hot. 'Never,' she said. 'But don't just wear them, make sure you work them- the hotter the better.' And Poonie always worked whatever she was wearing.

So now that I had reached the apotheosis, could I now let it go? But just before my 69$^{th}$ birthday I was in for a seismic shock. This would lead to an even deeper acceptance of me being sexy as well as spiritual.

Page intentionally left blank

# 19

## The White Tigress

Blood cancer! WTF! No not leukaemia- which is too many white blood cells – opposite – too many red blood cells and platelets. Rare, and also hard to pronounce- Polycythaemia Vera.

It is said that getting older is like experiencing one insult after another. I had heard of all the major diseases that could strike me in my old age. But I'd never heard of this. This was the latest health shock!

At the end of 2015, I was diagnosed with myeloproliferative disease. In the cancer wing of the hospital, the haematologist gravely told me that cells in my bone marrow were producing too many red blood cells. A mutant gene, called Jak-2, could not switch off and was involved in this proliferation. Untreated, this would lead to blood cells clumping together and causing thrombotic events like heart attacks and strokes. I was scared witless. As I was over 60, had type 2 diabetes and high blood pressure, I was regarded as high risk and the haematologist advocated that I immediately took a chemotherapy pill, hydroxycarbamide, to bring down my platelet and red blood cell count.

'I am very unhappy about taking these pills,' I said. 'Is there any other way of bringing down my platelet and red blood cell count?'

'No,' he said and prescribed the pills.

The box sat in the back of the cupboard with imaginary danger signs leaping out of its sides. I couldn't take them

Instead, I brought down my blood pressure, checked my diabetes and went into full-blown research on the Internet. I found a man in Brisbane who said my condition could be cured by auto-suggestion. I tried it for two hours a day for several months. In my world, anything was better than chemotherapy. I doubted that I could possibly tell my bone marrow to heal, but wanted to try.

Then I discovered Tao bone breathing. This was a technique that Chinese warriors used to strengthen their bones. I read about an old woman who cured herself of osteoporosis, using the technique. Mantak Chia, a Taoist master, had many videos on YouTube, so I learnt it and incorporated it into my two hours of meditation

I also ate a lot of raw garlic, onion, turmeric, gingko biloba and resveratrol, all substances reputed to bring down platelet numbers.

Two months later, my platelets had dropped to normal. I was ecstatic. However, my red blood cell mass was rising dangerously. Venesections, in which a pint of blood is removed, were one way to deal with this. I preferred this blood-letting to taking hydroxycarbamide, which was now relegated to a cupboard in the outside pantry. I even tried leech therapy but was too horrified by the leeches which seemed intent on draining **all** my blood. I stuck to venesections.

I resumed my meditation with vigour. In one of my daily sessions, I came in contact with Baba Yaga. She is my Russian bone witch- her house is made of bones and she has teeth as solid as iron. She seems the perfect archetype for me to visit and heal my bones.

Many years ago, I took my mother's ashes to her birthplace, Tarasivka, in Ukraine. She is buried in a plot among many generations of ancestors with our family name, Nesterenko. In my meditation, I visit this cemetery and call on my ancestors, as well as Baba Yaga, to heal my bones. These forebears ate lots of garlic and worked hard on the land, so I figured their bones would be strong. I imagined suffusing my bones with their strength.

I also immersed myself in Mantak Chia's many books on the Healing Tao. This new affliction, Polycythaemia Vera, along with Sciatica and Diabetes 2, has led me to whole new realms of inner exploration. Like with the seven tigers from sciatica, and seven dervishes from diabetes, I am being led to deeper and deeper levels of taking care of my body and discovering new avenues of healing. (Yes, I have even met seven dragons). I love concentrating on my bones- all 206 of them. I also do the inner smile meditation where you imagine a being in front of you who smiles at each organ. The joyful tree spirit I met in Peru, is now doing the job. Sometimes he is joined by all the other tree spirits. It is very beautiful and organs like my heart and liver really seem to appreciate being smiled at. How did I ignore them for so long? They are doing such vital work.

Mantak Chia advocates the use of sexual energy for healing. This is a new concept for me but makes sense of the healing I have experienced from sexual energy, as I did in India. I am willing to try anything and even bought a jade egg. If putting a jade egg in my cervical palace will heal my bones, so be it. Beats chemotherapy any day. But then I promptly lost the egg so this particular therapy is on hold.

Devouring the Taoist sexual system has led to something even more exciting, that has made sense of all my flirting during the previous ten years. I found a book called 'The Sexual Secrets of the White Tigress.' Yay, the tigers were still present. The White Tigress in ancient China was a woman who, within a particular branch of Taoist sexual healing practices, used the potent energy of men to lead her to enlightenment. I found the concept tantalising- a radical departure from prevailing images of men taking advantage of women. Here was a woman taking total advantage of men. No victim trip in sight here!  The White

Tigress used men specifically to advance her enlightenment. She usually lived with one man, the Jade Dragon, but within that relationship she sought other men, Green Dragons, to draw on their maleness. Through a variety of techniques, she was able to fuse with this Yang energy and transform it into her enlightenment.

I found this intriguing as it made sense of the energetic thrill I received when I engaged in a flirt with a willing man. It felt that the shot was like an electric infusion which enlivened me from head to toe. I liked the thought that Jake was my Jade Dragon and I was on the hunt for Green Dragons to advance my spiritual progress. This idea completely solved the split between my flirtatious and spiritual selves. They served each other. This seemed a great way to look at the world - it certainly helped me to cope with a rare blood cancer.

The White Tigress was always on the hunt for suitable Green Dragons. This emulated the tigress in the wild who, when on heat, stalked the jungle for male tigers and was voracious in her appetites. Wow, if I had been a much younger woman I would have loved to embark on that path. Would I, an ancient tigress way past her childbearing years, have any luck? It added a new delightful twist on the flirting game.

I decided to try it out. To look for a Green Dragon.

'Any excuse,' tut-tutted the crone lurking in the background.

The idea of a White Tigress superseding the Russian Bar Girl really appealed to me. She felt more sophisticated, and classy. An opportunity presented itself at a party of a friend who was turning fifty. I told Jake of the new plan and that I would be looking out for a suitable Green Dragon. Jake, as ever, was willing to go along with the game. In White Tigress terms, Jake was my Jade Dragon and my base, and it was from there that I could keep an eye out for Green Dragons. But where were these Green Dragons who pulsed with the male energy I wanted to harness? After nearly giving up, I had the good fortune to spot one near the bar- he was tall and good looking- we locked eyes. Yes, definitely Green Dragon material.

'Guess what?' I said to Jake. 'I have found a Green Dragon!' I continued enjoying being with Jake, who was very loving, very attentive and danced with me in a sexy way. We interspersed our dancing with intimate chats.

A little later, I spotted the Green Dragon again so said to Jake. 'I really want to catch that Green Dragon's eye.' As Jake and I had been so close, I didn't want to do anything to dispel the magic. 'Do you mind?' Jake didn't mind at all, for as well as flirting beautifully with me, he was having several naughty flirts of his own. So, I sat down waiting to grab the Green Dragon's attention. I didn't have to wait long- he was in an animated discussion with several people when I caught his eye. All others disappeared. He swooped. The exchange was short, hot and really intense. His eyes were dancing mischievously and seemed a luminescent green (had I found a real, live Green Dragon?)- he also pursed his lips ever so slightly and blew me a kiss, so full of heat and promise!

'Wow!' I said to Jake as I staggered out of the room. 'That's it, phwoar! I have got what I wanted. Thank you.' I was energised from head to foot and was just buzzing, very similar to how I felt in the jungle when we were waiting to spot a real tigress. This felt like a mini version of the White Tigress trip. Her Jade Dragon would condone the exchange, and encourage it, as they were both committed to her working towards her enlightenment. The newness and freshness of it was so tempting- the dance of fire that unfolds within a fresh charged encounter- so heady- I could imagine bringing that heat from my sexual centre, up my spine and into an explosion of energy in the brain (the aim of such a liaison between the White Tigress and one of her Green Dragons). However, I knew that I would not do that.

My path to enlightenment was through my relationship with Jake. With him, I had hot sex in spades. What would be lacking in a sexual encounter with a Green Dragon, would be the 37 years of intimacy in the mix. Jake loves my essence- Jake licks the tips of my fingers so lovingly and looks deep into my eyes with such tenderness, causing everything to tingle. My good friend Philippa, who was the photographer at this party, caught our magic on camera.

So, the White Tigress model, which included carnal sex with others, wouldn't work for me, as attractive as the idea sounds.

This model did not include intimacy or development of the central male/female relationship. However, I did like some of the White Tigress techniques, especially the idea of using a man's semen as a face lotion. The semen is supposed to rejuvenate the skin and was one of the ways in which a White Tigress kept herself looking young.

But as I approached my 70th birthday, I noticed that withering in my arms and legs was happening fast. How long could the White Tigress feasibly continue hunting for new Green Dragons, or the Russian Bar Girl look for new flirts?

Time to let it all go was fast approaching

I feel fulfilled and replenished- and it was a tough road to get to this place but I feel I have got here just before it was too late. I am delighted that I have caught some of the last trills of the sweet bird of youth. My husband says the 17-year-old in me is always present and won't disappear. During lovemaking, we often have to prop each other up as our ageing limbs fail to keep ourselves up in some sexual positions, but when the electric magic happens, weary old age is banished and we dance in a radiance that extends beyond time.

I said to Jake.

'Wow- I can't imagine our lovemaking getting any better than it is. I can't imagine that the bad boy you are, will at some point fail to thrill me anymore.'

I looked at him expecting him to say something like-

'Well, our sexual passion will diminish gradually but we will have fun riding it out.'

But no, he looked straight at me with a devilish look in his eye and said,

'You ain't seen nothin' yet!'

'Wow,' I said, wondering if my old body could keep up. I laughed. 'I think I've seen enough!'

It was this closeness with Jake that has led me to the resolution of my dilemma.

One evening a few weeks before my 70$^{th}$, Jake said he wanted to redefine our flirting boundaries.

'Uh oh!' I wondered about the next HOH party I was going to with Lorca.

Jake continued, 'There are two reasons for this. Firstly, as we get older and wrinklier, it is less appropriate for both of us to continue our outrageous flirting with others. And secondly, I want to contain our sexuality more so that it smoulders mainly between us. And claim you more as mine.'

As I listened, the Russian Bar Girl and the White Tigress were freaking out. While I liked Jake's sexual claiming of me, I now had to distinguish this from him curtailing my freedom. No, he was not my father. So, I thought long and hard and said,

'Okay I am willing to stop finding new young men to flirt with at HOH, but I still want to flirt with my usual flirting buddies.'

'Yes, that would work. It is the hunting I would really like you to stop!'

'Oh, I find the idea of that really hard. I LOVE having a roving eye.'

'I know,' he said. 'You learnt from me how to flirt. And I find the thought of me giving it up is just as hard.'

'Well, I am two and a quarter years younger than you.' Was I ready to give up?

'But I haven't been to a party in that long. You have.'

'Ah, but you did come to the party where I met a Green Dragon. At that party, you managed to flirt outrageously with seven young women!'

'Oh yes,' remembered Jake. 'That was fun and I could still get away with it. I want to stop before it becomes inappropriate. It is also part of me retiring from the world and withdrawing my energy.'

'But what about our experience that flirting with others keeps us sexually alive and feeds the juice between us? I personally experience that.'

'Me too. I suggest that if we find the fire dwindling between us, we can rethink our positions and go back to finding new flirts and see if (a) we can still pull, and it feeds our fire or (b) we are genuinely getting past it.

'And I thought you said I would be able to go on flirting till my 90s!'

'You will with me and our friends. But I like the fact that you are willing to give up hunting.'

'Did you feel threatened by the Green Dragon scenario?'

'No, that was very clear but I think it was you yourself who didn't want to go down that route because you preferred the intimacy between us.'

Yes, I had to concur. The best thing about our relationship was the forever increasing intimacy between us. There was no place to hide – Jake loves the glory that is me- the real me- wrinkles, age spots and all! And he will tell me when I look dreadful, which I do at times. So, I trust him totally when he says I look beautiful.

So where does this leave RBG and White Tigress? I have offered (a free choice) to give up hunting. That is sad as I am such a good huntress, but I am sure ageing tigresses and ageing huntresses have to give up hunting at some point. I would be 70 in one month's time. It was only ten years before that, I had seriously begun learning how to flirt and hunt. Now I have agreed we will flirt with the people with whom we have established well-defined flirt boundaries, but no new people. Oh, Noooooooooo!

'But what if Federico brings his sexy Italians to HOH? I wish I had met them before as now they could be classed as old flirts!'

'You and your Russian Bar Girl are really incorrigible!' Jake sighs.

'I know,' I said. 'Do you think I could just look at them? Get a buzz that way?'

'That might work. Like you, I don't want to give up eye candy.'

'Phew,' I said. That's good. Oh well, that was fun while it lasted.'

The good thing about this renegotiation was that we were doing it together and it has involved quite a bit of discussion and exploration.

'But Jake, I feel I have mastered the art of flirting. Now I must give it up??'

'Well,' said Jake. 'It is always good to quit when you are at the top of your game.'

Yes, I am at the top of my game; especially after all those fumbling attempts at the start. I am proud that I just kept going. And it became easy- I just had to be really honest- if a guy thrilled me, I just let him know. With a look, a touch, fanning myself, a swish of the skirt or just the words, 'Mmmm, I like the look of you!' It required confidence and total belief in myself as a juicy, sexy woman. And garnering a bunch of flirt buddies, both male and female, was fun. I was delighted with how many variations of the flirtatious game there were. The spontaneous ones were the best. As I get older my eyesight gets worse but with this comes opportunities. I had met Apollo, a circus artist at a HOH party last year, and we had a sexy banter. Later I thought I saw him again and went up to him with a welcoming 'helloooo'. As I got closer he didn't look the same- so I opened his coat to see if he had his circus top on- he didn't- but the bare chest before me was rather delicious, so I said 'Oh dear, I am so sorry, I thought you were someone else.' I noticed his appreciative look, so I said, 'But so what? You'll do.' And we flirted. Men love it. It's a game and those who want to play, play beautifully.

Do I give that up?

While I ponder the ramifications of redefining my flirt boundaries, the Dowager of Decrepitude is ecstatic.

'Oh, I am so relieved. Finally, you are facing the truth. You are getting old, honey. You are nearly a septuagenarian. You have 6 beautiful grandchildren. (I say 6, as like you, I feel a spiritual connection to Harper, your first grandson). Embrace being a babushka even more. And as Jake says, it is good to leave when you are at the top of your game.'

Page intentionally left blank

# 20

## The Future

As I enter my 8$^{th}$ decade, I think back to my 7$^{th}$ and am happy that I ignored all the rules and accepted what I am in essence, a Russian Bar Girl and a party queen. I certainly did not become invisible, about which many post-menopausal women complain. I have even become famous on Facebook for my outrageous outfits. And I have mastered the art of flirting. Gratitude plays a big part too. When Poonie was dying, she put the following message on Facebook, 'Gratitude is the Attitude: It will set you free.' Poonie has so inspired me and I am so grateful for her influence on me, that I could become what I am today, sexy and spiritual. I can fully own that I am Woman Incarnate.

I don't really know what my seventies hold, but I think it will be a lot less flamboyant. We have now become small-holders, which means growing most of our food and raising chickens for eggs and meat. And yes, I am a lot less lazy and am pulling my weight. We may branch out into pigs, ducks and pheasants. This is a far cry from the party queen, but with its own delights. The chicken liver pate I make from our hens is NOTHING like what you get from a supermarket, and as for the coq au vin and home-made ice-cream, wonderful! The brilliant thing about having diabetes is that we bought an ice-cream maker so I can eat ice-cream, made without sugar. A little xylitol combined with our garden fruits and cream is like something in a gastronomic fairy tale - blackcurrants, blueberries, cherries, strawberries, raspberries, peach, cherries, apricots. Eating our apricot ice-cream is like dying and going to heaven.

A big part of our 8th decade will be Epicurean feasts a-deux, and with close family and friends. And I will continue to bring out my Russian Bar Girl and do sexy dances for my husband. I am blessed with a man who not only provides me with youthful elixir for my soul but also with fresh food all year round, cosy wood fires and joyful abundance. This year, Jake has grown me 90 celeriac, and several cauliflowers, (these blended with cream are a great substitute for mashed potato) and he does most of the cooking and housework. With this in store for me, I think I can hang up my dancing shoes. That's not to say I will stop dancing- my closest, dearest friends are dancers, dreamers, Shamans and musicians, who like us, are pursuing the path of relationships.

A couple of years ago I was immensely moved by a photo from a Syrian capital city where thousands of people were standing in a queue for food. They did not look thin and starving- but were ordinary people in suits and nice clothes. I knew then that what was happening in Syria was horrific. So, I said to Jake,

'We have a lovely converted barn that we hardly use (for visiting family and party clothes!) – why don't we offer it to a Syrian family? I know it is just a drop in the ocean but it would make so much difference to that particular family.'

We seriously considered it. At our age, it is usual to start thinking about what we can give back in terms of good works. This could be it. But on reflecting further, I decided that my privacy was very important to me- selfishly perhaps, but that is the way it is. I started contemplating what other 'do-gooder' things we could do. How could we be of service?

'How about working with couples?' We had been couples' therapists in my psychotherapy years with much success. Jake had put up a free website which described the many things that had made our relationship work. This was getting a lot of favourable responses from all over the world.

We decided that we wouldn't charge for the work and invite couples who need help into our home. It would only be for a couple of days and then we would have our blissful privacy back. We would provide a beautiful environment with delicious meals from the garden and everything to enhance comfort and intimacy. It didn't take long. We had discovered many times that once you put an intention out into the universe, it coughed up. Within a few days, some friends of ours took us up on our offer.

It was heavy-going. When a relationship goes wrong, it goes badly wrong. The emotional entanglement has become bitter and infested and requires a lot of patience and love to help heal. In comparison, a Syrian family living in the barn felt as easy as collecting eggs from our chickens. However, it did help, and soon we had another couple on our doorstep.

This time we experimented with MDMA. This had been such an amazing tool in helping heal our own relationship (as had happened at the party where I faced my betrayal of Jake). After uncovering the sticking points in the relationship (and there are always many- and in this case, it looked like divorce!), we helped set up a safe atmosphere where the couple, armed with questions and a written guide, took a small therapeutic dose (supplied by them) and we left them to themselves.

The results were nothing short of miraculous. It turned the relationship around.

We did the same protocol with other friends a few weeks later. I said to Jake, 'It won't work this time around. The obstacles are too huge.' But I was pleasantly astonished. Another miracle had unfolded in our own home. The people opened their hearts to each other so simply and easily under the influence of the drug and cleared up huge levels of misunderstandings. And it seemed permanent.

A few weeks later. Another couple. Another miracle.

The morning after was always a time for reintegration- to look at the notes they had made and for the couple to come up with simple procedures to keep the loving momentum. One example was that each day (after a favourite radio programme and the kids in bed) the couple would touch base, scan the pluses and minuses of the previous day and put themselves back on track. Another couple decided to put aside an afternoon a week to just be together, no internet or phones and enjoying the intimacy. Every few weeks couples will recap what they have discovered, see what had lapsed or what is going well. We have asked for updates, and so far, the signs are excellent. This drug, which has been hijacked by the rave culture, is proving to be an effective tool for steering couples back into re-establishing harmony with a practical way of going forward. And it is as close to a magic bullet as I have ever witnessed.

MDMA for couples was used extensively in the US in the 1980s until it was driven underground by being made illegal. Now it is making a comeback in many research centres all over the world, especially in Switzerland where it is legal for medical and therapeutic purposes. The DEA in the USA is approving trials using MDMA for people suffering from post-traumatic syndrome.

We do not ask for payment for these services but Jake's requirement is that people offer this service to other couples- (we provide detailed instructions) to spread the protocol. My requirement is to receive a present. So far, I have a beautiful painted ostrich egg light and some wooden chimes that sound like tinkling goat bells. These always remind me of the look of love in those people's eyes when they re-opened their hearts to each other.

The future is promising. We love our relationship and want to pass on the opportunity for fulfilling relationships to other people; a good thing to do while expanding the nourishing delights of our garden and luxuriating in the simple pleasures of retirement.

I continue with my Taoist meditation. In this way, I feel I am in charge of my illnesses and not a victim of them. Mantak Chia is the best kind of teacher who teaches me to master myself. I find the lack of spiritual mumbo jumbo refreshing. The body is the source of spiritual regeneration and Chia teaches thousands of techniques, rooted in ancient Tao teachings, to heal the body. And there are sexual practices to actually heal the bone marrow, which I look forward to trying. I have also decided to blend these practices with weekly interferon injections. Interferon is a naturally occurring substance in the body that helps the immune system and works on repairing the bone marrow. It took me a while to come to terms with this. I wanted desperately to heal myself naturally. So far, the interferon is working well, and keeping my abnormal cell proliferation down. Without any input from me, my acupuncturist said he felt two dragons fighting inside my stomach and said I had to take charge of them. Funnily enough, I had already felt the presence of dragons, so decided to go with it and began an inner dialogue with them. They were large and fierce and it took me two weeks before they consented to bow to me. Then another two weeks to bow to each other. Now we are all on the same side. They have fallen in love with each other and have named their first dragon child, Pegasys (the medical term of the type of interferon I am injecting). I imagine Pegasys flying through my bones and healing them.

But what about my flirtatious self? What of the Russian Bar Girl? She will always be part of me and will exist comfortably with the Babushka who makes bread, chicken and leek soup and gooseberry ice-cream. And I have a good store of flirt buddies to play with. For example, Apollo and I continue to flirt. He is 26, and as a circus artist, has a fabulous, fit body. I say, 'I love your muscles.' He answers. 'I developed them for you, baby.' I say 'I can't believe that I am in my late 60s and you make me swoon.' He says, 'surely you mean your late 20s.' I say. 'Oh, I feel like a 17-year-old and if I were younger, I would join your circus troupe.' He says, 'You can join it now.' Then he introduces me to a circus friend, a woman from Santa Fe who works high wire and stilts. She is riding a monocycle from Santa Fe to Montreal for her 70$^{th}$ birthday and 10 years after our 60/30 party, I have enjoyed a 70/30 rave with my son.

I also have a brand-new flirt line. Jake and I bought a Tesla- a reward for all the hard work we have done for our energy efficiency business. It is a dream car to drive. In it, I feel Queen of the Road, which goes a long way to heal the time when I was at the bottom of the heap as a young migrant. And my new flirt line? I go up to a guy at a party and say- 'I have drunk a little too much- do you think you could drive me home?' as I press a key in the shape of a small Tesla, into his hand.

I don't think I am ready for cronedom, yet. I have too much fire and sexual energy.

Jake and I are proud that we have succeeded in relationship- that we have created our relationship as a path to the divine. We feel that this is a present we can give the world- just by being ourselves, just by showing that it is possible. And giving practical help through our website and creating a protocol where couples can take an in-depth look at their relationship. Each couple has their own, unique journey. What can unfold between them is magic and is beautiful to see.

I feel so high on the love we share. We are on a path to God together. And contrary to many of my former beliefs, it is not a saintly, sexless path. The dance between us is hot. Smoking, in fact. We use the erotic charge between us to lead us to divine contact, where we can rest in the beauty of each other's presence. Many of our friends look to us when their relationships are rocky because they hold us up as a couple who have made it, who still adore each other and look like we are having a really good time.

And it is true.

One of the best things we have discovered is that we have created in each other our ideal lover. When I say to Jake, 'you are such a good snogger', his answer always is, 'I have an excellent teacher.' He and I have become the hero and the heroine in each other's movie.

I have become sexy and spiritual in his eyes. And also, in my own.

# Dr Eva Maria Chapman's Bio

A former teacher, psychotherapist, researcher and successful business woman, I became an author when nursing my stepfather, Sasha for the last 2 years of his life. After a 33-year estrangement, we totally forgave each other and he unburdened the harrowing story of his Jewish family in Ukraine in WW2, and died a happy man. This plus my mentally ill mother's equally harrowing life, led me to write S*asha & Olga,* 2006 Lothian Books. This launched my new career as a writer; *Russian Roulette 20:20*, Solaris 2010; *From Russia to Love*, Robson Press 2012; *Butterflies & Demons* (long-listed for

Mslexia novel prize 2017), DoctorZed Publishing, Adelaide 2019; *Sexy at 70, A Spiritual Journey,* Publishing Push 2019.

She lives in wildlife sanctuary on the edge of Exmoor England, which she shares with her husband Jake (40 years together) who are on their joint path to greater love.

https://relating-manual.com/

http://www.evachapman.co.uk/

https://www.facebook.com/evamariachapman and FB page, Sizzling into my 70s.

@sizzling70s Instagram

Twitter @sizzle70s

Printed in Great
Britain
by Amazon

31908400R00246